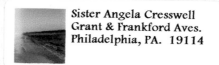

THE CRITICAL READING INVENTORY

D1232561

Assessing Students' Reading and Thinking

Mary DeKonty Applegate

St. Joseph's University

Kathleen Benson Quinn

Holy Family University

Anthony J. Applegate

Holy Family University

PEARSON

Merrill
Prentice Hall

Upper Saddle River, New Jersey
Columbus, Ohio

Library of Congress Cataloging-in-Publication Data

Applegate, Mary DeKonty.

The critical reading inventory : assessing students' reading and thinking / Mary DeKonty Applegate, Kathleen Benson Quinn, Anthony J. Applegate.

p. cm.

Includes bibliographical references.

ISBN 0-13-048619-1 (pbk.)

1. Reading—Ability testing. 2. Critical thinking. 3. Reading comprehension. I. Quinn, Kathleen Benson. II. Applegate, Anthony J. III. Title.

LB1050.46.A64 2004

372.48—dc21

2003054131

Vice President and Executive Publisher: Jeffery W. Johnston
Senior Editor: Linda Ashe Montgomery
Editorial Assistant: Laura J. Weaver
Production Editor: Linda Hillis Bayma
Production Coordination: Emily Hatteberg, Carlisle Publishers Services
Design Coordinator: Diane C. Lorenzo
Cover Designer: Jim Hunter
Cover image: Corbis
Production Manager: Pamela D. Bennett
Director of Marketing: Ann Castel Davis
Marketing Manager: Darcy Betts Prybella
Marketing Coordinator: Tyra Poole

This book was set in Galliard by Carlisle Communications, Ltd. It was printed and bound by Courier Kendallville, Inc. The cover was printed by Phoenix Color Corp.

Pearson Education Ltd.
Pearson Education Singapore Pte. Ltd.
Pearson Education Canada, Ltd.
Pearson Education—Japan

Pearson Education Australia Pty. Limited
Pearson Education North Asia Ltd.
Pearson Educación de Mexico, S.A. de C.V.
Pearson Education Malaysia Pte. Ltd.

10 9 8 7 6 5 4 3 2 1
ISBN: 0-13-048619-1

To Tony, who in love wrote this with me to help me heal.
To my Mom, Dad, sisters, and brothers who love and believe in me.

—*Mary DeKonty Applegate*

To my Mom and Dad, for teaching me to read and so much more.
To my children, for teaching me the meaning of life.
To my husband for teaching me to love.
To my teachers, students, and colleagues, for teaching me that
I have so much to learn every day.

—*Kathy Quinn*

To Mary: my colleague, my inspiration, my best friend, and my love.
In loving memory of my parents, Edmund and Anne,
who never failed to encourage me to love learning.

—*Tony Applegate*

Preface

In *The Critical Reading Inventory* (CRI) teachers will find many of the traditional and valuable characteristics of reading inventories, such as graded word lists, oral and silent reading passages, retellings, and comprehension questions. However, we feel strongly that it is crucial in today's educational environment to go beyond traditional assessment to the core issue of the thinking that children are doing about the reading they engage in. Thus, we have expanded our inventory to include retelling rubrics based on text structure; interviews with children, parents, and teachers; encouragement for teachers to delve into a deeper analysis of the reader's comprehension of text; and an audio CD that models how to administer the tests and story retellings.

Above all, in this inventory we offer the opportunity to assess a reader's ability to draw conclusions, make inferences, and critically respond to text. It is our hope that the users of the CRI will identify with confidence those children who do not think about what they read. Armed with that understanding, teachers will model thinking for their students and challenge them, through their own questioning, to understand their reading at new and deeper levels. It is our hope that more and more teachers will experience the thrill of hearing first graders discuss the mistakes that characters in their books have made or middle school students discussing the links between their reading and current events. Most of all, we hope that more teachers will experience the pure joy of seeing children learning to think about text and overcoming the firm belief that it is beyond their capability.

Ultimately, we must acknowledge the skill and insight of the teachers and reading specialists who use the CRI. No reading inventory can ever be better than the people who use it, and the CRI is no exception.

So many people have helped with this project along the way and deserve special thanks. Marjorie Seddon Johnson and Roy Kress, our major professors at Temple University, literally "wrote the book" on informal reading inventories. All three of us had the good fortune to be counted among their students. Eleanor Ladd Kress modeled instructional practices rooted solidly in diagnostic information. Elizabeth Davis taught us the principles of conscientious research. They were our mentors, our friends, and our inspirations; in short, everything that one can hope for in professors. Throughout the development of the CRI, we reread their words and reflected on their guidance. It is important to us that they know how much they empowered us.

Our editor, Linda Montgomery, has been a great help to us. Her enthusiasm for the project was infectious, and her guidance and encouragement of a trio of novices have been absolutely invaluable. Linda even went so far as to dream up the title for our fledgling text. Linda's assistant, Laura Weaver, has been a model of helpful and pleasant professionalism during our final stages of production. Her gently nudging e-mails and cogent advice have kept us on task. We would also like to thank Emily Hatteberg of Carlisle Communications for setting the bar so high in both her professional standards and her conscientious preparation of the text. Carlisle's production and art departments deserve special mention for their fine work and input.

The following professional reviewers provided wonderful encouragement and praise along with enormous insights and many valuable suggestions: Cathy Collins Block, Texas Christian University; Tim Campbell, University of Central Oklahoma; Paula Currie, Southeastern Louisiana University; Randal Donelson, The Ohio State University; Mary Ann Dzama, George Mason University; Alan Frager, Miami University; Marguerite Gillis, Southwest Texas State University; Michael Kibby, University of Buffalo; Roy A. Kress, Temple University, emeritus; Eleanor Ladd Kress, University of South Carolina, retired; Maria Meyerson, University of Nevada, Las Vegas; Nancy Mammarella Nagy, Marywood University; Barbara S. Pettegrew, Otterbein College; and Tim Rasinski, Kent State University. Their impact on *The Critical Reading Inventory* has been profound. We know from experience that book reviews can be a time-consuming and difficult task. Please accept our deepest thanks for your time and efforts on our behalf.

We are deeply indebted to so many colleagues who participated in the field testing of the CRI. We extend our thanks to Roger Gee and his preservice graduate students, Carleene Slowik and the reading specialists from Mount Laurel School District, along with Therese Garbett, Dawn Doheny, Pam Rothwell, Lucille Hager, Pat Erickson, Grace Hartman, Mary Tomlin, Betty Klear, Eileen Baker, Toni Spano, Gail Berkowitz, Sandra Peart, Donna Kennedy, and the graduate research group (Jackie Brobownicki, Cheryl Riddell, Susan Stackhouse, and Debbie Stein). We owe special thanks to Janine Sack and Lisa Freeman, who provided field testing for junior and senior high school students, and to Conne Broderick for her keen insights and suggestions. We owe particular thanks to Helen Hoffner and her staff and her inservice graduate students, to our graduate Reading Diagnosis students, and especially to the young students who so willingly gave their time and efforts during testing and who added so much to our understanding of the nature of the CRI.

In addition, we have had extensive and much appreciated technical assistance from Joanne DeBoy, Evan Nurse, Bob LaFond, John Tobin, and Thomas Quinn, Jr.; photography contributed by Pat Getty and Thomas Jenkins, Jr.; original artwork created by Walter Benson; and proofreading assistance from Kirsten Quinn. We are so grateful for the many special talents that have been contributed to this text and the accompanying *Reader's Passages* by so many special people.

Contents

Part II

Note: Every effort has been made to provide accurate and current Internet information in this book. However, the Internet and information posted on it are constantly changing, and it is inevitable that some of the Internet addresses listed in this textbook will change.

Part I

Section 1

Introduction to *The Critical Reading Inventory*

What Is Critical Reading?

If we examine the historical roots of reading instruction in the United States, we will find a long tradition of assessing the reading comprehension of children on the basis of how much of their reading they could recall and recite (Allington, 2001). Few reading experts would argue that a clear recollection of the points that an author makes is not important. But fewer still would argue that recall of information is sufficient to define a good and effective reader. Instead of a rather simple and passive gathering of information, reading is now viewed as "an active process that requires an intentional and thoughtful interaction between the reader and the text" (Report of the National Reading Panel, 2000, pp. 4–5). And, in addition to the text, the raw material that we use in that interaction is the collection of our past experiences and concepts, rooted in our culture and language (Anderson, Osborn, & Tierney, 1984; Pearson, 1992).

But as complex as this interaction of reading systems may be, it is still only the beginning of our job as readers. After we construct a plausible explanation of the text, we must react and respond to what we have read, and this reaction and response is the heart of what we describe as critical reading. C. S. Lewis described the literary experience in this way: "[I]n reading great literature I become a thousand men and yet remain myself . . . I see with a myriad eyes, but it is still I who see" (Lewis, 1961, p. 141). Critical reading of literature involves the exploration and analysis of characters, their histories, their motivations, their values, and their actions. As critical readers we react dynamically to characters, loving some and despising others, forgiving some and condemning others. In short, critical reading expands our knowledge of ourselves as it develops our understanding of others, enabling us to live vicariously through the lives of others (Rosenblatt, 1983). But we also assess the craft of the writer, analyzing techniques that the writer uses to elicit our responses and frequently judging the validity or quality of the writer's reasoning on the basis of that analysis.

And critical reading is not restricted to literature. When we react and respond to informational text, our aim is to incorporate new information into our existing frameworks of understanding. In many ways this task is more challenging than it is when we are reading narrative text. Informational text often presents ideas so new that we must create new schemata as we are reading in order to actively process the ideas (Bransford, 1984). We have all had the experience of effectively memorizing information and passing tests, only to find that the information is gone from our memories a few days later. But critical readers look for links between new ideas and their own experiences and may even make judgments or propose alternatives in response to informational text. When they do this, they arrive at a level of ownership that essentially insures that the information they have studied will be more easily accessible to them (Allington & Johnston, 2000).

In short, critical reading, as we are defining it for *The Critical Reading Inventory* (CRI), involves at its root a personal response to text that takes the reader far beyond mere memory for facts. Critical reading is thoughtful literacy, a dynamic process of thinking about what we read and how it fits in with our own ideas and values, the ideas of others, ideas we have encountered in the past, and ideas that we accept or reject. And critical reading for our purposes is also related to *engaged reading,* in that we must not ignore the simultaneous functioning of motivation, concepts, and social interaction during reading (Alvermann & Guthrie, 1993). The level of engagement in reading is predictive of the amount of reading that children do, and children who are engaged and read more are likely to continue to do so (Wigfield & Guthrie, 1997). Not surprisingly, research has suggested that engagement in reading is predictive of achievement (Anderson, Wilson, & Fielding, 1988; Cipielewski & Stanovich, 1992; Cunningham & Stanovich, 1997). At the core of critical reading is an interest and curiosity that leads readers to go beyond the surface of the text and to try to understand its meaning, its significance, and its relevance to their own lives (Schiefele, 1991).

It is not difficult to envision a reciprocal relationship between thoughtful, critical response to text and motivation to read. The more one is inclined to think about reading, the more one is likely to find it rewarding. The more one finds it rewarding, the more one is likely to engage in it. The more one engages in it, the better one is likely to become at it, which in turn enhances the level of thinking one brings to reading. At the center of this complex string of relationships is one's view of reading that must include at its very core thinking about and responding to what one is reading. Consequently, reading teachers and reading experts alike have called on assessment experts to expand their tools to include an assessment of the extent to which readers think about, not simply remember, what they have read. The response to this call has been broad and extensive.

Why Assess Critical Reading?

In response to reading research and theory, critical reading and thoughtful literacy are being more and more widely assessed on national, international, and state levels. At the international level, for example, the National Assessment of Educational Progress (NAEP) Reading Framework assesses four different stances or ways of responding to text: (a) forming an initial understanding; (b) developing an interpretation; (c) personal reflection and response; and (d) the critical stance. The Framework's target distribution of items for the fourth grade 2000 *NAEP Reading Test* was 33% critical stance, 33% personal reflection, and 33% combined initial understanding and interpretation (National Center for Education Statistics, 2002).

At the national level, the *Stanford Achievement Test–9 (SAT–9),* a widely used nationally normed achievement test, includes open-ended items as well as more traditional multiple choice measures. Each open-ended item on the *SAT–9* measures one of three reading processes: initial understanding, interpretation, or critical analysis (Harcourt, 2002). The *Terranova Performance Assessments in Communication Arts* assess the ability to establish understanding, explore meaning, extend meaning and examine strategies, and to evaluate critically (CTB McGraw Hill, 2002). A random sampling of 20% of the frameworks that guide the construction of state tests reveal that 90% of the statewide measures include open-ended or reader response items.

This increased emphasis on the ability to think about and respond to text represents a challenge for future success in reading instruction in the United States. For while the assessments are increasingly emphasizing critical thinking, classroom instruction does not seem to be responding. Allington (2001) reported that in study after study of the nature of classroom tasks, the overwhelming emphasis has been on "copying, remembering, and reciting with few tasks that engage students in thinking about what they have read" (p. 94). And while the NAEP performance of American students has risen to historically high levels of achievement with regard to literal comprehension, "only a few students can demonstrate even minimal proficiency with higher-order literacy strategies" (p. 8). It stands to reason that students who are asked more often to explain or discuss ideas from their reading are more likely than their counterparts to demonstrate proficiency in higher order tests (Donahue, Voelkl, Campbell, & Mazzeo, 1999). It appears that the challenge to develop thoughtful literacy is landing squarely in the schools.

But with the NAEP, national, and state tests acting as summative assessments, it appears that little is being done in the way of formative assessment, assessment that can redirect the teaching curriculum as it is being delivered. In fact, Black and Wiliam (1998) found that classroom assessment tends to be characterized by measures of rote and superficial learning. Questions that teachers use tend to be non-critical, focusing instead on the narrow learning that teachers mistakenly believe will assure short-term success on high-stakes tests (Black, 2000). If Black and his associates are correct, not only is there a gap between what is being assessed and what teachers are teaching, but there is also a fundamental misunderstanding on the part of many teachers about the kinds of learning that are now being assessed on national and state tests.

It is precisely this gap in formative assessment that *The Critical Reading Inventory* has been designed to fill. There appears to be widespread agreement among experts that reading involves a thoughtful response to and interaction with text (Flippo, 2001) and because of this agreement, the assessment of thoughtful response has been included in national and state assessments. But if there is indeed a mismatch between assessments that emphasize critical response and classrooms that do not address it, we must find a means for teachers and administrators to identify and approach the issue.

Why a Critical Reading Inventory?

The decision to add yet another reading inventory to a field where more than a dozen well-known and widely used inventories already exist was a difficult one. We had used several different informal reading inventories (IRIs) in our advanced diagnosis courses, courses that in our programs led to study in instructional strategies and techniques. Our orientation toward critical thinking and thoughtful literacy shaped our study of instructional strategies, but we perceived a heavy weighting toward literal comprehension in inventories that we had used. We even modified one such inventory, adding items that called for higher level thinking and thoughtful responses. But such modifications eliminated the benefits of any validity or reliability data that had been gathered on the original instrument. And so the mismatch between our concern for critical reading and our use of instruments that did not seem to measure it effectively led us to a more formal investigation of the problem (Applegate, Quinn, & Applegate, 2002).

We identified eight of the most widely used and cited IRIs and developed detailed descriptions of items that were text-based and items that were response-based. Text-based items called for readers to recall information verbatim from the text or to make simple and rather obvious low-level inferences. Response-based items required the reader to draw logical conclusions based on a combination of information from the text and ideas from their experience; or they called for readers to express and defend their ideas about the underlying significance of the key ideas in the text. From a sample of nearly 900 open-ended questions taken from the eight IRIs in the study, we found an overwhelming emphasis on text-based thinking (see Table 1–1). More than 91% of the items required only literal recall of information or low-level inferences. Items that required readers to draw a logical conclusion or to discuss the significance of a story occurred at a rate of less than 9%.

Needless to say, we found the results of our study disconcerting. We saw the use of open-ended questions to assess literal recall as a missed opportunity to make maximum use of the diagnostic potential of such items. Even aside from the fact that literal recall can be measured more easily and more reliably by objective test items, we concluded that the IRIs we studied were unable to distinguish between readers who could *remember* what they read and those who could *think about it*.

But even more crucial is the missed opportunity to use assessment data as a spur to instructional reform. If we cannot demonstrate that many of our children are unable to think about and respond to text, we will have no compelling reason to convince teachers that they need to adjust their instruction to address such needs. And because research suggests that

Table 1–1 Percentage of Item Types Found in Informal Reading Inventories

	Total Text-Based (%)	Total Response-Based (%)
Bader (1998)	92.5 (N = 136)	7.5 (N = 11)
Burns & Roe (1993)	88.1 (N = 111)	11.9 (N = 15)
Ekwall & Shanker (2000)	99.2 (N = 121)	0.8 (N = 1)
Flynt & Cooter (2001)	89.6 (N = 86)	10.4 (N = 10)
Johns (1994)	91.8 (N = 123)	8.2 (N = 11)
Leslie & Caldwell (2001)	81.6 (N = 93)	18.4 (N = 21)
Silvaroli & Wheelock (2001)	98.5 (N = 66)	1.5 (N = 1)
Woods & Moe (1999)	90.1 (N = 73)	9.9 (N = 8)
TOTAL	91.2 (N = 809)	8.8 (N = 78)

classroom questioning is largely literal (Allington, 2001; Brown, 1991; Elmore, Peterson, & McCarthey, 1996; Knapp, 1995; Tharp & Gallimore, 1989), the cycle of poor performance on assessments that call for thoughtful responses is likely to remain unbroken. Fortunately, the research into exemplary literacy classrooms suggests that teachers who engage children in reading, problem solving, and linking ideas across texts routinely obtain superior performance on standardized achievement tests (Gottfried, 1990; Pressley et al., 2001; Ruddell, Draheim, & Barnes, 1990; Taylor, Pearson, Clark, & Walpole, 2000). But we still must be able to provide a reason for teachers to learn and use effective literacy strategies in their classrooms.

The American Educational Research Association (AERA) has advised that "tests should be aligned with the curriculum as set forth in standards documents representing intended goals of instruction" (2000, p. 3). We noted that the experts agree, the developers of curriculum standards agree, and the writers of national and state tests agree that thoughtful response is a central part of the act of reading. We did not find an equal emphasis on critical response in the inventories we studied. We concluded that the challenge for reading specialists and experts is clear: We can lead the way toward fundamental changes in our approach to the assessment of thoughtful literacy, or we can wait until external assessments force us to follow.

Who Will Use *The Critical Reading Inventory*?

We envision the CRI as useful to three distinct groups: pre-service teachers, in-service teachers, and reading specialists/graduate students.

Pre-Service Teachers

The CRI can be useful in helping prospective teachers to develop the skills of diagnostic teaching rooted in the ability to identify student strengths and weaknesses. More specifically, we envision the CRI as a structured way to introduce students to the role of informal assessment as a guide to instruction. The diagnostic data they gather can be used as the basis for the development of instructional plans and programs. An important offshoot of the use of the CRI is the development of greater sensitivity to the notion of reading as thinking and the types of questions that can distinguish literal and critical readers. It is our hope that the study and use of these kinds of questions will promote the ability of pre-service teachers to develop thought-provoking questions for use in their own classrooms.

In-Service Teachers

The variety of uses to which in-service teachers may put the CRI calls attention to the flexibility of the instrument itself. Classroom teachers are frequently asked by their schools or districts to gather assessment data on their children. They may find it useful to use only a numerical or abbreviated version of the CRI, testing children, for example, only at their grade level, only on oral or silent reading passages, or to contrast performance on narrative and informational text. In other circumstances they may wish to assess critical thinking in response to silent reading for students at those grade levels selected for state or local assessments. But teachers may also need to confirm or estimate reading levels for students with specific needs, for example, new students. This task would call for a much different alignment of CRI features. It would be unusual for teachers to be asked to do a comprehensive diagnostic analysis on each of their students, but they may need to complete such analyses on some of their students.

As a consequence of these needs, we should approach the CRI as a tool to be tailored to meet a wide variety of demands and not as a rigidly formulated instrument. For example, if CRI results are being used as evidence of student growth, then steps should be taken to insure that the test is administered and scored as consistently as possible. If the CRI is being used to gather general diagnostic insights to inform a teacher about her program of instruction for a given child, then the teacher could exercise a good measure of latitude in selecting and administering those elements of the test that best meet her needs. Further discussion of the various uses of the CRI is included in section 4.

Reading Specialists/Graduate Students

Reading specialists and specialist candidates are or will be in the position of providing full-scale diagnostic analyses or estimating reading levels for students whom they assess. They may be called upon to provide instructional direction to classroom teachers or to instructional support groups. They may help school or district personnel to make decisions about instructional materials, programs, or strategies. Finally, they may also engage in research at a variety of levels and their need for reliable and valid assessment data may be met by the CRI. Reading specialists and graduate students or even those seeking master teacher status would normally use the CRI in its most comprehensive form, and it is to these individuals that the full-scale directions for test administration are generally directed. However, the flexibility of the CRI allows for decision making to be guided by the needs of the user and the demands of the situation (Bean, Cassidy, Grumet, Shelton, & Wallis, 2002; Bean, Swan, & Knaub, 2003).

Special Features of the Inventory

Three Measures of Comprehension

The most salient feature of the CRI is its use of three distinct item types in the assessment of reading comprehension. Text-based items require the reader to recall information from the text or to make fairly obvious connections between and among the ideas in the text. Factual information and readers' concepts comprise the building blocks upon which critical thinking is based. Thus text-based items are also included in the CRI for the purpose of contributing to differentiated diagnosis. Users of the CRI will discover, as we have, many students who can recall text and answer text-based items but who cannot think about the text in any other way.

The CRI measures higher level thinking in two different ways. Inference items require readers to draw conclusions by relating the information in the text to what they already know, for example, by predicting events, explaining ideas, or devising alternative solutions to problems. Critical response items require readers to address the "big picture" and arrive at statements of the broader significance of the text. They then must defend their ideas, based on information in the text and from their background experiences. A common Critical response item will, for example, require readers to make a judgment about a character or a character's actions and to defend that judgment. Thus the CRI can effectively measure a child's ability to recall the text, but at least 40% of the items assessing comprehension of a selection will require inferences and at least 20% of the items will require critical responses.

Complete and Extended Text

The CRI includes, as most inventories do, selections that can be used for oral as well as silent reading, and passages that are narrative as well as informational in nature (Johnson, Kress, & Pikulski, 1987). In the CRI we have developed original passages centered on topics that were chosen for their potential appeal to readers, but also so as not to be overly familiar. We were mindful of the criticisms leveled at the short and sometimes choppy passages that are used in reading assessment measures (Goodman & Goodman, 1994; Klesius & Homan, 1985). We were also aware that research had found that the nature of children's miscues changed as they began to develop a sense of the context of the text that they were reading (Goodman, 1970; Goodman & Burke, 1972). Because many informal reading inventories include passages that tend to be short or even incomplete in terms of story elements, children who read them do not always have an opportunity to develop a solid sense of the semantic and syntactic elements in the text. These observations create something of a dilemma for the constructors of IRIs because they must balance the demands for complete text with the demands of time spent in the diagnosis of reading difficulties. In the CRI, we opted for longer, more fully developed text, mindful of the need to match our assessment with the text that characterizes most instructional materials, as well as national and state standardized assessments in reading. Longer stories enable us to assess the reader's ability to construct meaning and develop a greater sense of story, content, and context. Because the longer and more fully developed text resembles actual reading tasks, we feel that they provide a higher level of validity in the assessment of comprehension.

Retelling Rubrics

The CRI includes for each narrative and informational passage a rubric to guide the user in assigning a relatively consistent numerical value to retellings. The rubrics are built around the central story elements of the narrative passages and the key factual data included in informational passages. The rubrics are thus designed to move users away from a reliance on verbatim recall as a measure of the worth of a retelling; the rubrics assign greater weight to the most significant ideas in the text. Included in the rubric is the element of student response to the text, which is factored into the final scoring. The use of the rubric to assign a numerical value to a retelling can in no way replace the careful analysis that can provide qualitative insights into a child's thinking. But it can lessen the wide range of values that might be assigned to retellings in the absence of any guidance. It can also provide another source of comparative data that may be useful, given the different purposes for which the CRI can be used.

Levels of Interpretation

The CRI includes instruction and case studies that illustrate three distinct levels of interpretation that are designed to serve the different needs and purposes of CRI users. For situations where assessment data is the primary objective of testing, examiners may choose to carry out a Level One Numerical Interpretation of the test data. This allows the examiner to compare a child's reading performance on several distinct dimensions of reading (e.g., performance on different item types, oral vs. silent, narrative vs. informational, unprobed comprehension vs. probed comprehension). Level One is far from superficial but it can save a great deal of time for users who must administer numerous assessments. A Level Two Analytical Interpretation is called for when the user needs detailed information about a child's reading performance. Level Two calls for users to expend the time to examine the child's responses in detail and draw conclusions about the nature of the child's thinking on the basis of those responses. A Level Three Comprehensive Interpretation is more detailed still, representing an attempt to piece together all available information that may be contributing to a child's reading performance, including personal view of and attitude toward reading, parental involvement, and classroom instruction. Levels of interpretation are simply another means of maximizing the flexibility of the CRI to meet the needs of a wide range of professionals involved in the reading assessment of children.

Interviews

Included as part of the CRI are interview forms that may be used for children (both older and younger), parents, and teachers. If the purpose of the CRI administration is to obtain a comprehensive picture of the child's entire reading situation, the interviews can provide some valuable insights. Under optimum conditions, the interviews are designed to support and supplement the CRI user's inquiry into the child's overall reading milieu, but they can also be used in their present form as stand-alone instruments. Ultimately, the interviews can, at the very least, give the CRI user information about children's view of and attitude toward reading, the level of parental support for and awareness of any reading problems, and the type of instruction that the children receive on a daily basis.

Reading Accuracy Index (RAI) and Meaning Maintenance Index (MMI)

The CRI includes, as do most inventories, a percentage score that reflects the sheer accuracy of a child's reading, the extent to which the reading is free from miscues. This we have termed the Reading Accuracy Index (RAI). But we have also acknowledged the research that suggests that not all miscues are created equal (Goodman & Burke, 1972). That is, less serious miscues, while they may deviate from the text, still represent a successful attempt on the part of the reader to make the reading meaningful. For other miscues, however, the need to preserve meaning breaks down and these miscues may violate the sense and syntax of the text. A significant number of this type of miscue may indicate a distorted view of the nature of reading itself. To differentiate between the two types of miscues, we have included a percentage of the reader's attempts to maintain meaning during reading, called the Meaning Maintenance Index (MMI). The MMI can provide at a glance an indicator of the extent to which the reader views reading as an active process of constructing meaning in response to text.

Scoring Aids

The CRI examiner's materials include charts to facilitate the calculation of comprehension scores as well as the calculation of the RAI and the MMI. Once the examiner has tallied the reader's responses, it is a relatively simple matter to locate the appropriate percentages on the charts that accompany every passage.

Potential Impact of *The Critical Reading Inventory*

It is our hope that the publication and use of the CRI will help educators focus on the wisdom and efficacy of assessing and teaching the ability to think critically about one's reading. If it is true that we are tending toward the assessment of traits that we are not effectively teaching (Allington, 2001), then accurate assessment is one of our most effective means of establishing the facts and stressing the need for change. Thus we envision the CRI as a potential change agent in that it can provide evidence that thoughtful analysis of and response to reading is not part of the view of reading held by a significant number of children. Without such data, it will be difficult to ask teachers to reassess the notion that literal recall is the central issue in reading assessment.

We acknowledge that teachers widely recognize the importance of critical reading and our hope is that the use of the CRI will add to that level of recognition. But if professional preparation programs have over-emphasized a linear conceptualization of reading, that framework may hinder some teachers from addressing thoughtful literacy. That is, some theorists and researchers believe that the process of reading involves a kind of taxonomy. Within the confines of that taxonomy, children must master all of the details of the text and acquire a baseline skill level before they can do any thinking about the text. Under these circumstances, some children may not progress to the point where they are ever required to engage in critical thought.

We also hope to spark debate about the link between thinking about one's reading and one's ability to find rewards in reading itself. We believe that the CRI can ultimately help teachers to distinguish between readers who can read and those who are likely to do so. Specifically, if children see reading as little more than storing and retrieving the details of text, they will have a very limited incentive to engage in the activity (Schraw & Bruning, 1999; Wigfield & Guthrie, 1997). Fortunately, a child's view of reading can be changed in response to effective instruction, but it must be identified first.

Ironically, the very tendency to read may well be at the heart of performance on reading tests. For example, research comparing the amount of reading that children do with their performance on achievement tests (Anderson, Wilson, & Fielding, 1988) revealed that students who scored in the 90th percentile read on average for more than 40 minutes per day. Students who scored in the 50th percentile read on average less than 13 minutes per day. And while correlational studies do not establish causal links, few experts will minimize the logical link between motivation to read and growth in reading (Guthrie, Wigfield, Metsala, & Cox, 1999; Meece, Blumenfeld, & Hoyle, 1988).

Conclusions

We believe that the CRI can be an effective measure of a child's ability to think about text at a variety of levels, an ability that is measured widely in summative but much less so in formative assessments. And because it is formative assessments that are designed to have a more direct impact upon classroom practice, it is at this level that we believe the CRI can make its greatest contribution. If the CRI can provide evidence that significant numbers of children are not thinking about what they read, then teachers will have the opportunity to develop both the tools and the incentive they need to effectively address the problem in their classrooms. Conversely, and even more important, the CRI may help to demonstrate to teachers that many of their children (about whom they may have presumed otherwise) can effectively think about what they read. Once teachers have recognized this potential on the part of their students, they may become more comfortable incorporating thoughtful literacy instruction on a regular basis in their classrooms.

Section 2

Description of *The Critical Reading Inventory*

Word Lists

The CRI, much the same as most traditional informal reading inventories, begins with an assessment of the child's word recognition level in isolation from text. A graded list of words is presented to the readers in 1-second flash and untimed formats, and their performance determines the starting point of the actual reading assessment.

Flash

The Flash administration of the graded words lists is designed to provide a relatively quick and easy estimate of the level of the child's sight vocabulary. Sight vocabulary is defined as the fund of words that the child can recognize immediately, without the need for any word analysis skills. To administer the Flash segment of the test, you will provide the child with a 1-second exposure to each word for a list of 20 words per grade level. The words have been chosen because of the frequency with which they appear in actual grade-level materials typically used in classroom instruction (see discussion in section 5). Because the Word Lists take very little time and are very easy to administer and score, we also use the results to obtain an estimate of the level at which we should begin the reading of graded passages.

This estimate is based upon an assumption that works most of the time: If children can identify all of the words in a given grade level given just flash exposure, the chances are good that they will be able to read materials written at that grade level with very little difficulty. Of course, there are always exceptions to that rule, but since you want the reading segment of the CRI to be administered with maximum efficiency, a fairly good estimate of the appropriate starting point will be well worth your while as you will see in greater detail when we discuss the process of estimating reading levels.

Untimed

If children do not immediately recognize a word (or do not respond after about 5 seconds), give them an opportunity to use their fund of word analysis skills to identify the word. This is the Untimed segment of the Word List test. Note that you are not assessing reading; there is no real text involved and thus no context. When you give children unlimited time (in reality 10 to 15 seconds) to decode a word, they can do one of two things. They can use either word analysis skills (breaking a word into component parts—prefixes, affixes, root words, etc.) or phonics skills (linking the correct sounds and syllables to the combination of letters). Obviously, there can be no syntactic (grammatical) or semantic (meaningful) clues involved if there is no real text.

Nonetheless, giving the Untimed word list can give you some additional information about the level of the child's decoding skills, how that child approaches decoding, how flexible the child is in trying different pronunciations or techniques, and even how effectively that child handles frustration. You can observe whether children try everything in their repertoire or whether they simply glance at a word, look up at you, and tell you they don't know what it is (and presumably will not know at any time in the near future). You can observe how the child deals with success as well as a lack of success. For all of these reasons, you will want to administer, despite its limitations, a list of graded, isolated words.

What Word Lists Cannot Do

We need as well to discuss what Word Lists cannot do. Word Lists cannot be used as the basis for the analysis of a child's pattern of errors in word recognition. We cannot develop a thorough program of word recognition instruction based on the Word Lists for one simple reason. The Word Lists are not actual reading. There is no coherent meaning in a list of words. Nor is there a grammatical structure in a word list; a reader cannot use context clues in word lists because the context does not exist. Frankly, based on the Word Lists alone, you will have no idea whether a child really knows what a word means. And until we observe children actually reading text, we will have no idea of the skills and strategies they use in the act of reading. All you are measuring at this point is whether the child can pronounce the word correctly. Needless to say, this is not the foundation upon which one wants to build an instructional program. We use the Word Lists because they can give us useful information about the starting point of *The Critical Reading Inventory*. But we cannot draw conclusions about a child's specific word recognition ability based solely on a list of words.

Form A: Narrative Passages

Form A of the CRI includes two narrative passages for each grade level, beginning with pre-primer and ending with senior high school. Narrative passages are designed to include the major story elements associated with a relatively simple story grammar. These include characters who experience a problem of some type, take action to solve that problem, and meet with varying levels of success in their progression toward a resolution. This action also occurs within a time frame and at a given place, either of which may influence actions or outcomes in the story. The story grammar structure enables the examiner to note which of the elements of a story are central and which are less so. Consequently, you will want to assess the effectiveness of a retelling by determining to what extent the child recalled or reacted to the central story elements. The scoring rubric for retellings that accompanies each passage is built upon these central story elements. In addition, we recommend that the first of the passages at each grade level be administered as oral reading and the second as silent reading. While acknowledging the contributions of miscue analysis research and the role of oral reading in that research (Goodman, 1970; Goodman & Burke, 1972), we also endorse Allington's (2001) observations about the authenticity of silent reading. Administering both oral and silent passages will offer you the opportunity to contrast the child's performance in two very different reading modes.

Form B: Informational Passages

Form B of the CRI includes two informational passages for each of the grade levels. These informational passages are designed to convey information to the reader, preferably information that is rather unusual so as to minimize the effects of prior knowledge insofar as that is possible. Informational passages tend to be more complex in structure than narrative passages, since they can be organized around one structure or a combination of structures, including comparison, contrast, cause–effect, examples, or enumeration, to name a few. Thus children's recall of and ability to react to informational text often depend upon the skills they demonstrate in organizing the information around a logical structure. This alone makes the evaluation of retellings of informational text both more challenging and a very rich source of diagnostic information about any given child's reading.

Oral Reading and Miscue Analysis

It is at this point that we are ready to make some judgments about the child's word recognition ability because there is a meaningful context and a somewhat authentic task involved. Now we can obtain some insight into how a child handles unknown words and uses (or fails to use) the meaningful context of a passage. We can, of course, make no claims that having a child read aloud in front of an adult who is furiously noting any deviation the child makes from the printed text is a very authentic reading situation. But it is the best you can do under the circumstances to gather some insights into the child's overall approach to word recognition. And it is the overall perspective on reading and word recognition that matters at this point, not the specific skills that the child appears to have deficiencies in.

It may be helpful to think that at least part of your work as test administrator will be to identify the child's place along a continuum of proficiency in word recognition during oral reading. At one end of the scale are those children who read with fluency, accuracy, good pacing, and expression and who use their ear for the grammar and meaning of the language to monitor their reading and insure that it "sounds right." These are the children who will immediately self-correct most miscues that violate the context of the passage, whether semantic (meaningful) or syntactic (grammatical). Consequently, they will earn consistently high marks when we assess their word recognition in the context of oral reading. Keep in mind that these high marks are no guarantee that these children have processed or critically reacted to what they have read. Rather, you will need to determine that later in the test.

Naturally, there are those children who stand at the opposite end of the word recognition spectrum. These children seem to see the task of oral reading as a one-word-at-a-time pronunciation task with little or no attention paid to the meaning or flow of the language. The oral reading of these children tends to sound as if they are reading a list of disconnected words with almost no intonation or inflection. The miscues that these children make are likely not to make sense in the context of their reading. These children may even create pseudo-words for the sake of attaching sounds to letters particularly if their instruction includes the use of non-words. Their self-correction and consequent monitoring for the sense of what they read may be virtually non-existent. Reading for these children appears to be word-by-word decoding and little more.

Of course, as you have probably suspected all along, there are innumerable gradations along the continuum of word recognition we have begun to define. But a key insight that you can hope to gain by engaging in *miscue analysis* of oral reading is that of the child's view of reading. And this is where self-corrections come into play. Self-corrections occur when children notice that what they have read aloud violates either the sense of the language (semantics) or the grammar of the language (syntax). That is, children who self-correct are indicating to us that they expect what they read to make sense and to fit in with the grammar of the language and that, when it does not, they know that they must do something to correct the situation. This is a healthy perspective on reading. For this reason, every self-correction is important for even if self-correction is inconsistent, it may indicate an emerging view of reading as a process of making meaning.

The Nature of Miscues

Aside from an overall assessment of a child's perspective on word recognition, you can also gain some insight into the child's view of the nature of reading by analyzing the miscues that have occurred (Goodman & Burke, 1972). Not all miscues are identical in terms of their importance or their interpretation. When you look at the overall pattern of a child's miscues (and a miscue is defined as any deviation from the printed text), you will find some that change the meaning intended by the author of the text but still fit in grammatically and make logical sense. For example, the text reads: *The boat was floating near the dock*, and Reader A reads: *The boot was floating near the dock*. The reader has clearly altered the intended meaning but has substituted a noun (boot) for a noun (boat) and thus has created a sentence that keeps the grammar of the language intact. The reader has also created a sentence that makes some logical sense. That is, it is entirely possible that a boot could be floating in the water near a dock. When we discuss the scoring of miscues in section 3, we will make the point that this type of miscue, even though it deviates from the actual text, can be classified as acceptable on the basis of both syntax and semantics. It can be viewed as the reader's attempt to make sense of the text. If a pattern of this type of miscue is evident, it suggests that the reader is developing some sensitivity to the structure of the language and expects what he or she has read to make sense. A pattern of these miscues does suggest that the reader is struggling to use words that fit logically or grammatically and is demonstrating some elements of a view of reading as meaning-making. In any case, you can observe whether the reader's confusion is cleared up by the context clues provided in the remaining text. If the story goes on to say that three boys jumped into the boat and the child continues to read "boot," then we have a different type of problem.

Reader B, on the other hand, may demonstrate a consistent pattern of miscues that violates both grammar and logic. For example, the text reads: *The man rode the horse into town*, and the child reads: *The man robe the horse into town*. In this case, the reader has substituted a noun (robe) for a verb (rode) and created a sentence that not only cannot exist grammatically but makes no sense at all. Such a miscue fails to maintain meaning and suggests that the reader is not attempting to make sense of the text. Readers who make significant numbers of such miscues and who do not self-correct are suggesting that they view reading as a simple decoding task wherein once the words have been pronounced, the task is over. The difference between Reader A and Reader B is significant. Children who demonstrate either of these patterns of miscues will require instructional programs that are very different from one another if you are to help them become better readers.

Of course, there are numerous variations in the nature of miscues. Our first concern at this point is to gather diagnostic information centering on whether children, in spite of the number and nature of their miscues, still attempt to make sense of what they read. Once we have answered that question, it will be worth our while to seek out patterns in the reader's approach to unknown words. In this case, the Miscue Analysis Worksheet (discussed in detail in section 3) will be helpful in that it provides a visual display of all of the miscues that the reader has made. It is then easier for us to identify when children use sounding out, for example, as their prime strategy in decoding words. Other children may take care to substitute syntactically appropriate words or word forms. Others may consistently attempt to identify word parts or break unknown words into syllables. When these strategies are used with some degree of consistency, it allows us to identify the reader's overall approach to the identification of unknown words and shed some light on the child's instructional needs.

We should note that readers will frequently use context clues and self-correct at reading levels that they find rather easy or only mildly challenging. However, when the reading becomes challenging they frequently focus more closely on graphophonemic cues and are much more likely to violate sense and language in their miscues. This is not a particularly unusual or alarming pattern.

In order to facilitate the analysis of miscues, we will ask the users of the CRI to calculate two different indices. The first of these is the Reading Accuracy Index (RAI). This is simply the percentage of the words in the passage that the child has read with complete faithfulness to the text. It is calculated by subtracting the number of scoreable miscues from the number of words in the passage and dividing by the number of words in the passage, then rounding off to the nearest whole number (see sample in Figure 2–1). The second of the indices is the Meaning Maintenance Index (MMI). This is calculated by subtracting the number of scoreable miscues that violate the sense or grammar of the text from the total number of words and dividing by the total number of words, then rounding off to the nearest whole number. Both of these indices will be discussed in greater depth in section 3: Administration and Scoring of the CRI.

Figure 2–1

Sample Calculations
of the RAI and MMI

Second Grade Silent: The Roller Coaster Ride is 244 words in length.

If Student A makes 13 scoreable miscues, the RAI is calculated in this way:

RAI

244 words − 13 scoreable miscues = 231 words read accurately

231 words ÷ 244 total words = 94.67%

= **95% is Student A's RAI for this passage (rounded off to the nearest whole number)**

If 7 of those 13 scoreable errors alter the grammar or meaning of the text, the MMI is calculated in the following way:

MMI

244 words − 7 meaning-altering errors = 237 words read in a manner that preserves meaning

237 words ÷ 244 total words = 97.13%

= **97% is Student A's MMI for this passage (rounded off to the nearest whole number)**

Note: To simplify the calculations, we have included a miscue calculator box with every selection in the CRI. Simply find the number of scoreable or meaning-violating miscues in that box and you will find the corresponding percentage for the RAI and the MMI respectively.

Comprehension Check and Retellings

We have included a statement in the Examiner's Copy of the CRI passages to introduce each assessment. In it we say, for example, prior to an oral reading passage: "*Please read this passage about ____ out loud for me. When you are finished, I'll take the passage away. Then I'll ask you to tell me about what you have read and what you think about it. After that, I'll ask you some questions about the passage.*" Once the reader has completed the oral reading, you will remove the Reader's Copy of the story and begin the assessment of comprehension.

There are several objectives for your use of the introductory statement. The most important of these is to give your readers a clear idea of what will be expected of them. Specifically, they will need to prepare to give a retelling and be ready to answer questions without the benefit of the passage in front of them. The objective in asking for the retelling is to try to determine which elements of the text that the reader felt were important enough to recall. You do not ask the child, for example, to "tell me everything you remember" about the story. You do not want to encourage the child to try to remember everything; at least some of the passage contains relatively incidental information or details. Instead you want to see what children decide to emphasize in their interaction with the text. If the retelling lacks logical structure or emphasizes elements that are really not central to the essence of the text (see examples of retellings and scoring rubrics in appendix B), then you have diagnostic information that can be very valuable in framing a course of instruction.

For each of the selections in the CRI, we have provided a Scoring Rubric. In it, you will find the elements of the text that are central to the intended message of the author, along with instructions for translating the retelling into a numerical value. We have found that most children will anticipate that you are asking for a verbatim recall of the details of the text. For this reason, you will extend an invitation ("Tell me about what you just read and what you think of it.") for the student to respond to the text. If the child does not provide a personal reaction in the initial retelling, we will repeat that invitation and specifically ask children what they thought of the story or text. Any hint of reaction to or interpretation of the message of the text is a very welcome sign of a child's development of a healthy view of reading. Even a laugh or grimace or any expression of like or dislike for the text can be viewed as a most encouraging personal response. But in order to receive credit for a personal response in the retelling scoring, readers must be able to support their responses.

Simply stating an opinion without an accompanying justification does not meet the criterion for a personal response.

After the unaided retelling of the selection, begin the open-ended questions that comprise the second phase of the Comprehension Check of the CRI. As we discussed earlier, we believe that remembering the details of what one has read is not a complete measure of one's understanding. Instead, comprehension involves the ability to remember what one reads, to think about it and to react to it. For these purposes, you will utilize three different types of items in our Comprehension Check.

Three Dimensions of Comprehension

1. *Text-Based Items*

As their name suggests, these items call for the children to recall information that they have read in the passage. In the CRI we have limited text-based items to include only information that is important in light of the central story elements or the key factual information related to the passage. Text-based items obviously have a single correct answer that is stated either verbatim in the passage or so nearly verbatim that the item would require little more than translation of the text into different words. In asking text-based items, you are attempting to find out if children can, without benefit of the passage in front of them, remember specific elements of what the author said. Text-based items assess memory for information, not the ability to use that information or even think about it. For example, in the narrative titled "The Race," the main character brags whenever he wins a race and he always wins. Consequently none of the other characters want to race against him. An example of a text-based item would be "Why didn't any of the other characters want to race against him?" Since the relationship between winning and bragging is stated explicitly in the text, an acceptable answer would be that the character bragged about his speed.

You will ask text-based questions because these items measure part of the reading comprehension process. Many children, however, have come to believe that memory of the facts is the essence of reading. Children with this view of reading are likely to perform much better in the text-based comprehension arena than they are at levels that require thought and analysis.

Specifically, text-based are those items that:
- require the reader to recall explicitly stated information from the text.
- involve the recognition of information in different words from those used in the original text. Such items require of the reader only a translation of the printed text.
- require the reader to identify relationships that exist between ideas in the text. Such items as these are not completely verbatim. For example, the text reads: *I was late for the meeting. My car wouldn't start.* A question such as: "Why was the character in the story late for the meeting?" would not be strictly verbatim only because the writer has not made the relationship explicit by using a grammatical marker (e.g., *because*). This is not to say that the skill of making such connections is unimportant. Classification of such an item as text-based is merely reflective of the fact that the writer assumes that at a given grade level, the reader can and will make the connection (Applegate, Quinn, & Applegate, 2002).

2. *Inference Items*

Inference items require children to draw logical conclusions about elements of the passage they have read. These items frequently demand that children draw upon experiences that they have, but the link between experience and text is more logical than interpretive. Consequently the inference items most often have a clearly identifiable link between experience and text. For example, in the narrative "The Race" cited above, the main character is finally beaten by a female cat who smiles when the main character challenges her to a race. An example of an inference item would be: "Do you think this is the first time this character has ever raced against anyone? Why or why not?" One can infer that the smile signifies a certain level of confidence that could be based on a record of prior successes. An inference item requires a response that is not stated verbatim in the text and that requires the child to do more than merely paraphrase the text. Children must link experience with the text to draw a conclusion about what they have read.

Inferences are those items that require the reader to:

- devise an alternative solution to a specific problem described in the text.
- describe a plausible motivation that explains a character's actions.
- provide a plausible explanation for a situation, problem, or action.
- predict a past or future action based on characteristics or qualities developed in the text.
- describe a character or action based on the events in a story.
- identify relationships between or among pieces of information in the text (Applegate, Quinn, & Applegate, 2002).

3. *Critical Response Items*

Critical response items require children to analyze, react, and respond to elements of the text based on their experiences and values. Because responses to these items can be based on the link between text and the child's unique experiences, critical response items do not generally lend themselves to single correct answers. What makes answers to critical response items correct is the children's ability to justify their responses by providing a clear and coherent rationale for their thinking. For example, in "The Race," the main character loses several rematches before he walks away angry. The cat who beat him is disappointed because she had hoped he would become her friend. An example of a critical response item would be: "Do you think he would have become her friend if she had let him win the race?" Both affirmative and negative responses could be justified, based on the character's actions and statements. Critical response items invite discussion about characters, situations, or ideas. But the reader must select information relevant to the question and ignore information that may be important in the story but not germane to the issue addressed in the question. If children can state opinions but are unable to discuss or support them, then their response is considered inadequate.

We regard critical response items as requiring the reader to:

- describe the lesson(s) a character may have learned from experience.
- judge the efficacy of the actions or decisions of a character and defend the judgment.
- devise and defend alternative solutions to a complex problem described in a story.
- respond positively or negatively to a character based on a logical assessment of the actions or traits of that character.
- use information in a passage in support of a judgment about the efficacy of an action or a solution to a problem (Applegate, Quinn, & Applegate, 2002).

The use of three types of items in the CRI will enable you to seek patterns of responses that give evidence of strengths and weaknesses. Many children will be able to answer only text-based items. Other children, particularly verbally proficient children, will respond effectively to text-based and critical response items, largely because they can link experiences to text and justify their thinking naturally. If that is all they can do, however, they will experience difficulty with inference items that require them to draw logical conclusions. Other children will recall and draw logical conclusions but may not have the slightest idea that they are supposed to think about and discuss ideas that are implied in the text. Thus the pattern of children's comprehension responses will often enable you to develop plans of instruction that are specifically geared to their needs.

Section 3

Administration and Scoring of *The Critical Reading Inventory*

Interviews

Student Interview

In the *Student Interviews* we distinguish between younger (kindergarten–4th grade levels) and older children (5th grade–senior high), but the overall intent is identical. The interview offers you an opportunity to develop a rapport with the child whom you are about to test. That rapport can often spell the difference between a thoroughly enjoyable intellectual interaction with a child or one that is terse or even unpleasant. In the course of the interview, you want to encourage the child to relax and to develop a sense of trust in you. For that reason, the interview should be conducted as an informal conversation rather than as an interrogation. But at the same time, the questions that you ask are not frivolous and the information that you obtain may be very significant when it comes time for you to piece together an educational profile of the child. Not surprisingly, the most significant items for you are often those that ask the child about reading, reading habits, and views of reading. The fact that you also interview parents and teachers gives you an opportunity to compare the child's responses to those of the adults who observe him on a regular basis.

You should record the child's responses to each interview question verbatim in the space provided on the Interview Form. You may also want to note any other interesting dimensions of the child's behavior in the margins of the form, such as the ease with which rapport was established, the level of confidence with which the child responded, or any signs of anxiety demonstrated by the child.

Parent/Guardian Interview

One objective of the *Parent/Guardian Interview* is to provide a counterpoint to the child's interview responses. But more important is your attempt to gain some insight into the level of parent awareness of, interest in, and support for the child's efforts in reading. The interview offers opportunities for the parent to react to the type of instruction and support the child is receiving at school as well as to demonstrate a level of awareness of any difficulties the child is experiencing in reading. The parent's responses should provide some idea of the extent of support that the child is receiving at home as well as some insight into the view of reading held by the parent. All of this information can become part of your overall picture of the child in a comprehensive analysis of reading performance.

Once again, the interview should be conducted insofar as possible as an informal conversation between a parent and a professional who is very much interested in helping that child to achieve higher levels of reading competence. Keep in mind that the interview questions are guidelines, and need not be followed slavishly. If conversations with parents or teachers are providing the information you need, you should feel free to abandon the interview format. The Parent/Guardian Interview would, of course, be most helpful if it were conducted face-to-face but you may often find yourself in situations where telephone interviews are the only viable option. Parent responses should be recorded in as much detail as is feasible on the Interview Form. Any observations about the parent's behavior, such as confidence level, willingness to elaborate, awareness of the child's school performance, etc. can be noted in the margins as well. Again we want to emphasize that the interview is not designed as a lockstep procedure. Any follow-up questions that can help to clarify responses will enhance the level of information you obtain from interviews. It is also worthwhile at this point to note that we need to avoid being judgmental about what we discover through the interviews. The more objective we remain in our analysis, the more value it will be likely to have for us and for the individuals whom we assess.

Teacher Interview

The *Teacher Interview* brings the third highly significant player in the child's reading journey into focus. You are most interested in gaining some insight into the teacher's view of reading, the instructional approaches regularly used in the classroom, and the match between that instruction and the child's needs. You will ask the teacher to briefly assess the child's ability, attitude, interests, needs, and behavior in the classroom and how these relate to reading. You will also ask the teacher to describe the instructional emphases that characterize her classroom, particularly with respect to the assessment of the child's reading comprehension. Your objective is to ascertain the level of the match between the child's needs as you determine them and the instruction that the child is receiving on a daily basis.

The Teacher Interview may need to be conducted via telephone, but personal interviews are always preferable. The interview is best conducted as a conversation between two professionals who have a mutual interest in the academic growth and achievement of a child. Responses should be recorded verbatim on the Interview Form, as with all interviews, along with any anecdotal observations that you may note in the course of your conversation.

Word Lists: Flash and Untimed

The technique for administering the *Word Lists* segment of the CRI is fairly straightforward. You will need the Reader's Copy of the Word Lists to show to the student and you will need the Examiner's Copy of the Word Lists to record the student's responses. Seated across from or beside the child (you will need to experiment here to decide which position is best for you), you will use a pair of 3×5 cards to expose each word for a 1-second period. We have found over the years that the easiest way to expose the words effectively is to drag the bottom card down the page far enough to expose the first word and then, after a silent count of "one thousand one," to drag the top card down to cover the word. You will need to be sure to cover the word after one second; a common error in the administration of this test is the tendency to leave the cards open for a period of time that exceeds one second. When that happens consistently, you are no longer gaining an estimate of sight vocabulary, the fund of words that the child instantly recognizes.

For younger elementary school children, begin the Word List assessment at the pre-primer level or, for upper level students, 2 or 3 years begin below their current grade level. It is good to begin the test at a level at which most children can achieve success so you will be able to observe them in a more relaxed situation. Of course, if your reader is a junior or senior high school student, beginning at the pre-primer level is not appropriate. If you have reason to believe that your reader is likely to be insulted by a list of very easy words, you will need to make the adjustment and choose a starting point that will, when possible, insure some level of success. There is, of course, always the possibility that some children will struggle even at the most elementary of levels.

In the interest of time efficiency, it is best to administer the Word Lists in this way:

1. Begin the Flash test at the point where you have reason to believe that the child will be successful but not insulted (usually 2 to 3 years below the child's grade

level). It is always possible, of course, that the child is a non-reader and must begin at the lowest possible levels.

2. Continue Flash exposure of words until the child makes a miscue. (Do not bother at this point to record each correct response.) Remember that if the child self-corrects in response to the Flash exposure of a word, we score the response as correct.

3. At the point of the miscue, open the cards that cover the missed word and say, "Let's take another look at that one."

4. While the child is trying to decode the word, record phonetically in the space next to that word in the "Flash" column what the child said in response to the Flash exposure.

5. Record the child's response after the Untimed exposure in the space next to that word in the "Untimed" column.

6. Discontinue the test once the child scores 70% or lower on the Flash portion of the lists.

6 wrong

Once you have selected a starting point, you are ready to begin the test administration. In the interest of conserving time, it really is not necessary to pause after each correct response to record a "+" on the examiner's copy of the Word Lists. Instead, record only what the child says that is incorrect; you can always fill in the plus signs later when you score the responses after the entire test has been completed. Some children may become overly concerned that you seem to be recording only when they respond incorrectly. If you see that this is happening, you may wish to place a mark on the line for every one of the child's responses.

During the test administration, if the child gives a response that is different from the word on the list, use the space provided next to that word in the Flash column to record what the child said. A phonetic spelling of the miscue will allow you or anyone reviewing your test materials to reproduce the child's performance later when you are analyzing test results. Any response that deviates from what is printed on the list and that is not attributable to variations in pronunciation or dialect is scored as a miscue. If the child responds with "I don't know," then record the letters DK in the space provided; if the child does not respond at all, record the letters NR for "no response."

Scoring of the word lists means simply calculating a percentage of words on the list that were identified correctly. Since every list has 20 words, the Flash score for a child who identifies 17 of the words in a list would be 85% for that particular level. If the child correctly identifies two additional words in the Untimed segment of the test, we simply add those two to the 17 correctly identified words in the Flash portion. Thus the child's score for Untimed at that level would be 95%.

20
÷0
14.0

Oral Reading

grade

Begin the Oral Reading segment of the CRI at the highest level where the child received a score of 100% on the Flash segment of the Word Lists. Again, your objective here is to arrive at your best estimate of a level that is unlikely to present great challenges because of oral reading and word recognition. Unlike the Word Lists, the reading segments at each level of the CRI take more time to administer and if you can acquire even a decent guess at an appropriate starting point, you may save yourself and your readers considerable time and effort. Once you have identified the appropriate level for your starting point, locate the Reader Copy of the story, present it to the child, and read the Introductory Statement that accompanies each passage to the child. Note that you are telling the child the topic of the passage but you are not engaging the child's background knowledge relative to the passage or attempting to help the child set a purpose for reading. At this point, you are in diagnostic mode and not in teaching mode and it is of great interest to you to observe for what purpose, if any, the child may read without any prompting. Furthermore, testing in this manner may predict how children will perform on formal, standardized measures where no activation of prior knowledge occurs.

It is a good idea to make use of a tape recorder to give yourself a second chance in case you should miss some elements of the reading. Even very experienced test users can find themselves hard pressed to keep up with a rapid reader who makes a significant number of miscues. In any case, it will take a significant amount of practice to master any notation system, but the effort will be worth it in terms of time saved and diagnostic information gathered.

Scoreable Miscues

With the Examiner's Copy of the story in front of you, listen carefully to the child's oral reading and carefully note any miscues the child makes in the albeit limited space provided. Because you are likely to be sharing some of your results with professors, teachers, colleagues, and/or fellow students, it is important to learn a common set of notations for different types of miscues. In this way, anyone looking at your Examiner's Copy will be able to reproduce the child's responses.

With this in mind, we need to identify during the test administration those miscue types that we will be noting for our miscue analysis. A miscue, once again, is defined as any deviation from the printed test, no matter how major or how minor. You will interpret the proportion of major and minor errors later when you score the measures. Miscues may be classified and noted as follows:

1. *Substitutions*—The most common type of miscue, a substitution occurs when a child reads a word that is different from the word in the text. To note a substitution, simply draw a line through the word that was read incorrectly and write the substitution in the space directly above the word. Once again phonetic spellings may be necessary for those occasionally creative substitutions that are not part of our language. *Reversals* are considered a variation on substitution.
2. *Omissions*—These occur when the child skips one or more words that are in the text. To note an omission, put an "X" through the word or words that have been skipped.
3. *Insertions*—These occur when the child includes in the oral reading a word or words that are not part of the text. Note insertions by writing the added words in the appropriate space in the passage and use an editor's carat: "^" to mark the place of insertion.
4. *Teacher-Provided*—Readers who cannot identify words will sometimes wait for help from the examiner. If a child cannot identify a word within a reasonable span of time (usually about 5 seconds or so), simply give the word to the child. When that occurs, note the event by circling the word that you have provided and noting it with the letters TP. Users of other informal inventories may note that examiners are often instructed to circle words that the reader has omitted. We have found that circling teacher-provided words gives the examiner a very useful visual cue to the presence of significant numbers of this particular miscue.
5. *Special Cases*—Occasionally a child will make *the same error on the same word* time after time throughout the passage. While you record every instance, you score only the first miscue. And so if a child reads *weather* for the word *water* and does so consistently for a total of 4 times throughout the passage, score it as only a single miscue. If a child *skips an entire line*, score it as only a single miscue although it is, of course, a very serious one.

Non-scoreable Miscues

There are several other types of miscues that we note during the oral reading but do not score. The most important of these is the self-correction. Self-corrections occur when readers notice that what they have said does not make sense or does not fit in with the grammar of the language. As we suggested earlier, self-corrections are indicators that the children are engaging in self-monitoring and that they may be developing or have developed a view of reading as something that must make sense. Consistent self-correction is an indicator that children, even if they are a bit sloppy in their oral reading, at least have a solid view of the act of reading as

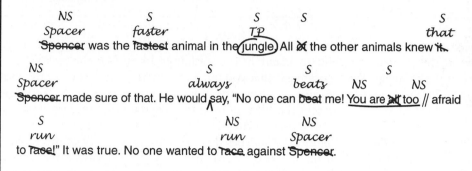

Figure 3–1

Sample Miscue
Notations

The child reads:

   Spacer was the faster animal in the . . . (waits for examiner to help) . . . jungle.
All the other animals knew that. Spacer made sure of that. He would always say, "No
one can beats me. You are too (long pause) You are too afraid to run!" It was true.
No one wanted to run against Spacer.

Miscue Notations

something that is supposed to make sense. In that respect, even a single self-correction is
significant and must be noted. Because of the speed of the Oral Reading test and the need for
the examiner to keep up the pace in noting miscues, you will almost certainly have begun to
note the miscue that the child eventually corrects. In the case of a self-correction, mark it
with a check mark or "SC" to indicate that the child has made the correction. Once again,
self-corrections are not scored as miscues.

   As noted in the discussion of the Word Lists, you should not score as miscues
variations in pronunciation or dialect and do not score miscues children make on *proper
names.* When readers *ignore punctuation marks* and read through the end of a sentence, for
example, without any change in pace or inflection we can note it by circling the skipped
punctuation mark. Do not, however, score it as a miscue. By the same token, you may note
in the margins of the Examiner's Copy certain characteristics of the child's oral reading, such
as word-by-word reading where the children read as if they are pronouncing a list of words,
or finger-pointing during reading, or pacing that is very fast or very slow. These notations
will prove useful if you are using the Oral Reading Fluency Rubric to assess the reader's fluency (see discussion of fluency, p. 27) but again these are not scoreable miscues. Children
will frequently *repeat what they have read* as they try to process information; again these can
be noted by underlining each part of the text that is repeated, but they are not considered
scoreable miscues. Hesitations or inappropriate pauses in reading can be noted with a slash
mark at the point of the hesitation as a mark of the overall fluency of the oral reading. In
Figure 3–1 we have included a sample of miscue notations with additional marks for scoreable miscues (S) and non-scoreable miscues (NS).

Miscue Analysis: Calculating and Interpreting the RAI and MMI

Scoring for the Miscue Analysis is a two-part process. First mark with an X in the margin
of the Examiner's Copy all scoreable miscues, whether they violate meaning and grammar
or not. Then tally all of these scoreable miscues. For a brief review of scoreable and non-
scoreable miscues, see Figure 3–2. Subtract this number from the number of words in the
passage to arrive at the number of words that the child has correctly identified in the context of the reading. Then divide the remainder by the total number of words in the passage, round it off to the nearest whole number, and that is the Reading Accuracy Index
percentage for that grade level. It is even easier to refer to the miscue chart that accompanies each passage. Simply find the number of scoreable miscues on the chart; the accompanying percentage will be the RAI.

Figure 3–2

Summary of Miscue
Scoring Conventions

Scoreable Miscues		Non-scoreable Miscues	
Substitutions	Self-corrections	Repetition of words	
Omissions	Repeated miscues	Ignored punctuation	
Insertions	Proper nouns	Finger-pointing	
Teacher-provided	Dialect differences	Subvocalization	

Next you must determine whether each of those scoreable miscues represents an attempt on the part of the child to maintain the meaningful sense or the grammatical integrity of the sentence. We recommend that you put a check mark beside any of the miscues that maintain a sense of meaning and leave the more serious miscues unchecked. The total of the checked X's will represent the MM (or meaning-maintaining) miscues while the total of the unchecked miscues will represent the MV (or meaning-violating) miscues.

Take the total MV, or the number of miscues that violated the meaning of the passage, and subtract that number from the number of the words in the passage. Then divide the remainder by the total number of words in the passage and round the result off to the nearest whole number. This will be the percentage for the Meaning Maintenance Index for that grade level. Once again, to simplify the calculation of both the RAI and the MMI, we have included a miscue chart for each reading passage in Form A and Form B. To use the chart, simply look up the total number of miscues to find the RAI percentage, and look up the MV or meaning-violating miscues to find the MMI. Then note the corresponding percentages on your recording form.

Note that the RAI and the MMI are simply screening devices that allow you to identify at a glance any potentially serious problems. They are not designed to replace the more detailed analysis that may be called for if a problem arises. The RAI itself is a fairly simple measure of the faithfulness of a child's oral reading with respect to the text. The RAI makes no attempt to distinguish between incidental miscues that do not change the meaning of the text and those that are more serious. That task is left to the MMI.

For example, a child who makes 10 scoreable miscues in a 200-word passage would have an RAI of 95% (200 words − 10 miscues = 190, divided by 200 total words). If each of those miscues turned out to be a fairly minor variation from the text, and each one indicated an effort to maintain both the sense and the syntax of the passage, we would have no MV miscues that distorted meaning. Thus our MMI would be 100%. If, however, 6 of those 10 miscues were MV and altered the meaning of the text, we would have an MMI of 97% (200 words − 6 meaning-violating miscues = 194, divided by 200 total words).

As the test progresses, you will need to pay attention to the reader's word recognition and comprehension levels in order to guide your decisions about whether to continue to test. In the interest of the most efficient use of testing time, you will not have the opportunity to calculate actual scores while the reader waits for the testing to resume. Calculations will have to wait until you have completed the testing and you have the opportunity to score responses and even to listen to tape recordings as needed. But as a rule of thumb, when readers begin to struggle seriously with general word recognition and when they begin to comprehend only half of what they read, it is probably time to end the testing.

Miscue Analysis Worksheet

The *Miscue Analysis Worksheet* (MAW) is an optional form that may be used to visually represent patterns in the child's word recognition strategies. It can also indicate at a glance whether there are significant changes in these strategies as the reading material becomes more challenging. Some users of the CRI may find it most useful to facilitate the analysis of miscues by summarizing them on the Worksheet.

In order to use the MAW effectively, you must have estimated tentative reading levels for the Highest Independent, Highest Instructional, and Frustration levels. To facilitate the analysis of miscues, as well as to prepare for the use of the Worksheet, we suggest that you use the margins on the Examiner's Copy of the selections to tabulate all miscues.

The child reads:

Spacer was the faster animal in the . . . (waits for examiner to help) . . . jungle. All the other animals knew that. Spacer made sure of that. He would always say, "No one can beats me. You are too (long pause) You are too afraid to run!" It was true. No one wanted to run against Spacer.

Miscue Notations	Type	Explanation
Spacer *faster* *TP* ~~Spencer~~ was the ~~fastest~~ animal in the (jungle).	✗ ✓ S ✗ TP	Spacer/Spencer is non-scoreable—proper noun faster/fastest jungle
that Spacer All ✗the other animals knew ~~it~~ ~~Spencer~~ made sure	✗ ✓ O ✗ ✓ S	of that/it
always *beats* of that. He would ⌃say, "No one can ~~beat~~ me! <u>You are</u>	✗ ✓ I ✗ ✓ S	always beats/beat
run ~~All~~ too//afraid to ~~race~~!" It was true. No one wanted to	✗ ✓ O ✗ ✓ S	all run/race
run *Spacer* ~~race~~ against ~~Spencer~~.		repeated substitution—non-scoreable

Figure 3–3

Sample Miscue Analysis

As a quick review, you should complete the following steps:

1. When you come to a scoreable miscue, record it with an X in the margin of the Examiner's Copy of the text.
2. Evaluate each miscue and determine the extent to which it reflected an attempt on the part of the child to make sense of the text.
3. If the miscue was an attempt to make the reading meaningful, place a check mark next to the X.

When you complete this process, you will be able to easily tally the scoreable miscues and meaning-violating miscues. Locate those numbers in the Miscue Chart, and determine the student's RAI and MMI. In the example in Figure 3–3, the first scoreable miscue was a substitution of *faster* for *fastest*. Since the substitution maintained meaning, you would record X✓. Keep in mind that teacher-provided miscues reflect no attempt on the part of the reader to utilize context or make meaning so they cannot be evaluated from a meaning-making perspective. However, all other miscues must be analyzed to determine if they do reflect attempts to use the context. You then *total all of the unchecked* (meaning-violating) miscues and locate the number of miscues and the accompanying percentage figure in the Miscue Chart on the Examiner's Copy of the texts. This percentage represents the MMI.

Examining Miscues: Using the Miscue Analysis Worksheet

After you have administered the entire test and you have completed the initial calculations of the RAI and MMI, you are ready to perform an even more careful analysis of the miscues that the child has made. The first thing you do is record the miscues that the reader has made at his Highest Independent, his Highest Instructional and his Frustration level in the first two columns (see another sample in Figure 3–4) of the Miscue Analysis Worksheet

Miscue Analysis Worksheet

Student __John__   Grade __5th__   Age __10.8__

Highest Independent Level __2nd__   Highest Instructional Level __N/A__   Frustration Level __3rd__

Miscue	Text	MM	MV	Non		Miscue	Text	MM	MV	Non		Miscue	Text	MM	MV	Non
again	against	X	-	-								hears	heard	X	-	-
and	But	X	-	-								vis-iting	visiting	-	X	X
Growled	grown	X	-	-								ez-cited	excited	-	X	X
												a	his	X	-	-
												he	-	X	-	-
												ru-sha	rush	-	X	X
												ju-lupt	gulped	-	X	X
												touring	Turning	-	X	-
												po-sto-les	Postholes	-	X	X
												tru-dy-ing	Trudging	-	X	X
												to	toward	X	-	-
												her	to	X	-	-
												early	eager	X	-	-
												too	so	X	-	-
												rep-lied	replied	-	X	X
Totals																

RAI __96%__   MMI __100%__   RAI ____   MMI ____   RAI __95%__   MMI __98%__

RAI: Count the number of scoreable miscues from Column 1 and use the Miscue Chart for that passage to obtain the RAI.
MMI: Count the number of meaning-violating miscues and use the Miscue Chart for that passage to obtain the MMI.
Non: The number of meaning-violating miscues that were Non-words.
MM: Miscue that represents an attempt to maintain the sense of the text.
MV: Miscue that violated the sense of the text.

Figure 3–4

Sample Miscue Analysis Worksheet

(MAW). Be sure to record only scoreable miscues in these columns. For those miscues that you have checked to indicate that they are meaning-maintaining, place a check in column 3 under MM. Since all remaining miscues are those that have violated meaning, put a check in column 4 under MV. Remember that teacher-provided words are always regarded as meaning-violating. If any of these meaning-violating miscues are non-words, place a check mark next to that word in column 5 under Non.

At this point you will have a complete visual display of the reader's miscues and the nature of many of those miscues. It will now be a fairly straightforward process to examine those miscues and determine if the reader is using a particular pattern of strategies in the decoding of unknown words. We will want to determine if the reader is: (a) over-using phonological clues in decoding, (b) attending to syntactic relationships by substituting nouns for nouns, etc., or (c) utilizing word analysis strategies by attempting to break words down into their smallest component parts. For instance, we find in the example in Figure 3–4 that the reader experiences few difficulties at his independent level but uses non-words frequently when he attempts to read at his frustration level. Some users of the CRI may be able to obtain the same information by analyzing the miscues as they are noted on the Examiner's Copy. But the MAW can be particularly useful for teaching miscue analysis techniques or for simply providing an overview of the bigger picture of an important dimension of the child's reading.

Fluency

Allington (1983) has identified reading fluency as an important factor for reading comprehension. In his view, a child's fluency and automaticity of word identification contributes to comprehension by freeing up mental resources that would otherwise be occupied with word identification. Once these resources are available, readers can then utilize them to concentrate on comprehension and thoughtful response. Fluency is composed of rate, accuracy, and expression and has been cited as an important goal for reading instruction (Allington, 1983, 2001; Rasinski, 1989).

Teachers using the CRI can easily evaluate fluency in a qualitative manner by taking anecdotal notes during the student's oral reading. Particular attention should be paid to the reader's expression, phrasing, and attention to punctuation during oral reading. CRI users can also time oral reading and compare a reader's rate to well-established average reading rate tables (Harris & Sipay, 1990, p. 634). Qualitative analysis and measurement of reading rate can contribute, along with the RAI and MMI, to a thorough assessment of a reader's fluency.

For users who prefer a more structured approach to the assessment of fluency, the CRI includes an Oral Reading Fluency Rubric (see p. 122) designed to help users assign a numerical value to a reader's fluency. Oral reading fluency should be assessed at the reader's instructional level, the level that presents challenges to, but does not overwhelm, the reader. It is difficult to see how the assessment of fluency in response to very easy reading or very difficult reading is likely to add a great deal to the overall assessment of any reader.

But most important of all, fluency should never be discussed in isolation from comprehension. Although fluent readers often comprehend materials effectively, that is not always the case. Nor is it true that children who are "disfluent" are necessarily weak in comprehension. For a specific example, listen to the reader on the audio CD that accompanies the CRI. Word recognition and comprehension function in a complex interaction that can vary widely among readers. It is tempting to conclude that we must teach all readers fluency before they can "free up the resources" to truly comprehend, but such a conclusion would be a profound oversimplification. It is because the interaction between fluency and comprehension is so complex that we must avoid conceptualizations that are simple and linear. It is equally tempting to conclude that poor readers need more intensive drills in sound, letter, and word instruction. Research has suggested that good readers are more likely to be given instruction that focuses on meaning and to have their teachers emphasize the need for oral reading to make sense and sound right (Allington, 1983). In short, fluency assessed apart from comprehension and language is likely to be of little value in contributing to the picture of any reader's functioning.

Silent Reading

Asking children to read passages silently offers them the chance to focus more of their attention on comprehension since they are relieved of the need to demonstrate their ability to pronounce aloud the words in the text. It also offers users of the CRI the chance to observe whether readers can take advantage of the situation and focus more effectively on comprehension. Silent reading forces readers to read without the help that can be obtained through teacher-provided words; it is not unusual for younger children or children with severe word recognition problems to demonstrate an inability to deal with text silently. Subvocalization during silent reading is common in such circumstances. But above all, silent reading offers the CRI user the opportunity to observe children reading alone, to note their habits and idiosyncrasies, and to compare their comprehension performance after oral reading and silent reading.

Comprehension Assessment: Retellings

After you have read the Introductory Statement and the children complete either the oral or silent reading, ask them to "Tell me about what you have just read and what you think about it" and record their retellings verbatim. Note that we specifically ask the child to respond to the text, express an interest in it, or react to the content. We are simply issuing an invitation to do so. It is of vital interest to you to determine if the children will themselves see reading as a task that requires them to use their background knowledge and thinking skills. Children who view reading as a passive activity will almost never accept the invitation to comment about "what they thought" of the passage or its content. If they do not, we repeat the invitation after the initial retelling as noted on the Examiner's Copy of the test.

We would advise you to have a tape recorder available for this part of the test because children who speak very quickly or give a lengthy retelling can severely challenge your hand and wrist strength as you try to write everything down. The purpose of the retelling is to ascertain, without the benefit of the jog in memory that accompanies the asking of open-ended questions, what the child has determined is important enough to remember and how it is organized. When you score the test, you will analyze the retellings both qualitatively and quantitatively as another window into the thinking of the child during and after reading. As an aid to analysis of the retellings, use the rubric provided in the Examiner's Copy of each story and look for signs of how the child perceived the structure of the text, the level of importance of the ideas included in it, and any personal response to the text the child may have expressed. You will often gain a great deal of insight into the organizational processes used by the child in your analysis of the child's retelling (see examples in appendix B).

Scoring Retellings

Scoring of retellings in the CRI follows the point scale summarized in the Retelling Rubric Box that accompanies each reading passage (see sample scoring in Figure 3–5). Use the story structure rubric (narrative) or the macro concept structure (informational) to calculate the student's retelling score. We suggest that you mark a "+1" next to each category listed in the rubric that you judge as having been addressed in the retelling. If the category is partially covered, you may find it necessary to award partial credit. Use the score descriptions to locate the appropriate numerical value for the child's retelling. Once again, because there are several variables involved in the calculation of the final score, you may find it necessary to award half-credit scores such as 2.5 or 3.5.

A retelling that receives a 4-point rating is one that includes all key story elements and a well-supported personal response. A score of 3 represents a retelling that includes all or nearly all major elements but no supported personal response; it is, by that definition, a complete literal retelling and no more. A score of 2 points includes at least one logical connection between two elements of the story. A 2-point retelling will include some minor errors in the details of the story, and some of the elements of the story may be somewhat disjointed. One-point retellings are largely disjointed or disorganized renderings of literal elements of the story that contain errors or significant omissions. Finally, no points are given for a retelling that bears little or no resemblance to the text, or that provides a story title

Child's Retelling:

"Spencer brags to the other animals about how fast he is and tries to get them to race so he can brag more. Then a new family moves in, and he asks them to race and Annie races him and wins. All the animals were happy 'cause they thought he would stop bragging but Spencer was mad and he went away. He came back the next day and bragged about how high he could jump and all the animals rolled their eyes and groaned." *Examiner:* "Tell me what you thought about the passage." *Child:* "It was about a cat who bragged a lot."

Scoring and Discussion

This is a very good retelling that includes the key characters, the character's goal, and all five steps in the problem-solving process. The only piece that is missing is the personal response; in its place the reader simply relates a very brief summation of the story.
Score: 3.0

1.	**Key Characters and Setting:** Spencer, other animals, and Annie who moved into jungle.	+1
2.	**Character's Problem or Goal:** Spencer wants to be the fastest runner in the jungle and to brag about it	+1
3.	**Problem-Solving or Goal-Meeting Process:**	
	• Spencer brags and gets others to race with him so that he can brag more.	+1
	• Annie moves in and Spencer races with her.	+1
	• Spencer loses the race.	+1
	• Spencer walks away angrily and Annie is sad because she had wanted a friend.	+1
	• Spencer returns the next day and brags about jumping.	+1
4.	**Personal response:** Any positive or negative response to the characters or events in the story; any reaction to the humor or sadness in the story; any indication of positive or negative reaction to the story as a whole.	0

Rubric:
4 = Complete retelling includes characters, problem/goal, and all five steps in the problem-solving process and a well-supported personal response.
3 = Retelling includes characters, problem/goal, and all five steps in the problem solving process but has no personal response.
2 = Retelling includes characters, problem/goal, and three or four steps in the problem-solving process; some key factual errors or omissions. Add ½ point for a well-supported personal response.
1 = Retelling omits either characters or problem; includes one or two steps in the problem-solving process, but the account is disjointed and includes factual errors or serious omissions. Add ½ point for a well-supported personal response.
0 = Provides a title or topic statement but shows no real awareness of the character's problem and how the problem is worked out.

Figure 3–5

Sample Retelling Scoring Rubric

that the reader cannot elaborate upon. For more examples of retellings and application of scoring criteria, CRI users can consult appendix B.

The Nature of Retellings

The optimum retelling, that done by our hypothetical ideal reader, includes all of the important elements in the text and also includes a well-supported personal response to the text. This is a rather tall order for most children in that surprisingly few children respond spontaneously to what they read. Most children who are familiar with the concept of an unaided retelling will strive to faithfully reproduce the information that they have read. They will often do so without commenting on whether they enjoyed reading it or not, whether it matched their belief system, or whether they found it in any way interesting. For this reason, we will often find it necessary to remind readers that we would like to hear their personal response.

While you will use the Retelling Rubric Box that accompanies each passage as a means of assigning a numerical score to each retelling, it is important to emphasize that the retelling is only one piece of information that you can use in the analysis of a child's reading performance. Seldom is the retelling sufficient in itself as a diagnostic tool although it can offer you glimpses of the child's thinking processes that can be gained in no other way. Retellings are often insufficient in themselves because of extraneous variables that may affect a child's performance on any retelling. For example, the child's confidence and willingness to elaborate on responses may be affected by the rapport developed with the examiner. If a child is characterized by a fear of making incorrect responses, you may obtain nothing more than minimal retellings from that child. Children with little confidence in their ability to verbalize or explain their answers may score very poorly on retellings. Children who are simply unaccustomed to doing a retelling and more comfortable with the memory jog that comprehension questions provide may do poorly as well. In any of these cases, it is not necessarily the child's reading ability that is affecting the retellings. For this reason alone, it is important that we verify, insofar as possible, any observations we make in one area of the test with performance in all other related areas.

Comprehension Questions

You then ask the comprehension questions that accompany each passage in the order in which they occur. For each question, record the child's response verbatim in the space provided on the Examiner's Copy. This is another instance of furious writing on your part but it is well worth it in the long run. We have found that at this point a tape recorder provides an excellent and sometimes very necessary backup system. It is an impossible task to try to rely on your memory when it comes time to analyze the child's performance on the CRI. You can take one shortcut, however. If the child's response is the same as the suggested sample response that accompanies each item, simply underline that part of the suggested answer that the child used. This is likely to save you at least some writing, particularly for the literal items for which there is usually only one correct response.

There is yet another major difference between the CRI and most standardized tests and that is the extensive use of open-ended questions on the CRI Comprehension Check. Open-ended questions are really an attempt to open a window on the child's thinking processes. In the course of responding to open-ended questions, however, children may be vague, evasive, fuzzy in their thinking, or simply lacking in confidence in their ability to express themselves verbally. In these cases the examiner is encouraged to ask follow-up questions or probe to elicit more information or more clarity from the children. When you do ask a probe question, you should note the question by a circled question mark when you are recording the child's responses. Then record the child's response to the probe immediately after the question mark. Because the CRI is an assessment that attempts to measure the maximum performance of the reader, we do give the child credit for any correct answers given in response to a probe. (See sample probe questions in Figure 3–6.)

A need for many probes may be evidence of imprecision in thought or expression that may be addressed in your instructional plan for that child. In order to know when it is appropriate to probe for more information, it is absolutely essential that the examiner be familiar with the CRI selections and the range of acceptable answers for at least the oral and silent passages at all levels. For this reason, you are likely to become a more effective diagnostician the more that you administer the CRI. If you are a beginner with the CRI, time allotted for reading and studying selections, questions, and sample responses will be time well spent. The more familiar you are with the test materials, the more efficient and effective your testing will be. And because your time with any given child may be limited, you will need to be aware of testing techniques that make the best use of that time. An examination of the probe questions noted in the Case Studies in section 6 will also be helpful to you in identifying appropriate times to ask probe questions.

Once you have completed the Comprehension Check for the oral reading selection for a particular grade level, you progress immediately to the silent reading selection in that same grade level. Once again, you *use the printed introductory statement to introduce the reading* and then you observe while the child reads silently. You may note at this time any behaviors that suggest themselves as worthy of note, such as subvocalization, fingerpointing at words and lines, unusually fast or slow pace of reading, etc.

Figure 3–6

Sample Probe Questions
on the CRI

Example 1
In the second grade story entitled "The Race," the child is asked, "What did the animals do when Annie won the race?" She responds, "They were happy." The examiner notes that the child is correct based on the information in the story, but that she has not really addressed the text-based question about what the animals do. She follows up with a probe question: "Good, but can you tell me what the animals did that let you know they were happy?" When the child responds, "They cheered her," the examiner records the response as correct.

Example 2
In the same story, the child is asked, "Do you think this was the first time that Annie had ever raced against anyone?" She responds, "No, because she knew she would win." This response hints that it was confidence behind Annie's smiling acceptance of the challenge to race, but the link is not clear. Thus the examiner follows up with the question: *"But why would Annie think she would win?"* When the child responds with, "She had probably raced other people before and so she knew she was fast," the logical link is complete.

The Comprehension Check after silent reading is identical to that following oral reading. That is, you ask the child for a retelling and then follow with the open-ended comprehension questions.

Scoring Comprehension Questions

Scoring comprehension questions can range from the very simple to the very complex depending upon the nature of the reader's responses. Most scoring of text-based items is quite straightforward. Either the child remembers the details or does not. One notable exception occurs when readers interpret a text-based question as calling for an inference or critical response. A probe question redirecting the reader to "what the passage said" is usually very effective in eliciting an appropriate response. But inference and critical response items can often be quite another matter. Even in those inference items that have a single correct response, the range of creative ways in which the children can express their ideas can often present a challenge to scorers.

For this reason, we include sample correct responses in the Examiner's Copy for each item in the CRI but we encourage you not to follow them slavishly. They are by no means the only answers that can be correct. Often you will find yourself considering a logical interpretation of both the question and the response. This individual variation in scoring is the most often cited of the weaknesses of any informal reading inventory but it is also its most valuable strength. You simply need to keep in mind that the ultimate objective for the user of the CRI is to gather diagnostic information that will make your instructional program more effective in the long run.

Scoring critical response questions can be even more challenging than scoring literal and inferential ones. A good answer to a critical response item is one that provides solid and logical support from the text for one's ideas. It is not sufficient to answer a critical response item by stating an opinion; in the CRI, opinions are of no consequence unless readers can back them up with reasons. It is up to you to make judgments about the extent to which readers have supported their responses. CRI users may wish to consult appendix A for sample responses and scoring. An examination of a few sample responses should clarify what is meant by effective and ineffective responses.

As we have noted, you may at any time choose to ask children probe questions in search of more complete or precise responses. Readers are not penalized when they arrive at a correct response as a result of a probe. We are interested more in gaining insights into how the child is thinking than in the "fairness" of the scoring. You are also free to assign partial credit to any of the child's responses. It is often possible for the examiner to recognize in retrospect that a child's response may be logical but also incomplete.

Scoring involves once again the calculation of a simple percentage. For both the oral and silent passages, simply add the number of correct responses (or partially correct responses) and divide by the number of comprehension questions used at that grade level. To arrive at the average comprehension for a grade level, add the oral and silent percentages, divide by 2, and round off to the nearest whole number. For your convenience, we have included percentage boxes in section 7 to facilitate your calculations.

Administering the Listening Comprehension Test

You should administer the Listening Comprehension assessment of the CRI to those children whose Instructional Level is lower than their current grade level placement. In such cases, administer the Listening Comprehension test by selecting a passage at the grade level where the child is currently placed. Your purpose is to assess whether children are able to comprehend adequately in their current classroom and thus if they are benefiting from oral instruction in the classroom. You may also use the Listening Comprehension for children whose word recognition problems appear to be overwhelming their ability to comprehend text.

We have found that the easiest way to phase into the listening comprehension test is to simply say to the child, "Since you have read to me it is only fair that I should read to you for a change. When I'm finished, I'll ask you to tell me about what you've heard and I'll ask you questions, just as I did when you read." Then you proceed to read one passage per grade level, followed by a retelling and the comprehension questions.

Lookbacks

It is clear that the practice of taking the text from students and then asking them to retell and to respond to questions about what they have just read taxes the memory. It is equally clear that as diagnosticians we want to know how and where readers have allocated their memory resources in response to text. But it is also enlightening to assess the extent to which readers are able to function when the sheer memory task is relieved and they are allowed to look back at the text they have just read. In other words, we want to see if their test performance has been largely due to difficulties with memory or difficulties with comprehension.

Users of the CRI may wish to expand their assessment to include *lookbacks*. To do so, you would simply return the text to students after they have responded to all comprehension questions related to the passage. Since a student who has responded correctly to all questions has already demonstrated a solid level of comprehension, we would normally use lookbacks only when a reader has experienced some difficulty with several of the comprehension questions. Lookbacks are likely to be particularly helpful in assessing the comprehension of students who tend to respond frequently with "I don't know" or "I don't remember." To utilize lookbacks, simply return the passage to the reader and say, "Let's see if looking back at the passage can help you with some of these questions." Then we would repeat those questions with which the reader experienced initial confusion. Any additional responses the student makes can be noted on the Examiner's Copy. A simple slash and a notation of L will make it easy for you to distinguish between unaided responses and responses that followed lookbacks (see example in Figure 3–7).

Figure 3–7

Sample Notations After Lookback

> **Comprehension Questions**
>
> 1. Why was everyone in the family excited about the vacation in Florida?
>   Text-based: It was their first family vacation; first trip to Florida.
>   *I don't really remember.*
>   *L // It was their first trip to Florida*
>
> Located information quickly and efficiently.

Our objective in utilizing the lookback convention is, of course, to add to our overall diagnostic profile of the reader. During lookbacks, we want to see if the reader is able to make use of the text in a meaningful way. Some readers will, for example, quickly and easily locate information relevant to the comprehension item, particularly if the item is text-based. Others will struggle and may even read the entire passage in search of helpful information. Some readers will demonstrate clearly during lookbacks that they believed their initial response to be more than sufficient to answer the question. Still others will read in an attempt to locate answers directly in the text, even when the item calls for them to draw conclusions or respond to ideas in the text. All of these types of behaviors, of course, add valuable information to our overall diagnostic profile of any reader.

It goes without saying that rereading the entire passage in search of answers to questions is a poor strategy and we would normally stop using lookbacks with students who consistently reread passages. We would gain little or no further information about these readers as a consequence of lookbacks.

Comprehension after lookbacks can be considered a more authentic type of assessment since it replicates more closely the kind of reading that a student will normally engage in. But we must realize that lookbacks will provide some readers with clues that their responses are wrong or incomplete. For readers with a great deal of confidence, or readers who project a high level of confidence, the realization that all is not well may be disconcerting. In these cases we would generally stop the use of lookbacks as well.

But while lookbacks may give us information that will help us in the process of estimating a student's reading levels, scores after lookbacks should not be used as the basis for these estimates. While the authenticity of such reading is not in question, we simply do not have available data that relates comprehension after lookbacks to actual classroom performance in reading. Nor are traditional criteria for estimating reading levels based on comprehension after lookbacks.

Lookbacks are particularly valuable in the assessment of students who over-rely on memory in their attempts to comprehend text. Retellings that include scattered details, significant gaps or clear attempts at verbatim recall of the text are telltale signs of such readers. If their inferential and critical response comprehension improves significantly after lookbacks, then we can include in their instructional program tools to help them use their memory more effectively. These might include story grammars, graphic organizers, sketch to stretch, the use of post-it notes to encourage self-questioning, or even more extensive prereading activities during instruction. Readers who do well in text-based comprehension but who do not improve in response-based comprehension after lookbacks will require a different approach. They are likely to benefit from prereading that builds on an examination of their own experiences as these relate to the text and their own ideas related to the underlying significance of the text. Such an approach is designed to lead readers to a full-scale reexamination of their view of reading itself.

Using the Recapitulation Record

The Recapitulation Record simply provides a summary of the child's overall performance on the CRI and facilitates some relevant analyses of those scores as well. The Recapitulation Record, as the name suggests, provides a recap of the child's performance that is useful for what we will discuss in section 4 as Numerical Interpretation. An examination of the Recapitulation Record can provide us with an overview of any child's performance. But the Recapitulation Record should actually be used in conjunction with a careful analysis of the child's comprehension responses. The more sources of information you bring to bear on the case, the more effective your proposed program of instruction is likely to be. And, as we will see, there is far more information available to you in the CRI beyond the numbers alone that can give you valuable insights into any child's strengths and weaknesses in reading. After you have graded and calculated all scores for the CRI, you are ready to begin to fill out the Recapitulation Record.

Word Lists. Simply transcribe the Flash and Untimed percentages you have calculated and place them in the appropriate boxes under the heading Word Lists, as illustrated in Figure 3–8.

Word List				
Level	Flash	Untimed	RAI	MMI
Pre-Primer	100	100	99	100
Primer	90	95	98	99

Figure 3–8

Sample Box 1 From
Recapitulation Record

Comprehending and Responding to Text				
Oral Comp. %	Retelling Score	Oral Text-based	Oral Inference	Oral Critical
		3/3	2/3	2/2
		3/3	1/3	1.5/2

Figure 3–9

Sample Box 2 From
Recapitulation Record

Comprehending and Responding to Text

Oral Reading. After you have analyzed the miscues the child made during oral reading, you can calculate an RAI and MMI score for each level the child has completed. Place these numbers in the appropriate columns on the Recapitulation Record (see Figure 3–8).

After you have graded the oral comprehension questions, calculate the overall oral reading comprehension percentage score and put it in the first column as illustrated in Figure 3–9. Then move to the retelling. Place the score you have assigned in the box labeled Retelling Score. Then fill in the number of questions that were correctly answered in each of the three question types.

When you have completed the oral comprehension, simply move on to the silent passage and follow the same procedures (see Figure 3–10). Then calculate the average percentage value of the Oral and Silent Comprehension and put it in the appropriate column. Repeat the process for all additional passages, oral and silent. Finally, identify the grade level used for Listening Comprehension (if administered), and fill in the comprehension percentage and number of items in each category for that level.

Estimating Reading Levels. After the completion of the recapitulation table, you use the recorded data to identify tentative reading levels (see section 4 for a complete discussion of level-setting). We suggest that you use the Betts' criteria listed in Table 3–1 as the basis for these levels.

Recording Scores in the Analysis Table. Once you have estimated reading levels, you are ready now to transcribe the scores from the examiner's copy of the CRI to the Level One Numerical Interpretation tables in the lower half of the Recapitulation Record (see Figure 3–11). At this level you will be looking primarily at the story told by the numbers you have gathered and not necessarily at the reasons why the reader obtained these scores. That will occur in the Level Two Interpretation. The Level One table is structured so as to

Silent Comp. %	Retelling Score	Silent Text-based	Silent Inference	Silent Critical	Average Oral & Silent	Listening Comp. %
81	2.5	3/3	2/3	1.5/2	85	—
75	2.0	2/3	2/3	2/2	73	—

Figure 3–10

Sample Box 3 From Recapitulation Record

Table 3–1 Betts' Criteria for Estimating Reading Levels

Level	Average of Oral and Silent Comprehension	Reading Accuracy Index (RAI)
Independent	90%	99%
Instructional	75%	95%
Frustration	50%	90%
Listening	NA	75%

promote a systematic look at the data and to raise some important questions about contrasts in reading performance.

Word Lists and Miscue Analysis. After you have estimated the child's reading levels, transcribe these levels in column 2, 3, and 4 for the Highest Independent, Highest Instructional, and the Frustration level, respectively. Begin with scores from the Highest Independent level and transcribe the Flash, the RAI, and the MMI for that level from the main body of the Recapitulation Record. Then retrieve the MM and MV scores from the record of miscues in the oral reading Examiner's Copy for that level. The same data will be included on the Miscue Analysis Worksheet if you used that instrument. The only additional analysis that we ask at this point is that you identify the number of MV or meaning-violating miscues in the child's reading that represented non-words and list that number under the Non heading. Repeat this process for the Highest Instructional level and the Frustration level.

When this part of the table is complete you will have at a glance a contrast between the child's performance with words in isolation and words that the child has encountered in the context of actual reading. This part of the table will also facilitate the contrast between attempts to make meaning and failure to do so, with particular attention to the use of non-words. These contrasts are designed to provide insight into the child's view of reading.

Comprehension Scores and Retelling. For this part of the analysis, transcribe the oral and silent comprehension percentage score for the independent level and average the two. Then take the oral and silent retelling scores for the same level and average the two. Repeat this process for the instructional and frustration levels.

The key contrast that this part of the table is designed to highlight is the difference that might exist between the child's unaided recall of the text (the retelling average) and the structured assessment provided by specific comprehension questions. You can also compare at a glance the differences that might exist between the child's oral and silent reading comprehension. This contrast is becoming increasingly important as national, state, and local measures rely more and more on silent reading as their means of assessment. Any significant changes that occur in the child's pattern of comprehension between independent and instructional or even frustration levels can be invaluable in setting up an effective program of instruction for the child.

Oral Comprehension and MMI. Transcribe the oral comprehension score and the MMI from the body of the Recapitulation Record for the Highest Independent level, the Highest Instructional level, and the Frustration level.

This segment of the table facilitates the observation of any discrepancy that might exist between overall comprehension following oral reading and attempts at meaning-making on the part of the reader. For example, a child who directs most of her energy toward accuracy and fluency and fails to comprehend effectively may be signaling us about a view of reading that does not include thinking about or responding to text. While MMI and oral comprehension are generally quite similar at the independent level, discrepancies at the instructional and/or frustration levels are usually a clear signal of the need for instructional intervention.

Level One Interpretation

Level:	Highest Independent Level _____			Highest Instructional Level _____			Frustration Level _____		
Word List and Miscue Analysis:	Flash _____ MM _____	RAI _____ MV _____	MMI _____ Non-words _____	Flash _____ MM _____	RAI _____ MV _____	MMI _____ Non-words _____	Flash _____ MM _____	RAI _____ MV _____	MMI _____ Non-words _____
Comprehension and Retelling Scores		Comp. % _____	Retelling _____		Comp. % _____	Retelling _____		Comp. % _____	Retelling _____
Oral Comprehension, Fluency, and MMI	Oral: _____ Silent: _____ Average: _____ Oral comp.% _____ MMI _____			Oral: _____ Silent: _____ Average: _____ Oral comp. % _____ MMI _____ Fluency _____			Oral: _____ Silent: _____ Average: _____ Oral comp. % _____ MMI _____		
Question Type:	Text-based: _____ Inference: _____ Critical: _____	Oral _____	Silent _____	Text-based: _____ Inference: _____ Critical: _____	Oral _____	Silent _____	Text-based: _____ Inference: _____ Critical: _____	Oral _____	Silent _____

Figure 3–11

A Method for Systematically Examining and Comparing Numerical Data from the CRI

Question Type. Transcribe the fractions from the body of the Recapitulation Record for the three different question types for the oral and the silent reading at the independent, instructional, and frustration levels.

This segment of the table is designed to provide at a glance the extent to which comprehension is balanced across the ability to recall, the ability to infer, and the ability to respond. Once again, it is important to look for discrepancies that might exist across different reading levels.

The analysis table at the bottom of the Recapitulation Record is the basis for what we will define in section 4 as the Level One or Numerical Interpretation of CRI data. While the numbers are largely redundant with respect to the body of the Recapitulation Record, their juxtaposition allows us to isolate issues that will be of the greatest interest to us during our Level One Interpretation.

Section 4

Interpretation of Test Results

Levels of *The Critical Reading Inventory Analysis*

Teachers and reading specialists will use the CRI for a variety of different purposes and so the type of interpretation they use will vary as well. If, for example, you use the CRI to investigate the reading needs of children with whom you will be working on a daily basis, you may not need a thorough and detailed analysis of results. You can presume that your daily teaching and observation of the children will provide you with ongoing insights into their needs. If, on the other hand, you are administering the CRI at the request of a teacher who needs comprehensive and structured input as to strengths, weaknesses, and optimum instructional strategies, your analysis will need to be thorough and detailed. The chances are good that you will not encounter those children in an instructional setting on a regular basis and so the more insights you can share with the teacher, the more helpful you are likely to be.

Because of your different needs for depth and detail of analysis, we have designated three different levels of interpretation of the CRI. These levels, while distinct, are by no means mutually exclusive. They are simply an attempt to address specific purposes.

Level One: Numerical Interpretation

The first level of analysis we have identified is *numerical interpretation*. Numerical interpretation is, in some respects, a concession to the fact that a rather artificial assessment constrained by time and circumstances can never replace the insights you can gain by means of daily interaction with children. But some schools and districts use informal reading inventories for the purpose of gathering assessment data on the reading performance and growth in reading of their children. If the CRI is used for this purpose, it can provide a broader cross-section of a child's comprehension performance than can most inventories. It can do this because of the distinction among question types and the Retelling Rubric that is included with each passage. Numerical interpretation will include comparisons of a child's performance on several different dimensions of the CRI, such as performance on different comprehension item types, on oral versus silent reading, on reading in relation to grade level, on retellings, etc.

It is important to note that numerical interpretation is by no means superficial, but that it seldom stands completely alone. Any insights you gain from a comparison of numbers should be verified on the basis of your observations of the child's actual performance. But numerical analysis can save a great deal of time and enable less experienced professionals to use the CRI effectively, while still providing a solid level of diagnostic information.

Level Two: Analytical Interpretation

In cases where teachers or reading specialists will require a higher level of insight into a child's strengths and weaknesses (a situation that is nearly universal), we recommend the *analytical interpretation* of CRI results. The analytical interpretation goes beyond numbers to an examination of children's actual responses and their significance as evidence of processing skills, thinking strategies, or reading habits. For example, you will frequently find children who are capable of answering virtually any text-based item but who experience difficulty with inference or critical response items. The fact that there is a significant numerical difference in their performance on these items is important to note. But if you want to delve deeper into the nature of their difficulty, you must examine their responses to the questions that they could not answer. Many children, for instance, will regularly respond to difficult items with "I don't know." (Possible translation: "I have no idea how to approach this item or how I would even arrive at an answer.") Others may reply with "It didn't say in the passage." (Translation: "I expect every question to have a clear and direct answer and I expect to find it stated in the text") Still others will respond with marvelously detailed and creative answers that have absolutely no connection to what they have just read. (Translation: "I have no idea that I must use information from the text to support my thinking.") Clearly there are different problems implicit in the patterns of responses elicited from these three types of children.

An analytical interpretation of CRI results will note signs of frustration or annoyance on the part of readers. It will attempt to describe the strategies that a child uses in response to unknown words, ranging from the lack of strategy indicated by frequent teacher-provided words to an overemphasis on graphic cues from text, to the detriment of context clues. While Level One Interpretation can tell us, for example, that the child is making numerous meaning-violating miscues, including non-words, level two interpretation can give us insight into the source of those problem areas. We can find out if the child is over-emphasizing syllabication rules in his creation of non-words. Or we might observe insensitivity to the syntax of the language that is reflected in the child's oral reading performance. Analytical interpretations also require us to examine retellings in detail, looking for signs of strategies such as attempts to memorize every detail as if they were equal, inclusion of extraneous details, or the inability to logically link ideas presented in text. It will include observations such as very fast oral or silent reading, a reluctance to elaborate on responses, a lack of enthusiasm or inflection in reading, or even the lack of an emotional response to text.

Analytical interpretation of all of these factors, and many more, will play a part in the detailed analysis of any child's responses. Coupled with creative insight and a firm grasp of the nature of reading, analytical interpretation will enable teachers and specialists to draw up a much clearer picture of any child's needs. It will, of course, also enable them to justify and explain more effectively the differences in the programs of instruction most likely to address those different needs.

Level Three: Comprehensive Interpretation

Finally, there is a third level of analysis which we have termed *comprehensive interpretation*. Comprehensive interpretation goes one step beyond the qualitative assessment of children's responses to the inclusion of the multiple sources of data that are available as a consequence of the time we have spent administering the CRI. For example, the children who consistently respond to inferential and critical response items with "I don't know" may be telling you that they have no idea how to respond. But your examination of their retellings during your Level Two analytical interpretation may indicate that they do not have a strategy for recalling or responding to text in an organized way. Your observation of these children during the CRI administration may lead you to conclude that they are reluctant to attempt anything associated with a risk of failure. Interviews with teachers, parents, or the children themselves may provide evidence of a regular avoidance of reading. Performance on district and state assessments of reading may provide further insights into the nature of the child's view of reading. In other words, comprehensive analysis is, as its name suggests, an exhaustive examination of all relevant factors that may be contributing to a child's performance on the CRI. More specifically, it is an attempt to piece together any and all facets of a child's performance to arrive at an educational profile that underlies that child's performance as a reader. Comprehensive interpretation is the most challenging and in many respects the most rewarding use of the CRI. And needless to say, the greater your depth of understanding of the nature of reading and the factors that influence it, the more valuable your analysis is likely to be. Examples of all three levels of CRI interpretation (numerical, analytical, and comprehensive) can be found in our discussion of case studies in section 6.

The Analysis of Reading Performance:
What a Good Reader Does

Any analysis of a child's reading performance on the CRI must begin with an examination of the fundamental elements of good reading. At the same time, we need to be aware of the ways that these traits are evidenced throughout the administration of the CRI. We will first identify those traits of the good reader that we regard as axiomatic and then identify elements of CRI performance that may act as "red flags" relative to each trait.

1. *Good readers achieve a balance among text-based, inference, and critical response items in their comprehension of text.*

High achievement in text-based reading to the exclusion of inference and critical evaluation often indicates a reader whose view of reading is rooted in remembering factual information (Durkin, 1978–79; Guthrie, 2001; Singer & Donlan, 1982). Inference items require the reader to draw logical conclusions based on both text and experience. Success in this arena is often associated with precision in concepts. Critical response items require that the reader express a point of view and defend it logically using both experience and information from the text.

Warning signs:
- consistent and large differences in percentage scores on text-based, inferential, and critical response items (for example, text-based scores that are consistently 20 or more points higher than inference or critical response scores)
- inability or unwillingness to elaborate on or explain responses to higher level items
- annoyance or frustration in response to items that have no clear answer stated in the text
- retellings that may be characterized by attention to less significant details or that may reflect attempts to memorize the passage
- reports from parents and/or teachers that proficient literal readers are viewed as "good readers"

2. *The good reader demonstrates solid comprehension in both oral and silent reading relative to his or her grade level.*

A consistent pattern of higher performance after oral reading may indicate that children are overly dependent upon listening skills (Armbruster & Wilkinson, 1991; Lynch, 1988; Miller & Smith, 1990; Stauffer, 1969). This pattern is more likely to occur among younger children, particularly those with limited experience with silent reading. A pattern of higher performance after silent reading is more common among older children (Allington, 2001). Weak silent reading may suggest that the reader lacks strategies to approach word recognition and comprehension independently.

Warning signs:
- consistent and large differences between average oral versus average silent reading comprehension scores (for example, average oral comprehension scores that are consistently 20 or more percentage points higher or lower than silent comprehension scores)
- very fast or unrealistically fast silent reading
- consistently high MMI coupled with low comprehension after oral reading
- frequent teacher-provided miscues during oral reading
- expressions of annoyance or frustration at the need for silent reading

3. *The good reader responds or reacts to the ideas included in text.*

Other than the acquisition of knowledge, there is little purpose or joy in reading if one does not think about text, evaluate its messages, compare its ideas to one's own, or respond to it, whether positively or negatively (Anderson, Wilkinson, & Mason, 1991; Cross & Paris,

1988; Hansen, 1981; Morrow, Tracy, Woo, & Pressley, 1999; Stauffer, 1969). Such thoughtful response to text lies at the heart of active thinking and construction of meaning.

Warning signs:
- admission of a dislike for reading in the course of the interview
- inability or reluctance to elaborate upon or explain responses
- frequent questions about when the testing will be over, sometimes even at the start of the testing
- negative response to the testing situation
- report from parent or teacher that the child is uninterested in reading

4. *The good reader detects the logical structure inherent in text and uses it as an aid to the organization and retrieval of ideas.*

Sensitivity to the ways that the writer has linked ideas together can go a long way toward promoting a reader's ability to process and retrieve those ideas (Beck & McKeown, 1991; Carnine & Kindler, 1985; Kameenui, Carnine, & Freschi, 1982). Passive reading or attempts to memorize ideas in text are far less effective because the ideas are not linked to existing schemata in the reader's mind.

Warning signs:
- frequent responses of "I don't know" to higher level questions
- no demonstration of personal response to text.
- obvious demonstrations of frustration or anxiety as reading materials become more challenging
- low retelling scores and higher comprehension scores on the same passage (child may make use of the actual questions as an aid to memory rather than the organization of ideas)
- recall of extraneous details in retellings or attempts to memorize passage
- omission of major story elements or central factual information
- little or no evidence of logical links between ideas in retellings

5. *The good reader uses a range of strategies for recognizing unknown words and frequently self-corrects miscues that alter the sense or grammar of the text.*

Monitoring for comprehension is a hallmark of good reading and when a reader does this type of monitoring, miscues that make no sense are immediately detected and corrected (Adams, 1990; Allington, 1983, 2001; Biemiller, 1994; Clay, 1979; Eldredge, Quinn, & Butterfield, 1990; Foorman, Novy, Francis, & Liberman, 1991; Goodman & Burke, 1972; Gray & Moody, 2000; Stahl, Duffy-Hester, & Stahl, 1998). By the same token, miscues that do not fit the grammatical structure of text simply do not "sound right" and will be corrected.

Warning signs:
- lack of inflection in reading or word-by-word reading
- overemphasis on graphic cues in word recognition
- infrequent correction of even serious miscues
- frequent teacher-provided miscues during oral reading, particularly at more challenging reading levels
- identification by parents and/or teachers as a struggling reader (may even be labeled as "learning disabled")
- history of avoiding reading

6. *The good reader has developed an extensive sight vocabulary relative to his or her grade level.*

Sight vocabulary tends to grow as a consequence of solid attention skills and frequent reading. Much of a child's sight vocabulary is learned incidentally as a consequence of that reading. The broader the sight vocabulary, the easier and more fluent one's reading tends to be and the more likely one is to engage in the activity (Adams, 1990; Allington, 1983, 2001; Betts, 1954; Morrow et al., 1999). Thus the level of a child's sight vocabulary tends to be a classic case of the rich getting richer (Stanovich, 1986).

Warning signs:
- Flash percentage at child's current grade level lower than 70%
- word recognition that does not improve significantly when reading in the context of the actual selection (Flash consistently higher than MMI)

- no demonstration of a systematic or consistent strategy for recognizing unknown words
- infrequent or sporadic independent reading on the part of the child
- low self-concept related to school

7. *The good reader enjoys reading and engages in it regularly for a wide variety of purposes.*

The ultimate goal of reading instruction is to help children to arrive at the conclusion that reading is a rewarding and enjoyable activity (Allington, 2001; Baker & Wigfield, 1999; Gray & Moody, 2000; Guthrie, 2001; Wigfield & Guthrie, 1997). In order to arrive at this belief, children must experience the joys and rewards of seeing their own lives mirrored in those of characters about whom they read. They must be drawn in (Langer, 1995) to the transaction that will demand of them a full participation in the world of ideas that reading represents.

Warning signs:
- failure to elaborate upon or explain responses to test questions
- lack of ease or comfort in the testing situation
- tendency toward low sight vocabulary relative to grade level
- expression of a dislike for reading in the interview
- avoidance of reading in classroom and home settings

We can use these seven characteristics of the good reader as a starting point in the analysis of reading performance.

Reading Levels in *The Critical Reading Inventory*

As we mentioned earlier, setting reading levels with the CRI (as with any IRI) requires thoughtful attention to a fairly wide range of factors. Not only do we have to consider the children's reading performance on the CRI itself, but at the very least we must also take into consideration the type of instruction and the teacher expectations that the children will encounter on a daily basis. It goes without saying that any diagnostic information you gather about the child's reading and thinking, no matter what level of interpretation you use, will matter little if the child is expected only to recall details of the text in the classroom. If you do not have all necessary information related to the instructional milieu, level setting can be tricky. Still, you must recognize that level setting is one of the most common uses of informal reading inventories, particularly because standardized test performance is unlikely to provide you with a great deal of help in determining at what reading level you should instruct a child.

Independent Level

Informal reading inventories are generally used to distinguish among three different reading levels (Johnson, Kress, & Pikulski, 1987). The first of these is the *independent level*. This is the level where children can identify the vast majority of the words they encounter without difficulty, they can develop a sense of the semantic and syntactic content of the text, they can grasp the meaning intended by the author, and they can think about and respond to what they have read. And they can do all of this without the help of either a teacher or a parent. The independent level is, of course, the level where homework should be assigned as well as the level where children should be doing a great deal (but by no means all) of their leisure reading. It is important for you to observe, when possible, your readers on the CRI reading at their independent level, most particularly to see if the strategies they are using when the material is fairly easy for them differ from the strategies they use when the material is more challenging.

Instructional Level

The second reading level that you want to estimate through the use of the CRI is the *instructional level*. This is the level where you can achieve the optimal match between the child's needs and the instruction that you provide in response to those needs. The instructional level is very much akin to Vygotsky's oft-cited Zone of Proximal Development (Vygotsky, 1978) in that the instruction that you provide matches the child's needs so well that you help the child achieve a just slightly higher level of competence in reading. Of course, your first requisite is a firm grasp of your students' needs and those needs are best demonstrated when they are reading material that challenges them and stretches their reading competence beyond their comfort level. In other words, children experience Piagetian disequilibrium (Piaget, 1973) in the instructional setting; otherwise they will have no reason to accommodate and change their way of doing things. A savvy observer who is in the presence of children reading at their instructional level will soon be able to spot shortcomings, confusions, strategic gaps, or distortions that are preventing children from progressing to the next stage in reading achievement. But of course this type of diagnostic insight can be gained only when children are reading at their instructional level in the presence of a skilled teacher of reading. Consequently, instructional level reading is most often meant for instructional situations, situations where skilled professionals can guide children and help meet their needs.

Frustration Level

The third level that you want to identify through the CRI is the *frustration level*. Children reach their frustration level when the reading material, whether by virtue of difficulty in word recognition or comprehension, becomes too difficult for them to handle and too complex for them to even benefit from instruction. There are simply too many things going wrong at the frustration level for teachers to address at one time. In the course of the administration of the CRI, you will ask children to read materials at their frustration level. You do this simply for the sake of the insights that you may gain when you observe how (or if) the children adjust to frustration in reading. For example, some children may revert to less sophisticated views of reading and attempt to use only graphophonemic clues when they encounter unknown words. Others increase their use of non-words, simply attaching sounds to collections of letters with no attention to syntactic or semantic fit. Still others will revert to attempts to memorize instead of think about what they have read. Still others may shut down completely and give up any attempt to read what they perceive as materials that are beyond their scope. In any and all cases, you can gain some insights into their view of reading, their motivation to succeed, and the strategies that they fall back on when the going gets tough. It is our hope that the short-term discomfort of reading at one's frustration level will yield enough diagnostic information to make it worthwhile.

You must keep in mind that your ultimate goal is to help every child to read those very materials with a high level of success as soon as possible. The diagnostic information you gain may help to bring about this ultimate success. It also never hurts to tell the children whom you test that no one expects them to succeed at every level, that you know they are reading at very high levels and that mistakes are OK. You should even feel free to tell them that the authors who created this test insist that you make them read such difficult materials. Anything you can do to reassure the children may eventually pay off in solid diagnostic insights.

Listening Level

The fourth reading level that we can use in certain circumstances is the *listening comprehension level*. You estimate the listening comprehension level by reading the passages yourself to the children and then measuring their comprehension just as you would if the children themselves had read the text. You will undoubtedly encounter children whose word recognition skills are so seriously problematic that they become insurmountable obstacles to comprehension. In such cases, it is very beneficial to know what kinds of materials or conceptual levels the children could handle if they were relieved of the burden of sheer word recognition. When you observe that children are struggling mightily with word recognition and you suspect that they can comprehend at a much higher level if the materials are read to them, it is time to try to estimate the listening comprehension level.

Setting Reading Levels With the Inventory

The traditional approach to level-setting utilizes a combination of: a) the overall percentage of successful word recognition during oral reading, or the Reading Accuracy Index (RAI), and b) the percentage of accurate responses to comprehension questions averaged across oral and silent reading at any given grade level (Betts, 1954). Thus the numbers associated with different reading levels look like this:

	Reading Accuracy	Average Comprehension
Independent Level	99	90
Instructional Level	95	75
Frustration Level	90	50
Listening Level	N/A	75

questions

Even given the frequently stubborn refusal of numbers to fit neatly into the patterns described above, it is often a fairly straightforward process to estimate a child's reading levels using a combination of these two data sources. But we must also consider the nature of the reader's word recognition problems. Even though reading experts long suspected that not all miscues were equal in importance (Johnson, Kress, & Pikulski, 1987), that realization did not have widespread impact until the work of Goodman and Burke on miscue analysis became widely disseminated. Now the equation becomes a bit more complicated: One reader with 95% accuracy in oral reading at a given grade level may have made no serious miscues while another reader with an identical score may have made many. In spite of the identical numbers, the problems experienced by each reader are very different and so, of course, are the instructional strategies that we would use to address them.

And so in the CRI we will ask you to consider not only the pure percentage of words that a child reads correctly (RAI), but also to consider the percentage of the words the child reads that preserve the sense of the text (MMI). Significant discrepancies between these two numbers accompanied by problems with comprehension may signal a failure to monitor for meaning that may severely hinder a child's growth in reading. Under these circumstances, the word recognition problems are often more severe and will affect the judgment we make about a child's ability to handle materials at any given reading level.

For example, the Reading Accuracy Index for a child who reads a 200-word passage and who makes 12 scoreable miscues would be 94%. This is so because the RAI is calculated by subtracting the number of scoreable miscues from the number of words in the passage and then dividing by the number of words in the passage ($200 - 12 = 188$; $188/200 = 94\%$). Then we calculate the Meaning Maintenance Index by first examining each of the miscues and determining whether the miscue altered the meaning intended by the authors of the text. In this case, the child exhibited the tendency to look at the first part of any difficult word and simply guess at the rest. He frequently used non-words in these cases and 8 of the 12 miscues noted were serious; that is, they distorted the meaning of the text. Therefore the MMI for this child would be 96% since the MMI is calculated by subtracting the number of meaning-altering miscues from the number of words in the passage and then dividing by the number of words in the passage [$200 - 8 = 192$; $192/200 = 96\%$].

A Meaning Maintenance Index score of 96% coupled with reading comprehension problems is a red flag. It suggests that readers are not actively monitoring the reading to ensure that what they read makes sense. Note that the MMI in this child's case is actually higher than the RAI. This will happen frequently. The RAI is based on the sum of the meaning-maintaining and meaning-violating miscues; the MMI is based only on meaning-violating miscues. Thus the MMI can never be lower than the RAI. But we are less concerned with the absolute value of the MMI and more concerned with the fact that it represents a departure from the quintessential purpose of reading: making meaning. It will be our hope that every miscue a child makes will be relatively minor and will not affect the overall sense of the text. In such cases, the child will score at 100% on the MMI every time. If the child does not score 100% then we would do well to examine the nature of the miscues that took place during the oral reading and to contrast the MMI with overall comprehension scores as well as performance on different comprehension item types.

Another consideration in the setting of levels is the fact that the CRI attempts to identify not only the absolute comprehension of passages but also three different types of thinking called for by comprehension questions: text-based, inferential, and critical response. We have found that it is fairly common for children to demonstrate solid proficiency in text-based comprehension but serious difficulties with inferential and critical response comprehension. On a typical reading inventory, such children might be expected to perform quite well (Applegate, Quinn, & Applegate, 2002). If these same children are taught in a classroom where the primary emphasis is on the recall of the details of text, they would be likely to perform equally well. However, their inability to think about or respond to text would be a significant disadvantage on the CRI (not to mention in their growth as readers and their performance on state and national reading tests) and would clearly lower their overall reading level identified by any user of the CRI.

Thus users of the CRI would be well advised to think of diagnosis and level-setting, whenever possible, as an interaction between the child's instructional situation and the child's test performance. For example, many children are instructed in classrooms where teachers expect them to critically respond to ideas in text, discuss those ideas, and defend their interpretations. For these children, the CRI would be an effective diagnostic instrument that could provide a prediction of a child's performance in that class. If, however, the child is instructed in a classroom where text-based reading assessment is the norm, then that child's level may be underestimated by the CRI. Because research suggests that a significant amount of the nation's classroom reading instruction is characterized by text-based assessment (Allington, 2001; Brown, 1991), this is an issue that should be included in our thinking about the estimation of reading levels.

It is our hope that users of the CRI become change agents who can effectively address the preponderance of literal thinking in the reading classroom. It is becoming increasingly important for teachers to foster a greater balance between thoughtful responses to text and memory for text details, particularly in light of the emphasis on the former that is beginning to emerge in state and national assessments of reading.

Technical Features of *The Critical Reading Inventory:* Development and Validation

Field Testing

The primary purpose of the CRI is to assist teachers and reading specialists in their assessment of children's reading ability, strengths, needs, and interests. To determine the extent to which this purpose is met, we conducted field testing of the original test materials, including word lists, interviews for children, parents, and teachers, narrative and informational text selections, three types of comprehension questions, retelling rubrics, and a fluency rubric.

Test materials were evaluated by 22 practicing reading specialists, who averaged 15 years of experience and who administered informal reading inventories an average of 100 times per year. All had at least one master's degree and two were enrolled in doctoral programs. All were certified reading specialists, with 14 also certified in elementary education, 6 in secondary education, 4 in special education, 2 in early childhood education, and 7 seeking educational leadership certification. Their current teaching assignments included urban, suburban, and rural districts ranging in grade level from K–12, ranging in family income from low to high, and including several schools with diverse populations. Twelve novice pre-service teachers enrolled in an elementary M.Ed. program also administered the CRI during the field testing, as did the authors. All participation was voluntary.

Seventy children who participated in the initial tryout ranged in grade from K–8, with 60% White, 21.4% African American, 11.4% Asian American, and 7.2% Hispanic. Approximately 7% were classified as receiving special education and 20% were receiving services for reading difficulties. The group was 45% female and 55% male and was mixed evenly for socioeconomic status.

Input from the initial field testing led to changes in passage wording, readjustments of levels, increased clarity of directions for administration and scoring, and rewording or revision of questions. After the initial revision, further field testing was conducted by an additional 10 reading specialists as well as by the authors. Fifty-three graduate students seeking reading specialist certification administered the CRI twice under the supervision of two of the authors. Additional adjustments to wording and clarity of directions for administration and scoring were made. The CRI was deemed worthwhile and valid during extensive field testing based on its usability and on the extent to which it accurately assessed reading strengths and difficulties that had been identified by teachers participating in the study.

Constructing the Word Lists

The word lists were compiled using high frequency word lists such as Fry Instant Words, the Dolch word lists (Dolch, 1948), and Frances and Kucera's list (1982), along with graded basal reading series and content books, (particularly for the grade 3–senior high school lists) and graded vocabulary study texts.

A regression analysis was completed on data collected from field testing, comparing entry point based on the word lists (highest level at which the child attained 100 percent on the Flash portion) and performance (instructional or independent) on the passages. The high correlation ($r = .83$) led us to conclude that the word lists are functioning accurately to predict entry-level performance on the passages. Those who completed the field test also participated in a survey where they evaluated whether the word lists provided accurate starting points in the graded passages for each child tested. More than 90% reported a match between the starting point suggested by the word lists and the child's performance on the CRI.

Constructing the Interviews

We created the student interview questions as a means of gathering: (a) background information on the child, (b) information about the child's view of reading, and (c) information about the child's interests and attitudes. Our intent was to add a more balanced and affective dimension to the data collected. To enable users to obtain multiple perspectives rather than just a self-report, we included both a Parent and Teacher Interview form. Teacher information includes their perception of the child's ability and classroom performance, a description of the classroom reading program, and an indication of the teacher's theoretical orientation to reading instruction. Parent information includes the parents' perception of their child's reading and classroom performance, the level of parental involvement, and literacy/school activities in the home. These sources contribute to a triangulation of key information to lend to the CRI's credibility and practical value in diagnosis. Interviews were also used during field testing and were deemed a valuable source of information in the survey completed by the users. Examples of typical responses to interviews are included in the case studies discussed in section 6.

Constructing the Passages

All graded passages were written by the authors based on 5 years of observational notes in classrooms and clinics for grades K–12 and over 20 years of professional experience in classrooms per author, including supervision of reading practicum experiences at their respective institutions. These observations included notes regarding curriculum, materials, topics, themes, and children's interests and children's developmental responses to the curriculum and activities, in addition to personal experience. Key ideas for the content of the passages were brainstormed among the authors; then each author wrote several passages on agreed upon themes or content for a particular age/grade level. We then met, shared, and revised the passages collaboratively. Two narrative and two informational passages were written for each level, pre-primer through senior high school. At the lower levels, pre-primer through grade 1, we made an effort to include repetitive text and structural elements that would be appropriate for the emergent reader (Fountas & Pinnell, 1996). Throughout the CRI, but particularly at the higher level of the informational passages, we attempted to include high interest but less familiar topics in order to avoid potential reader overexposure to topics, a difficulty we had noted in other recently published IRIs.

Readability

We initially evaluated passage readability using the multiple formulas included in the Micro-Light Software for readability, but we found many inconsistencies across formulas. We decided to use the Flesch Kincaid Formula found on Microsoft Word software (1997). The formula itself is similar to the Fry Readability Scale and the Smog Readability Formula in its method of formulation (http://www.med.utah.edu/pated/authors/readability/html, 3/10/02). Furthermore, its use would allow the CRI users easy access for checking the readability of materials they wish to use with their students. It is important to note that the 1997 software package was used for the purpose of determining CRI passage readability. Subsequent versions of the Flesch-Kincaid formula on later editions of Microsoft Word tend to significantly overestimate readability. For exact information regarding readability and length, see appendix C. Passages were written to maintain a .2 or less difference between the readability estimates at each level and to insure that there would be "equal intervals" in readability between levels (Gerke, 1980; Klesius & Homan, 1985).

In addition to readability considerations, we used content, appeal, interest, background knowledge, text structure, overall length, and print format/layout in determining appropriateness for each passage at each grade level. It is well established that sentence length, word frequency, and number of syllables and words per sentence are not the only factors that should be considered in evaluating the difficulty of text (Jitendra et al., 2001; Johnston, 1997; Kinder, Bursuck, & Epstein, 1992; Lynch, 1988).

Pictures were included at pre-primer through grade 1 for one selection at each level on the narrative passages, and photographs were included at the same levels for one selection at each informational passage. Thus the examiner can compare a child's performance with and without "picture clues" at each of these three levels. The pictures and photographs were specifically created to support the text in a meaningful way.

For the narrative passages, we used a variety of genre types, including familiar childhood experiences as well as folktales and fable-like stories. All passages were created by the authors in order to eliminate the concern for past exposure to stories by our intended audience. Passages were written with an eye toward gender fairness and ethnic diversity. The informational texts include original social science and science content as well as biography. All informational selections were researched for accuracy of the facts presented.

During field testing, we also assessed children's interests, background knowledge, and performance on the materials as a means of determining level appropriateness. As a result, several passages were modified for ease or difficulty. Two passages were exchanged and rewritten for the more appropriate grade and developmental level. Originally, "The Race" was written as a fourth-grade narrative, and "Autumn Leaves" was written as a second-grade narrative. After field testing and evaluating the affective response and performance of age-appropriate children, we determined that these should be modified and exchanged. We also noted that a third-grade passage which was written with a first-person narrator frequently had a confounding effect on estimates of reading levels. We revised the passage to reflect a third-person narrator and thus resolved the leveling issue.

Selection length was also an issue that we discussed and examined. Based on previous recommendations (Jitendra et al., 2001; Johnson, Kress, & Pikulski, 1987; Jongsma & Jongsma, 1981; Klesius & Homan, 1985), it is important to have adequate length (more than 125 words) at each level except for pre-primer so that there will be substantive content to serve as the basis for comprehension assessment. In addition, passage length is important in that the majority of materials that children will be expected to read in their classrooms (from mid-first grade on) will have well over 100 words. State and national assessments also tend to include longer passages. Research has suggested that shorter Informal Reading Inventory (IRI) selections tend to overestimate children's reading ability for regular classroom materials and show inaccurate miscue patterns (Bowden, cited in Klesius & Homan, 1985). Jitendra and colleagues also found that most recent basal series have selections that are well over 100 words in length and most content text chapters also fit this pattern. Because one of the primary intentions of informal reading inventories is to estimate placement into curriculum materials, suitable length was an important factor in the development of the CRI.

Assessment of Comprehension

Since comprehension is the most important aspect of reading that is being evaluated, we have developed two tools to assess comprehension: Retelling Rubrics and Post-Reading Questions. An Oral Reading Fluency Rubric is included to accompany assessment of the reader's comprehension.

Retelling Rubrics

Rubrics for the scoring of retellings are included for each passage in the CRI. In the case of narrative selections, the elements assessed in the retelling are based upon essential story grammar components, that is, characters, character goals or problems, and the key steps characters take toward the solution of the problem or the attainment of the goal. The final component of the Retelling Rubric is the presence or absence of a well-supported personal response to the text.

Rubrics for informational passages draw a distinction between macro concepts and micro concepts. Macro concepts are defined as superordinate ideas that are central to the information presented in the text and which are supported, illustrated, or further explained by additional information in the text. The supporting details are defined as micro concepts, not because they are unimportant but because they act as support for the more general and inclusive macro concepts.

In the case of either narrative or informational text, test users will consult the rubric provided, note the presence or absence of text elements, and match score descriptions to arrive at a numerical score ranging from 0 to 4 for the reader's retelling.

In addition, because reader response to text is central to our definition of critical reading, we have included an invitation to readers to discuss their personal response to the text. Assessment of the personal response is included in the rubric used for scoring retellings. During field testing of the CRI, this component was identified by participants as a positive feature that provided reliable data with regard to a reader's view of and attitude toward reading.

Post-Reading Questions

After examining several Informal Reading Inventories and analyzing their methods of comprehension assessment, we determined there was a need for a more structured assessment of retellings and the development of questions that would assess higher level thinking in the forms of inferential and critical response items (Applegate, Quinn, & Applegate, 2002; Manzo, Manzo, & McKenna, 1995; Nessel, 1987). We then applied the criteria we had developed (see Table 5–1), along with the recommendations from Klesius and Homan, to create text-based, inferential, and critical response questions for each passage. All questions are labeled as to type and possible correct responses, many of which were actually given by children during the field testing. These are included on the Examiner's Copy of the CRI.

For levels pre-primer through grade 1, there are 8 questions for each passage at each level and for each type of text. For levels grade 2 through senior high school, there are 10 questions for each passage at each level for each type of text. For narrative passages, when there are 8 questions, there are 3 text-based, 3 inference, and 2 critical response items; when there are 10 questions, there are 4 text-based, 3 inference, and 3 critical response items. For informational text, when there are 8 questions, there are 3 text-based, 3 inference, and 2 critical response items; when there are 10 questions, there are 4 text-based, 4 inference, and 2 critical response items. There are more critical response items for narrative text at the upper levels because there is more opportunity for this type of thinking in response to this type of text (Rosenblatt, 1983). No direct assessment of vocabulary was done since these types of questions are often dependent on a child's background knowledge and language ability (Puffelmeyer, Robinson, & Squier, 1989).

Virtually all questions require that the child actually read the passage and use information from it in order to avoid one of the pitfalls of many IRIs regarding passage dependency (Klesius & Homan, 1985). No questions rely totally on a child's past experience or background knowledge, although we know that some children will and should make use of their experiences in order to help them comprehend and respond to the passages. Passage dependency of questions was also evaluated by asking six children and four adults the comprehension questions without affording them the opportunity to read the passages. More than 85% of the questions could not be answered. Questions from the informational passages at the lower levels (pre-primer through grade 2) were more readily answered correctly without reading the passages; however, this was done more frequently by older children and adults who for the most part would not be evaluated by those passages.

We also noted that lookbacks could be utilized as an additional dimension of the assessment of reading comprehension. Lookbacks can be most useful with students who have recurring difficulty with literal recall and who frequently respond with "I don't know" or "I don't remember." Lookbacks enable the user to assess whether the reader is experiencing difficulty with remembering or with comprehending the text. It also enables you to

Table 5–1 Criteria for Determining Question Types

Text-Based Question Types (TB):

1. **Literal Items**: Answers to these items are stated explicitly (verbatim) in the text. They simply require that the readers recall what they have read.

2. **Low-Level Inference Items**: The answers to low-level inferences are not stated verbatim in the text but may be so close to literal as to be very obvious. All inference items require that the reader draw a conclusion on the basis of the text and use his or her background experiences to some extent as well. However, low-level inferences require very little in the way of drawing conclusions. We classified as low-level inferences, for example, items that:

   • involve the recognition of information in different words from those used in the original text. Such items require of the reader only a translation of the printed text.

   • require the reader to identify relationships that exist between ideas in the text. Such items as these are not literal only because the writer has not made the relationship explicit by using a grammatical marker (e.g., *because*). This is not to say that the skill of making such connections is unimportant. Classification of an item as low-level is merely reflective of the fact that the writer assumes that at a given grade level, the reader can and will make the connection.

   • deal with details largely irrelevant to the central message of the text.

   • require that the reader draw solely on background knowledge or to speculate about the actions of characters without the benefit of information in the text that may transform speculation into a logical prediction.

Inferential Question Types (I):

3. **High-Level Inference Items**: These items call for the reader to link experience with the text and to draw a logical conclusion. Answers to these items require significantly more complex thinking than low-level inferences. Examples include those items that require the reader to:

   • devise an alternative solution to a specific problem described in the text.

   • describe a plausible motivation that explains a character's actions.

   • provide a plausible explanation for a situation, problem, or action.

   • predict a past or future action based on characteristics or qualities developed in the text.

   • describe a character or action based on the events in a story.

Critical Response Question Types (CR):

4. **Response Items:** These items call for a reader to express and defend an idea related to the actions of characters or the outcome of events. Response items differ from high-level inference items in that they are usually directed toward broader ideas or underlying themes that relate to the significance of the passage. While high-level inference items are directed toward a specific element or problem in the passage, response items require a reader to discuss and react to the underlying meaning of the passage as a whole. Examples include items that ask the reader to:

   • describe the lesson(s) a character may have learned from experience.

   • judge the efficacy of the actions or decisions of a character and defend the judgment.

   • devise and defend alternative solutions to a complex problem described in a story.

   • respond positively or negatively to a character based on a logical assessment of the actions or traits of that character.

assess the reader's ability to quickly locate information relevant to questions that he or she had been unable to answer (Alvermann, 1988; Bossert & Schwantes, 1995–96; Swanson & De La Paz, 1998).

Estimating Levels: The Betts' Criteria

The criteria in Table 5–2 are used to estimate reading levels based on the combined results of the oral reading miscue scores and the average oral and silent comprehension score at any given level.

We have chosen to use the Betts' criteria even though there have been studies that have both supported (Bader & Weisendanger, 1989; Johns, 1991; McKenna, 1983) and critically examined them (Johns & Magliari, 1989; Lowell, 1969; Pikulski, 1990). Because it is the most frequently used set of criteria, we believe that it is useful for comparative purposes. In

Table 5–2 Estimating Levels

Level	Average of Oral and Silent Comprehension	Reading Accuracy Index (RAI)
Independent	90%	99%
Instructional	75%	95%
Frustration	50%	90%
Listening	NA	75%

addition, many of the other criteria that have been tried are very close to Betts' original set. We wish to emphasize that, in any case, these criteria are only guidelines for estimating levels. There are many other factors that enter into such estimates, including qualitative information, knowledge about the student's actual performance in the classroom, and observations about reading strategy use and behavior (Goodman, 1997; Harris & Lalik, 1987).

Reliability

Interrater reliability for scoring the CRI was assessed using a primer narrative selection and a fifth-grade level informational selection. Participating were 22 experienced teachers and reading specialists as well as eight college faculty ($N = 30$). Each participant listened to the oral reading, retellings, and comprehension question responses of a child who was administered the CRI. Each participant listened to each selection twice before scoring and calculating the RAI, MMI, retelling, and comprehension scores. There was very high agreement for each area (90% agreement for RAI, MMI, and comprehension items, and 85% agreement for retellings). The oral reading scores all fell within $+/-1$ point (RAI mean $= .98$; MMI mean $= .99$), with a range from 97–99 for the RAI and a range of 98–100 for the MMI. The retelling scores were all within $+/-.5$ point (Retelling mean $= 1.5$) ranging from 1 to 2 for each. When there was disagreement, the comprehension scores for each passage all fell within $+/-1$ question (Comprehension mean $= 75$).

The key components of reliability for any informal reading inventory are readability and the appropriateness and accuracy of passage content and levels. But also crucial to reliability considerations is the preparation of examiners. Through guided practice and coaching (including the use of the Audio CD-Rom), examiners will be expected to integrate their understanding of the reading process, their observations of children's reading behaviors, and their thorough knowledge of the assessment tool to arrive at a clear picture of children's reading strengths and weaknesses. We have attempted to ensure that these components are in place and we hope that the users of this tool will continue to share with us their concerns and insights.

Section 6

Case Studies

The following two case studies represent a very detailed analysis of test data by three very experienced test administrators. The detail you include in your analysis will reflect the purposes for which you are using the CRI. We are not suggesting that every reader's performance will be, or even should be, analyzed in the same detail. We are merely illustrating the depth of analysis that is possible through the use of the CRI.

Case Study 1
Tamika
(pp. 54–87)

5th Grade Student
10 years, 4 months

Student Interview
Parent/Guardian Interview
Teacher Interview
Graded Word List Assessment
Oral and Silent Reading Assessments
Discussion of Case Study 1: Interpreting the Data

Case Study 2
John
(pp. 88–118)

5th Grade Student
10 years, 8 months

Student Interview
Parent/Guardian Interview
Teacher Interview
Graded Word List Assessment
Oral and Silent Reading Assessments
Discussion of Case Study 2: Interpreting the Data

Student Interview:
Fifth Grade–Senior High

Name: _____Tamika_____ Date: _____11/25_____

1. What kinds of things do you like to do when you're not in school?
   I watch TV and I mess with the computer; I like the computer games.

2. How about reading? (If reader does not volunteer the information, probe for how often, what kinds of materials, topics of interest, where materials are obtained, etc.)
   I'm really good at reading. (Teacher probe) When we get our projects I go to the library for the books. Now I find lots of stuff on the Web. I'm pretty good at searching.

3. How do you think you do with reading in school? What about writing?
   I'm really good. I get good marks on all my writing projects.

4. What have you read recently for enjoyment? For school? Did you find them enjoyable? Were they easy for you to understand?
   I read Missing May, Chasing the Redbird, and I forgot the other one. It was the third one on the booklist we had; we had to pick three. As soon as I got my homework done, I could do whatever I want for the rest of the summer. I did it right away.

5. What is the hardest part about reading?
   There's nothing hard about reading for me.

6. What are the best and worst things about school?
   I like doing our projects and displaying them. I don't really like our health book.

7. Is writing hard or easy for you? What do you think makes it that way?
   I get good grades on my writing projects. I pick out good books and I just use them.

8. Are you on any clubs or teams at school? Do you have any hobbies? Do you have a job?
   No clubs; not really; no, I don't have one.

9. How are your grades in school? Do you have any concerns with any subjects?
   Really good; no.

10. Have you ever thought about what kind of job you'd like to have when you're older?
    Not really.

11. Is there anything else that you'd like to share about yourself?
    Not really.

Parent/Guardian Interview

Name: _____Tamika_____   Date: ___11/25_____

1. What made you think that it would be a good idea for ___Tamika___ (student's name) to be tested at this time?
   We were devastated when we saw her scores on the state test.

2. How is ___Tamika___ doing in school, particularly in reading?
   She's doing great; she always has.

3. What kind of reading does ___Tamika___ do at home?
   She always does her assigned reading from school. (Any reading for pleasure?) I think she does read for pleasure, but I'm not sure what she really likes to read.

4. How would you characterize ___Tamika___ 's:
   a. **Ability**—*she's very bright.*
   b. **Attitude**—*it's always been great.*
   c. **Interests**—*she seems to enjoy whatever they study in school; they vary with the different topics they study.*
   d. **Needs**—*we didn't think she had any; that's why we were so shocked.*
   e. **Behavior**—*very well behaved; she's a typical 5th grader and periodically she has arguments with her younger sister but that's only natural.*

5. What would you say is the major reason for ___Tamika___ 's school performance?
   We thought that she was a very good student; she works hard at her schoolwork, all of it. She's very conscientious!

6. How long has he/she had this difficulty?
   Not applicable.

7. What kinds of help has he/she gotten so far?
   Not applicable.

8. What are you currently doing at home to help ___Tamika___?
   Not applicable.

9. Is there anything else you think might be helpful for you to do?
   Not applicable.

10. What is the school or the teacher doing this year to help ___Tamika___?
    Not applicable.

11. What else do you think it would be helpful for the school or teacher to do?
    In the 4th grade when she went down on the district test, we met with her teacher so we could figure this out. But she said that Tamika's a very good reader. Apparently something is wrong.

Teacher Interview

Name: _Tamika_   **Date:** _11/25_

1. What would you say are the greatest needs in reading of the class you have this year?
   Applying multi-syllabic rules and developing vocabulary.

2. Could you describe for me a typical reading/language arts period in your classroom (this should include time spent, materials used, methods, and grouping techniques)?
   Introduce words from the story in literature basal; have children take turns reading the story and then answer journal questions; break children into groups to complete skill sheets that accompany the story. This takes about one hour and a half.

3. How does _Tamika_ (student's name) generally react to your instruction?
   She has no trouble with multi-syllabic words; she's very quick picking up meanings and definitions.

4. In your comprehension instruction and assessment, do you tend to emphasize recall of information, student response to the text, or both equally?
   The journal questions do both; students get a chance to tell their personal responses and they also answer questions that do check their comprehension.

5. How would you characterize _Tamika_ 's:
   a. **Ability**—*she's very bright*
   b. **Attitude**—*she's strongly motivated*
   c. **Interests**—*they vary; I know she's great at using the Web to research whatever topics we study. She amazes me!*
   d. **Needs**—*I don't see any. I assumed she'd be one of my highest scorers; I can't figure this out.*
   e. **Behavior**—*Outstanding student; she's a real pleasure to have in class.*

6. What kinds of activities or strategies have you tried specifically with _Tamika_? What seems to work best? What doesn't seem to be working?
   I have never needed to do anything special for Tamika.

7. What do you know about the type of support _Tamika_ gets at home?
   I know that her parents are pleased with her work habits. They were as surprised as I was. In fact, they were the ones who insisted on the testing.

8. If there were one thing that you could recommend that you think would help _Tamika_, what would it be?
   I can't think of anything at all.

Word Lists: Examiner's Copy

Third Grade

	Flash	Untimed
1. enter	+	
2. change	+	
3. lesson	+	
4. think	+	
5. music	+	
6. trust	+	
7. human	+	
8. pencil	+	
9. mail	+	
10. phone	+	
11. fright	+	
12. unusual	+	
13. they'll	+	
14. bread	+	
15. forest	+	
16. early	+	
17. hurt	+	
18. water	+	
19. because	+	
20. hour	+	

Score	20/20	20/20
	100%	100%

Fourth Grade

	Flash	Untimed
1. doesn't	+	
2. concern	+	
3. sample	+	
4. official	+	
5. given	+	
6. present	+	
7. decorate	+	
8. windshield	+	
9. exercise	+	
10. finish	+	
11. enjoyable	+	
12. wrong	+	
13. daughter	+	
14. quiet	+	
15. morning	+	
16. huge	*hug*	+
17. covered	+	
18. thought	+	
19. creature	+	
20. people	+	

Score	19/20	20/20
	95%	100%

Word Lists: Examiner's Copy

Fifth Grade	Flash	Untimed		Sixth Grade	Flash	Untimed
1. bravely	+			1. athletic	+	
2. embarrass	+			2. psychology	+	
3. important	+			3. realize	+	
4. guarantee	+			4. ridiculous	NR	+
5. magical	+			5. successful	+	
6. prevent	+			6. reluctant	+	
7. typical	+			7. consideration	+	
8. vision	+			8. mountain	+	
9. handle	+			9. partial	+	
10. ledge	+			10. graceful	+	
11. wounded	+			11. applause	+	
12. defend	+			12. survival	+	
13. jungle	+			13. materials	+	
14. seasonal	*season*	+		14. pressure	+	
15. different	+			15. license	+	
16. through	+			16. vehicle	+	
17. interesting	+			17. definite	+	
18. necessary	+			18. experience	+	
19. medicine	+			19. predictable	+	
20. mysterious	+			20. conform	+	

Score	19/20	20/20		Score	19/20	20/20
	95%	100%			95%	100%

Word Lists: Examiner's Copy

Junior High   **Senior High**

	Flash	Untimed		Flash	Untimed
1. continuous	+		1. acquiesce		
2. uncertainty	+		2. discrepancy		
3. imperative	*imperial*	+	3. figurative		
4. precious	+		4. connotation		
5. appreciation	+		5. reiterate		
6. regularity	*regular*	+	6. vehement		
7. disregard	+		7. subsidiary		
8. encyclopedia	+		8. innocuous		
9. computerized	+		9. mandatory		
10. prognosis	+		10. tangential		
11. synthesize	+		11. fathomable		
12. journalist	+		12. cursory		
13. opportunity	+		13. impervious		
14. participated	*participation*	+	14. poignant		
15. employment	+		15. exuberant		
16. nucleotide	*nuclear*	*nuclear; DK*	16. ambidextrous		
17. occurrence	+		17. suave		
18. holocaust	+		18. officious		
19. obsolete	+		19. ultimatum		
20. irony	+		20. limpid		

Score	16/20	19/20	Score	/20	/20
	80%	95%		%	%

Second Grade Oral: The Race

Reader's copy on p. 24 of the Reader's Passages.

Introductory Statement: "Would you read this passage about two cats who race each other out loud for me? When you are finished, I'll take the passage away. Then I'll ask you to tell me about what you read and what you think of it. After that, I'll ask you some questions about the passage."

Story

Spencer was the fastest animal in the jungle. All of the

Others ✔ *SC*

SC other animals knew it. Spencer made sure of that. He would say, "No one can beat me! You are all too afraid to race!" It was true. No one wanted to race against Spencer. He always won. Then he would brag even more.

One day another family of cats moved in. Spencer ran up to the new family. He said, "I'm the fastest animal in the jungle. Do you want to race?" The father said, "No, thank you. But maybe our daughter Annie will race with you." Annie smiled and said, "Yes. I'd love to race." Soon the two cats <u>were</u> / running for the finish line. Spencer was winning as always. But Annie was very fast. She raced past him and crossed the finish line first.

The other animals cheered in surprise. But Spencer cried, "I want another chance!" They raced again and again. But the result was still the same. There was a new champion in the jungle and her name was Annie.

All the animals came over to talk to Annie. But Spencer went away angry. Annie was a little sad. She hoped that Spencer would be her friend. "Well, at least we won't have to listen to him brag again," said the fox. The next day Spencer was back. The first thing he said was, "I can jump higher than anybody in the jungle! No one can beat me!" The other animals groaned and rolled their eyes. Nothing had changed after all.

(256 words)

Miscues

__0__ N of miscues that maintained meaning (checked). This is the MM.

__0__ N of miscues that violated meaning (unchecked). This is the MV.

Reading Accuracy Index: <u>100</u> %
(N of words – N of miscues, checked and unchecked)/ N of words

Meaning Maintenance Index: <u>100</u> %
(N of words – N of meaning-violating miscues, unchecked only)/N of words

The Race: 256 words

Miscue Chart

Miscues	%	Miscues	%	Miscues	%
1	100	13	95	25	90
2	99	14	95	26	90
3	99	15	94	27	89
4	98	16	94	28	89
5	98	17	93	29	89
6	98	18	93	30	88
7	97	19	93	31	88
8	97	20	92	32	88
9	96	21	92	33	87
10	96	22	91	34	87
11	96	23	91	35	86
12	95	24	91	36	86

Retelling

Examiner: "Tell me about what you just read and what you thought about it."

Spencer told everybody that he was the fastest animal in the jungle and they kind of got tired of it. Then a new cat Annie moved in and he asked her to race. She beat him and the other animals were surprised. Spencer ran away after the race and then he came back and bragged about how high he could jump. So nothing changed after all.

If there is no spontaneous response, repeat the request, "Tell me what you thought about the passage."

It shows that he didn't change.

NOTE: Use the Retelling Rubric on the next page to assess the child's retelling performance.

Retelling Rubric

Story Structure:	
1. **Key Characters and Setting:** Spencer, other animals, and Annie who moved into jungle.	+1
2. **Character's Problem or Goal:** Spencer wants to be the fastest runner in the jungle and to brag about it.	+1
3. **Problem-Solving or Goal-Meeting Process:**	
• Spencer brags and gets others to race with him so that he can brag more.	+1
• Annie moves in and Spencer races with her.	+1
• Spencer loses the race.	+1
• Spencer walks away angrily and Annie is sad because she had wanted a friend.	+1
• Spencer returns the next day and brags about jumping.	+1
4. **Personal response:** Any well-supported positive or negative response to the characters or events in the story; any reaction to the humor or sadness in the story; any well-supported positive or negative reaction to the story as a whole.	0

Rubric:

4 = Complete retelling includes characters, problem/goal, all five steps in the problem-solving process, and a well-supported personal response.

3 = Retelling includes characters, problem/goal, and all five steps in the problem-solving process, but has no personal response.

2 = Retelling includes characters, problem/goal, and three or four steps in the problem-solving process; some key factual errors or omissions. Add ½ point for well-supported personal response.

1 = Retelling omits either characters or problem; includes one or two steps in the problem-solving process, but the account is disjointed and includes factual errors or serious omissions. Add ½ point for well-supported personal response.

0 = Provides a title or topic statement but shows no real awareness of the character's problem and how the problem is worked out.

Retelling Score: ___3.0___

Comprehension Questions

1. Why didn't any of the animals want to race against Spencer?

   Text-based: He always won and he bragged afterwards.

   He was bragging because he won all the races.

   +10

2. What did the animals do when Annie won the race? (Must identify one.)

   Text-based: Cheered; talked with her.

   They cheered.

   +10

3. Why would Spencer want to race against Annie again?

   Inference: He couldn't accept the fact that someone was faster; thought he could win.

   He thought that he could beat her.

   +10

4. Why did Annie agree to race against Spencer when no one else would?

   Inference: She knew she was very fast; she probably knew she could beat him.

   She knew she would win.

   +10

5. What would have been the best thing for Spencer to do after Annie beat him? Why?

   Critical Response: Be a good loser and admit that she was faster; try to be her friend since he didn't have any friends; stop bragging about himself to the other animals.

   Be a good loser, maybe shake hands and say "let's be friends."

   +10

6. What did Spencer do when he came back the next day?

   Text-based: Started bragging about something else; bragged that he could jump higher than anyone else.

   Started bragging that he could jump higher than them.

   +10

7. Do you think that this was the first time Annie had ever raced against anyone? Why or why not?

Inference: No, she smiled when Spencer challenged her; she probably knew she could beat him.

No, that's why she knew she could beat him. ?(Examiner probe: So what does that show about Annie?) She did it before so that's why she knew she'd beat him.

+10

8. What did the other animals hope would happen after Spencer lost the race?

Text-based: That Spencer would stop bragging.

That he'd stop bragging.

+10

9. If another new family moved into the jungle, do you think Spencer would ask them to race or not?

Critical Response: Yes, he did not seem to have learned anything; still bragged even after he lost. No, he has lost once; he may still brag but he didn't like to lose and he may not be as confident as he was once.

Yes, because he used to brag and he didn't stop so he won't stop asking for a race either.

+10

10. If Spencer stopped bragging, do you think he would be a good friend for Annie or would he still have to change?

Critical Response: Yes, he wouldn't annoy people; others would give him a chance; others would like him better. No, has to be a better loser; shouldn't be so selfish; must admit she is a better runner.

Yes, because Annie and the other animals could like him then.

+10

Comprehension Analysis:

Text-Based: _4/4_
Inference: _3/3_
Critical Response: _3/3_

Total Comprehension %: _100%_

Second Grade Silent: The Roller Coaster Ride

Reader's copy on p. 25 of the Reader's Passages.

Introductory Statement: "Would you read this passage about a ride on the roller coaster to yourself? When you are finished, I'll take the passage away. Then I'll ask you to tell me about what you read and what you think of it. After that, I'll ask you some questions about the passage."

Story

Today it was finally Jessie's birthday. She jumped out of bed and called to her mom, "Mom, can you come here and see how tall I am?" She ran to the wall and waited. Mother marked the spot where Jessie had grown since her last birthday. "I made it!" shouted Jessie. "I'm tall enough to ride the roller coaster now!" On Saturday, Jessie, her mom, and Aunt Jane would go to the park. Then she could take her first ride!

Mom was too afraid to ride so Aunt Jane took Jessie to the line to wait their turn. Jessie and Aunt Jane jumped into a car and pulled the bar over their heads. Then they waited for the ride to start. "Let's get going," thought Jessie. Soon the ride started and Jessie was really excited. She felt very grown up. Then the car climbed higher and higher. It came down and went faster and faster. Jessie was so afraid that she thought she was going to die.

Jessie held Aunt Jane's arm. She covered her face and screamed. Jessie prayed that the ride would end. "Don't let me die," she prayed, "and I'll never ride a roller coaster again." Aunt Jane hugged Jessie. Jessie opened her eyes and she saw people laughing and screaming. Aunt Jane was laughing too. They were all having fun.

The car slowed and then stopped. The ride was finally over. "Aunt Jane," said Jessie, "Can we do it again?" (244 words)

Retelling

Examiner: "Tell me about what you just read and what you thought about it."

It's Jessie's birthday and she gets out of bed and calls to her mother to check how tall she is. Her mother tells her she's tall enough to ride the roller coaster. She went with her Aunt Jane because her mother was afraid but she got scared when the roller coaster went so fast. She held her aunt's arm and screamed for a long time. Then they both laughed when the ride was over and Jessie asked her to take another ride.

If there is no spontaneous response, repeat the request, "Tell me what you thought about the passage."

She found out she liked the roller coaster ride.

NOTE: Use the Retelling Rubric on p. 64 to access the child's retelling performance.

Retelling Rubric

Story Structure:

1. **Key Characters and Setting:** Jessie, Aunt Jane, and Mom at amusement park.   +1
2. **Character's Problem or Goal:** Jessie wants to finally be big enough to ride the roller coaster.   +1
3. **Problem-Solving or Goal-Meeting Process:**
   - Jessie is finally tall enough to ride the roller coaster.   +1
   - Aunt Jane goes with her on the ride.   +1
   - Jessie becomes frightened.   +1
   - She promises she will never ride again.   0
   - She realizes that the ride is safe and fun.   +½
   - She decides to go on the ride again.   +1
4. **Personal Response:** Any well-supported positive or negative response to the characters or events in the story; any reaction to the humor or sadness in the story; any well-supported positive or negative reaction to the story as a whole.   0

Rubric:

4 = Complete retelling includes characters, problem/goal, and all six steps in the problem-solving process and a well-supported personal response.

3 = Retelling includes characters, problem/goal, and five or six steps in the problem solving process, but has no personal response

2 = Retelling includes characters, problem/goal, and three or four steps in the problem solving process; some key factual errors or omissions. Add ½ point for well-supported personal response.

1 = Retelling omits either characters or problem; includes two or three steps in the problem solving process, but the account is disjointed and includes factual errors or serious omissions. Add ½ point for well-supported personal response.

0 = Provides a title or topic statement but shows no real awareness of the character's problem and how the problem is worked out.

Retelling Score: __2.5__

Comprehension Questions

1. Why did Jessie want her mother to see how tall she was?

   Text-based: Wanted to see if she was tall enough to ride the roller coaster.

   So she could see if she was tall enough to ride the roller coaster.

   +10

2. Why didn't Mom want to ride on the roller coaster with Jessie?

   Text-based: She was afraid of roller coasters.

   She was afraid of roller coasters.

   +10

3. Do you think that Jessie had ever been to an amusement park before? Why?

   Inference: Yes, She knew that she had to be a certain height to go on certain rides; may have seen a roller coaster at an amusement park before.

   Yes, because she wants to ride the roller coaster. ?(Examiner probe: Does that tell if Jessie has been to an amusement park before?) *She must have seen one there.*

   +10

4. Why would Jessie want so much to ride the roller coaster?

   Inference: Sign that she was growing up; was something she wasn't allowed to do before; she thought it would be fun.

   She thought she'd love the ride.

   +10

5. How do you think Mom felt about Jessie taking her first roller coaster ride? Why?

   Critical Response: Proud that she had grown up; afraid she might be hurt; happy that Aunt Jane would be with her.

   She was happy that Aunt Jane took her.

   +10

6. How did Aunt Jane help Jessie during the ride?

   Text-based: Hugged her; held her close.

   She hugged her.

   +10

7. Why did Jessie decide to ride the roller coaster again?

   Inference: She wanted to have more fun; may have wanted to prove to herself that she wasn't afraid; made her feel grown-up; she ended up liking it.

   Because she liked it so much.

   +10

8. What did Jessie do during the ride to help herself stop being afraid? (Must identify one.)

   Text-based: Hugged Aunt Jane; saw others having fun; prayed; screamed out loud.

   She prayed.

   +10

9. Do you think it was right for Jessie to get back on the ride after she promised never to ride again?

   Critical Response: Yes, she didn't really mean what she had said. No, she gave her word and probably shouldn't break it.

   Yes, by the end she had changed her mind and wasn't afraid.

   +0 (missed point of critique of action)

10. Do you think the story would end the same way if Jessie took the ride with her mother instead of Aunt Jane? Explain.

    Critical Response: No, her mother might have been afraid too and neither one would ever ride again. Yes, her mother probably would hide her fear for Jessie's sake.

    No, her mother wouldn't go on the ride. ?(Examiner probe: But how would it end if her Mother did?) *She wouldn't have.*

    +0 (missed hypothetical relationship needed)

Comprehension Analysis:

   Text-Based: _4/4_
   Inference: _3/3_
   Critical Response: _1/3_

Total Comprehension %: _80%_

The Roller Coaster Ride: 244 Words

Reader's copy on p. 26 of the Reader's Passages.

Introductory Statement: "Would you read this passage about a boy's visit to a farm out loud for me? When you are finished, I'll take the passage away. Then I'll ask you to tell me about what you read and what you think of it. After that, I'll ask you some questions about the passage."

Story

It was five o'clock in the morning when David heard his grandfather call. David never got up this early before but he didn't mind at all! He was visiting his grandfather's farm for the first time and he was excited. He had always wanted to be a farmer and now he would have his chance. Besides, Grandpa had horses too and David looked forward to learning how to ride.

to ✔SC

SC   When David ran into the kitchen, Grandfather said, "Eat a good breakfast, Dave. We've got a lot to do this morning. We'll start with the hay."

"Don't rush him!" said Grandma. "Are you sure you want to work with Grandpa all day?" she asked David.

"Sure am!" said David. He gulped down his breakfast and dashed out to help load the hay wagon. He never knew hay was so heavy.

"You finish up here while I get the tractor. We've got some work to do in the garden," said Grandpa.

up ✔SC

SC   David walked over to the garden and <u>climbed on to</u> the tractor. Up and down they drove, row after row, turning up the soil as they went.

"Lunch time," said Grandpa when the sun was overhead.

"When do the horses get fed?" David asked Grandma as he walked into the kitchen.

"Do you want to do that after lunch? You've worked so much already," said Grandma.

"Don't forget, honey," said Grandpa, "We've got lots to do. That's how life is on the farm."

"That's OK," said David. "Maybe I better stay and help Grandpa."

After lunch, David worked under the hot sun, helping Grandpa dig postholes for a new fence. Then David and Grandpa picked corn and brought it to their roadside stand. David was trudging slowly back toward the *to* ✔SC SC house when Grandma called, "Do you want to feed the horses?"

David ran to the barn and helped to feed the horses. "I wish I could ride you," he said to each one as he rubbed its nose. "Maybe Grandpa will teach me!" David fell asleep immediately that night but when the sun rose the next morning, he was not so eager to get up. He had the feeling that today would be another day just like yesterday. As it turned out, he was right.

"Do you still want to be a farmer?" asked Grandfather at the end of the week. "I'm not so sure," David replied. "If the sun rose at ten o'clock and there wasn't so much hard work, then maybe farming would be more fun." (417 words)

Miscues

__0__ N of miscues that maintained meaning (checked). This is the MM.

__0__ N of miscues that violated meaning (unchecked). This is the MV.

Reading Accuracy Index: __100__ %
(N of words − N of miscues, checked and unchecked)/ N of words

Meaning Maintenance Index: __100__ %
(N of words − N of meaning-violating miscues, unchecked only)/N of words

The Farm Vacation: 417 Words

Miscue Chart

Miscues	%	Miscues	%	Miscues	%
1	100	12	97	23	94
2	100	13	97	24	94
3	99	14	97	25	94
4	99	15	96	26	94
5	99	16	96	27	94
6	99	17	96	28	93
7	98	18	96	29	93
8	98	19	95	30	93
9	98	20	95	31	93
10	98	21	95	32	92
11	97	22	95	33	92

Retelling

Examiner: "Tell me about what you just read and what you thought about it."

At five o'clock Dave woke up because his grandfather was calling him. He went to the kitchen and his grandfather told him they had lots to do. His Grandma wanted him not to work so much. David wanted to be a farmer and this was his first visit to the farm. They did a lot of hard work together so David didn't ride the horses. He did feed them so he probably got a ride too but now he doesn't want to be a farmer anymore.

If there is no spontaneous response, repeat the request, "Tell me what you thought about the passage."

David changed his mind about being a farmer and he probably never learned how to ride horses.

Retelling Rubric

Story Structure:

1. **Key Characters and Setting:** David and his grandparents on the farm. +1
2. **Character's Problem or Goal:** David visits farm to learn about farming and to learn to ride horses. +1
3. **Problem-Solving or Goal-Meeting Process:**
   - David wants to learn about farming and to ride horses. +1
   - Grandpa has him working hard but Grandma wants him to enjoy himself. +1
   - David decides to work with Grandpa. +1
   - David never gets chance to ride the horses. 0
   - David reconsiders his choice. +1
4. **Personal Response:** Any well-supported positive or negative response to the characters or events in the story; any reaction to the humor or sadness in the story; any well-supported positive or negative reaction to the story as a whole. 0

Rubric:

4 = Complete retelling includes characters, problem/goal, all five steps in the problem-solving process, and a well-supported personal response.

3 = Retelling includes characters, problem/goal, and all five steps in the problem-solving process, but has no personal response

2 = Retelling includes characters, problem/goal, and three or four steps in the problem-solving process; some key factual errors or omissions. Add ½ point for well-supported personal response.

1 = Retelling omits either characters or problem; includes one or two steps in the problem-solving process, but the account is disjointed and includes factual errors or serious omissions. Add ½ point for well-supported personal response.

0 = Provides a title or topic statement but shows no real awareness of the character's problem and how the problem is worked out.

Retelling Score: 2.5

Comprehension Questions

1. Why was David excited about visiting the farm?

   Text-based: He always wanted to be a farmer.

   He always wanted to be a farmer.

   +10

2. How did David feel about farming *at the end* of the week?

   Text-based: He wasn't sure about it; he had changed his mind.

   He wasn't sure anymore.

   +10

3. Do you think that David lived near his grandfather? Explain.

   Inference: Probably not, he was visiting the farm for the first time.

   No, it was his first visit.

   +10

4. Do you think that Grandma was happy about how David's first week at the farm was going?

   Inference: Probably not, he was working very hard and having no fun; he should have been riding the horses.

   No, she wanted him to learn to ride the horses.

   +10

5. Do you think that Grandpa really wanted David to become a farmer? Why or why not?

   Critical Response: Probably not, made him work very hard, possibly because he wanted David to understand how difficult farming was. Probably so, wanted him to understand everything about farming, including the hard work.

   Probably not, he only made him work real hard.

   +10

6. What did David want most from Grandpa?

   Text-based: To learn how to ride the horses.

   To teach him how to ride the horses.

   +10

7. Do you think that David ever got to ride the horses that week? Why?

   Inference: Probably not, seemed that there was little time for play and Grandpa didn't appear too interested in seeing David ride the horses.

   Yes, his grandmother wanted him to ride them. ?(Examiner's probe: But did he ever get to ride them?) *I don't remember if it said that.*

   +0 (missed story connections to make inference)

8. Why did David change his mind at the end of the week? (Must identify one.)

   Text-based: Had to get up too early and there was too much hard work.

   He had so much hard work and he had to get up at 5 o'clock.

   +10

9. Do you think David and his grandfather had a close relationship? Why or why not?

   Critical Response: Yes, David cared for the grandfather; always helped him work even when he would rather ride the horses. No, seemed that they did not talk very much; Grandfather unaware that David wanted to ride the horses; didn't talk very much about farming.

   Probably not, this was the first time he ever visited him.

   +10

10. Was Grandpa fair to expect David to do so much work that first week? Why?

    Critical Response: No, he seemed to have one task right after another with no rest. Yes, David wanted to learn about the farming life; it would be dishonest to present it in any other way.

    No, he had to work too hard. ?(Examiner's probe: Could you explain what you mean?) *I don't know. The story didn't say anything about that.*

    +0 (unable to provide support for response)

Comprehension Analysis:

Text-Based: __4/4__
Inference: __2/3__
Critical Response: __2/3__

Total Comprehension %: __80%__

Third Grade Silent: The Championship Game

Reader's copy on p. 28 of the Reader's Passages.

Introductory Statement: "Would you read this passage about an important baseball game to yourself? When you are finished, I'll take the passage away. Then I'll ask you to tell me about what you read and what you think of it. After that, I'll ask you some questions about the passage."

Story

At the end of a long softball season, Jill's team made it to the championship game. They would play against the top team in the league, the Ramblers. Before the game, the teams had batting and fielding practice. Jill watched her teammates. She knew that they would have a hard time winning. Their shortstop kept dropping the ball during fielding practice. Their starting pitcher was as wild as she had ever been. Jill thought that if her team was going to win, she would have to be the one to step forward. Soon the coach called the players in to sing the national anthem. Jill thought to herself, "This is just like it will be when I get to the pros." She knew the other players were nervous but not her! She couldn't wait to start the game.

Early in the game, Jill's team took a 1–0 lead. Jill came up to bat with a runner on second. But the umpire called her out on strikes. She couldn't believe that he called such a terrible pitch a strike! She really wanted to say to him, "You just called out Jill, the best player on the team." By the third inning, the lead was 3–0. Things were looking good for the team. But Jill still didn't have a hit. Her next time up, she hit a long fly to left. When the ball was caught, she blamed a gust of wind for taking away her home run.

Then the Ramblers scored four runs in their half of the inning. Now Jill had her chance to be the star. There were runners on second and third. With two strikes she got the pitch she was looking for. She swung with all her might. She couldn't believe that she missed it. Jill sat down, angry that the sun had gotten in her eyes at the wrong time. She just couldn't see the ball. Then the shortstop lined a double to left field and scored the two runs that the team needed. The pitcher struck out their last batter and Jill's team won 5–4. The team went wild, but Jill didn't feel like celebrating. Even after the team picture, Jill felt terrible. It was her worst game all season and it was the biggest game of the season, too. She wished that she had done better in front of all those people. (399 words)

Retelling

Examiner: "Tell me about what you just read and what you thought about it."

Jill played in the championship game and was real excited when they played the national anthem because she wanted to be a professional player. When they were practicing a lot of the players were making mistakes. She struck out and the other team was getting hits but they won anyway. But they almost lost.

If there is no spontaneous response, repeat the request to "Tell me what you thought about the passage."

They did win even though they made lots of mistakes when they were practicing.

NOTE: Use the Retelling Rubric on p. 70 to assess the child's retelling performance.

Retelling Rubric

Story Structure:	
1. **Key Characters and Setting:** Jill and her team playing in the championship game.	+1
2. **Character's Problem or Goal:** Be the star of the game.	0
3. **Problem-Solving or Goal-Meeting Process:**	0
• Jill has no confidence that her team can win the game.	0
• Jill thinks she is better than the other players.	+½
• She plays badly but makes excuses for it.	+1
• Jill's team wins the championship.	0
• Even though her team wins, Jill is unhappy about her play.	0
4. **Personal Response:** Any well-supported positive or negative response to the characters or events in the story; any reaction to the humor or sadness in the story; any well-supported positive or negative reaction to the story as a whole.	0

Rubric:

4 = Complete retelling includes characters, problem/goal, all five steps in the problem-solving process, and a well-supported personal response.

3 = Retelling includes characters, problem/goal, and all five steps in the problem-solving process, but has no critical response.

2 = Retelling includes characters, problem/goal, and three or four steps in the problem-solving process; some key factual errors or omissions. Add ½ point for well-supported personal response.

1 = Retelling omits either characters or problem; includes one or two steps in the problem-solving process, but the account is disjointed and includes factual errors or serious omissions. Add ½ point for well-supported personal response.

0 = Provides a title or topic statement but shows no real awareness of the character's problem and how the problem is worked out.

Retelling Score: 1.0

Comprehension Questions

1. Why didn't Jill think that her team was going to win the game?

   Text-based: Practice was going badly; shortstop dropped the ball often and pitcher was wild.

   They made a lot of mistakes in practice.

   +10

2. Did the other players on the team feel the same way that Jill did about winning the championship? How do you know?

   Text-based: No. They were happy to win, while Jill was disappointed in herself.

   No, they went wild cause they won.

   +10

3. Do you think that Jill and her teammates were good friends or not? Why?

   Inference: Probably not. She didn't seem to know their names. She didn't care too much about the team; said that they wouldn't play well.

   Yes, they played a lot of games together.

   +0 (missed focus of relationship)

4. How important to Jill was winning the championship game? What made you think that?

   Inference: Not very important. She was more concerned that she didn't have a hit. When her team was losing she thought about herself, not winning the game.

   Real important; the national anthem made her think of being a pro.

   +0 (missed focus of relationship)

5. Do you think that Jill has a chance of becoming a professional player? Why or why not?

   Critical Response: Probably not, won't work hard if she thinks everyone else is responsible when she doesn't play well; not a team player. Yes, she is the best player on the team; everyone can have a bad game; she has the confidence she needs.

   Yes, she's the best player on a champion team.

   +10

6. What reasons did Jill give for playing poorly in the game? (Must identify two.)

   Text-based: Blamed umpire; blamed the wind; blamed the sun.

When she hit the long drive the wind made it an out. And the umpire called her out.

+10

7. Was Jill good at predicting how well her teammates would play? Explain.

   Inference: Not very good; both players that she thought would do poorly played well.

   Yes, she saw the players making mistakes.

   +0 (missed need for inferential thinking)

8. Why was Jill upset at the end of the game?

   Text-based: She played badly; she was embarrassed in front of the people; she wished she had played better.

   She felt bad cause it was her worst game.

   +10

9. Do you think that Jill needs help from her coach? Why or why not?

   Critical Response: Yes, she may not be as good as she thinks she is; she needs to stop making excuses and practice more; she needs to be more of a team player.

   No, she is already the best player on the team.

   Yes, coaches can help everybody. ?(Examiner's probe: Does Jill need help?) *Not any more than anybody else.*

   +0 (missed focus of relationship)

10. Why do you think that Jill didn't play as well as she thought she would in the big game?

    Critical response: May have been overconfident; big crowd may have bothered her; may have tried too hard to be the star; made excuses instead of trying harder.

    She knew she always played good so she thought she'd play good again.

    +10

Comprehension Analysis:

    Text-Based: __4/4__
    Inference: __0/3__
    Critical Response: __2/3__

Total Comprehension %: __60%__

The Championship Game: 399 words

Reader's copy on p. 29 of the Reader's Passages.

Introductory Statement: "Would you read this passage about a family vacation out loud for me? When you are finished, I'll take the passage away. Then I'll ask you to tell me about what you read and what you think of it. After that, I'll ask you some questions about the passage."

Story

Juan burst into his sister's room. "Only eight more days!" he shouted.

"I started packing already!" said Maria. "I can't wait to see what Florida is like."

Juan and Maria had started every day for the last two weeks talking about their Florida vacation. Mom and Dad were just as eager as they were.

But that evening, Father walked into the house, looking like a ghost. "What's wrong?" Mother asked. "No more overtime for the rest of the year," he stammered. Mother knew that they were going to use the overtime money to pay for the hotel rooms and the plane tickets to Florida. This was their first family vacation!

Mr. Ruiz struggled as he told the children that they would have to cancel their vacation. Juan ran up to his room crying while Maria hugged her father and sobbed.

"Let me see what I can do," said Mrs. Ruiz as she left the room.

She was smiling from ear to ear when she returned. "I just spoke with my brother Sal and he said that we could use his van to drive to Florida and we can stay with his wife's sister!"

SC   Maria was excited with the news but Juan was [*that* ✔SC] angry! That wasn't the fun vacation he had been dreaming of for weeks. He had never flown on an airplane and he had never stayed in a hotel.

During the trip, the family stopped to look at different sights along the way. But every time, Juan refused to leave the van. He was irritated with their/jabbering about what they had seen at each stop.

The following day, Juan again sat in the van while the others went out to see a nearby river. Suddenly, Maria came rushing back to the van. "Juan! Juan!" she called, "Hurry, there's an alligator!" Juan jumped out of the van and dashed the quarter mile to where his parents were standing.

"You missed it," said his father sadly. "It's gone!"

Maria, Mom, and Dad told Juan how they first saw the alligator sunning itself on the bank of the river. Maria had quietly run back to get Juan but a squawking bird startled the alligator and it dashed into the river.

Everyone saw how disgusted Juan was and no [*so* ✔SC / SC] one said a word for over twenty minutes.

"You know, Juan . . . " began Mother.

"I know, Mom." said Juan. "I've been missing one of the best chances I've ever had! But I won't do it again!" (412 words)

Miscues

__0__   N of miscues that maintained meaning (checked). This is the MM.

__0__   N of miscues that violated meaning (unchecked). This is the MV.

Reading Accuracy Index: __100__ %
  (N of words – N of miscues, checked and unchecked)/ N of words

Meaning Maintenance Index: __100__ %
  (N of words – N of meaning-violating miscues, unchecked only)/N of words

The Vacation: 412 words

Miscue Chart

Miscues	%	Miscues	%	Miscues	%	Miscues	%
1	100	13	97	25	94	37	91
2	100	14	97	26	94	38	91
3	99	15	96	27	93	39	91
4	99	16	96	28	93	40	90
5	99	17	96	29	93	41	90
6	99	18	96	30	93	42	90
7	98	19	95	31	92	43	90
8	98	20	95	32	92	44	89
9	98	21	95	33	92	45	89
10	98	22	95	34	92	46	89
11	97	23	94	35	92	47	89
12	97	24	94	36	91	48	88

Retelling

Examiner: "Tell me about what you just read and what you thought about it."

The family was going to fly to Florida and stay in a hotel but the father couldn't work overtime. But then they got a van somehow and so they could go. Juan wanted to fly so he was sad. He missed seeing an alligator because he wasn't with his family.

If there is no spontaneous response, repeat the request, "Tell me what you thought about the passage."

He didn't stay with his family so he missed the alligator.

Retelling Rubric

Story Structure:

1. **Key Characters and Setting:** Juan, Maria, his mother and father on family vacation. +½
2. **Character's Problem or Goal:** Juan is disappointed with a change in travel plans +1
3. **Problem-Solving or Goal-Meeting Process:**
   - Juan's family plans a trip to Florida. +1
   - Trip must be cancelled because of money problems. +1
   - Mother makes arrangements so trip can take place. 0
   - Juan is disappointed that the trip is not everything he wanted. +1
   - Juan does not participate in the family's fun. +½
   - Juan misses seeing the alligator and realizes that he has been wrong. +½
4. **Personal response:** Any well-supported positive or negative response to the characters or events in the story; any reaction to the humor or sadness in the story; any well-supported positive or negative reaction to the story as a whole. 0

Rubric:

4 = Complete retelling includes characters, problem/goal, all six steps in the problem-solving process, and a well-supported personal response.

3 = Retelling includes characters, problem/goal, and five or six steps in the problem-solving process, but has no personal response

2 = Retelling includes characters, problem/goal, and three or four steps in the problem solving process; some key factual errors or omissions. Add ½ point for well-supported personal response.

1 = Retelling omits either characters or problem; includes two or three steps in the problem-solving process, but the account is disjointed and includes factual errors or serious omissions. Add ½ point for well-supported personal response.

0 = Provides a title or topic statement but shows no real awareness of the character's problem and how the problem is worked out.

Retelling Score: _2.0_

Comprehension Questions

1. Why was everyone in the family excited about the vacation in Florida?

   Text-based: It was their first family vacation; first trip to Florida.

   It was their first one.

   +10

2. Why did it seem that the family would have to cancel their vacation?

   Text-based: Mr. Ruiz could get no more overtime at work.

   The father wouldn't have overtime.

   +10

3. Why didn't Mrs. Ruiz ask her brother earlier if they could borrow his van?

   Inference: The family planned to fly to Florida.

   They wanted their first airplane ride.

   +10

4. What reason would Juan have for being upset when his family talked about what they had seen?

   Inference: Jealous of them; didn't want to be reminded of what he had missed; wanted everyone else to suffer along with him.

   Because he was mad that they weren't flying.

   +0 (missed time relationship of the question)

5. Who do you think was older, Juan or Maria? Why do you think so?

   Critical Response: Maria—seemed more concerned with her father's feelings; handled the disappointment better than Juan did; was willing to enjoy the vacation with her family. Juan—Maria was just the messenger when the family saw the alligator; she would have teased him if he were younger.

   They could probably be the same ages. ?(Examiner's probe: But what one might be the older one?) *It didn't say that one was older.*

   +0 (missed hypothetical relationship of the question)

6. Why was Juan disappointed when he heard that the family would drive the van to Florida? (Must identify one.)

   Text-based: He was looking forward to flying and staying in a hotel for the first time.

   He wanted to take an airplane ride and stay in a hotel.

   +10

7. How did the family show that they cared about Juan's feelings after he missed seeing the alligator?

   Inference: They didn't force him to go with them; they didn't preach to him; they stayed silent for 20 minutes after he missed seeing the alligator; they gave him some think time.

   They took him on the first family vacation. ?(Examiner's probe: But how did they show this on the trip?) *It really didn't say.*

   +0 (missed time relationship required in the question)

8. Why was the family still able to go to Florida without the extra overtime money?

   Text-based: Mrs. Ruiz got help from her brother; brother gave her his van and found place for them to stay.

   The mother's brother helped them.

   +10

9. Do you think Juan's parents were right to let him sulk for so long?

   Critical Response: Yes, maybe they were trying to help him learn a lesson; you can't really force someone to have a good time; he learned something from the experience. No, he was trying to put a damper on everyone else's vacation; he had already made up his mind not to have a good time.

   No, he should be hollered at for not listening to his parents.

   +0 (made inappropriate relationship)

10. What lesson do you think Juan could learn from his experience?

    Critical Response: Don't sulk because you could miss some very good things; don't think the worst because sometimes things work out for the best; keep your mind on what is important in life.

    He should have gone with his family so that he could have seen the alligator because he liked alligators.

    +½ (very specific response to a question requiring a general application)

Comprehension Analysis:

Text-Based: __4/4__
Inference: __1/3__
Critical Response: __.5/3__

Total Comprehension %: __55%__

Reader's copy on p. 30 of the Reader's Passages.

Introductory Statement: "Would you read this passage about two sisters who have a job to do to yourself? When you are finished, I'll take the passage away. Then I'll ask you to tell me about what you read and what you think of it. After that, I'll ask you some questions about the passage."

Story

"Libby, come here quick," I called. "The leaves are all falling." It is fall and my little sister, Libby, and I will have to rake the leaves together every day. Mom said that Libby is finally old enough to help with the chores and that I have the job of showing her how to clean up the yard. If we don't rake up the leaves, they will clutter up the lawn, the sidewalks, and even the rainspouts. Mom says that falling leaves are messy and dangerous, especially when they are wet.

"Look at all the leaves, Sue!" shouted Libby. "I want to go out and play right now!" I told her that we couldn't play just then. "Mom wants us to rake the leaves up. If it rains, people walking by our house might slip and fall."

"Please, Sue. Let's just jump in them for a little while," she begged. So I told her that if she would help me clean up afterwards, we could pile them up into a big mound and jump in. She was so excited that she promised to help me.

We went out and raked the leaves into a big pile and then we shouted, "One, two, three, jump!" And we jumped on the pile of leaves again and again until the leaves were scattered over the entire yard. Then I told Libby that it was time to rake them up, but Libby just wanted to keep playing. While she played, I had to gather the leaves and put them in the trash bags myself. Then I had to drag all of the bags out to the sidewalk for the trucks to come and pick up the next morning. I knew that more leaves would fall tomorrow but I wondered if Libby would help me clean them up then.

The next day, I had piano lessons so I didn't get home until late. I was surprised to find that Libby had gone outside and raked the leaves herself. But then she remembered the fun she had the day before and she jumped in them and they flew all over the yard. When I saw the mess I told Libby that she would have to clean up the leaves. I even offered to help her rake them up before Mom came home. But Libby ran away to play with her friend and I was left to do all of the work again. I really wanted to just leave everything there in the yard but I knew that Mom would be disappointed. Falling leaves can be fun for kids but grown-ups don't see it that way. I think I'm starting to see the reason. (447 words)

Retelling

Examiner: "Tell me about what you just read and what you thought about it."

> *Sue had to teach her little sister how to rake up the leaves. The little sister said she'd help but then she didn't. Then she did the same thing the next day. Her mother was mad at her.*

If there is no spontaneous response, repeat the request, "Tell me what you thought about the passage."

> *It shows that the little sister said she'd help but she didn't.*

NOTE: Use the Retelling Rubric on p. 76 to assess the child's retelling performance.

Retelling Rubric

Story Structure:

1. **Key Characters and Setting:** Sue and younger sister (Libby) at home. [+1]
2. **Character's Problem or Goal:** Sue has difficulty getting her little sister to help her with the leaves. [+1]
3. **Problem-Solving or Goal-Meeting Process:**
   - Sue tells Libby about their job raking the leaves. [+1]
   - Libby wants to play and leaves Sue with the work. [0]
   - The next day it happens again. [0]
   - Sue does not know what to do about Libby. [0]
   - Sue begins to understand why parents look at leaves differently. [0]
4. **Personal Response:** Any well-supported positive or negative response to the characters or events in the story; any reaction to the humor or sadness in the story; any well-supported positive or negative reaction to the story as a whole. [0]

Rubric:

4 = Complete retelling includes characters, problem/goal, all five steps in the problem-solving process, and a well-supported personal response.

3 = Retelling includes characters, problem/goal, and all five steps in the problem-solving process, but has no critical response.

2 = Retelling includes characters, problem/goal, and three or four steps in the problem-solving process; some key factual errors or omissions. Add ½ point for well-supported personal response.

1 = Retelling omits either characters or problem; includes one or two steps in the problem-solving process, but the account is disjointed. Add ½ point for well-supported personal response and includes factual errors or serious omissions.

0 = Provides a title or topic statement but shows no real awareness of the character's problem and how the problem is worked out.

Retelling Score: **1.5**

Comprehension Questions

1. In what season does this story take place?

   Text-based: Fall

   The fall.

   +10

2. What chore do the children have to do in the story?

   Text-based: Raking the leaves up.

   Rake the leaves.

   +10

3. How much older do you think Sue is than her sister Libby? Why do you think this?

   Inference: Must be several years; older one is responsible for the other; tells her what Mom wants her to do; decides if they can play in the leaves or not.

   Not much—maybe about 2 years—she has the job but the sister didn't.

   +10

4. Do you think Libby might have a good reason for not wanting to work with Sue? Explain.

   Inference: Libby might think she is bossy; makes her do things she doesn't want to do; her sister nags her about their jobs.

   Kids don't like it when they have to work with their sister. ?(Examiner's probe: But do you think she had a reason?) *It really didn't say.*

   +0 (missed point of cause–effect relationship)

5. What do you think that Sue should do the next time Libby promises to help? Why?

   Critical Response: Should refuse to do it until Libby shows she can keep her promises; should talk to Libby about the importance of keeping your word.

   Make her keep her promise. ?(Examiner's probe: Could you tell me more?) *You're supposed to keep promises.*

   +0 (can't support response)

6. Why couldn't the two girls work together on Tuesday?

   Text-based: Sue had piano lessons.

   She had piano lessons.

   +10

7. What do you think Sue meant when she said that she's beginning to see why adults don't see falling leaves as fun?

Inference: They are a lot of work and responsibility; lot of work when no one helps.

Adults don't play in leaves.

+0 (pure background with no use of story)

8. Why wasn't Sue happy that Libby raked the leaves by herself while Sue was at her piano lesson?

Text-based: She played in the leaves and scattered them all over the yard.

She had messed them all over the yard.

+10

9. Do you think that Sue should have done Libby's work for her? Why or why not?

Critical Response: No, she will only do the same thing again if she gets away with it. Yes, because if she didn't do it, someone might be hurt; she is being responsible.

No, but she had to do what her parents told her to do.

+0 (inaccurate information)

10. Do you think that Sue should tell Mom that Libby did not help with the work? Why or why not?

Critical Response: Yes, Libby is not being fair or responsible and will not listen to her sister. No, that would be tattling; she should refuse to let her play until she helps.

Yes, the sister did make a promise. ?(Examiner's probe: Can you tell me more about it?) *You're supposed to keep promises.*

+0 (no support provided)

Comprehension Analysis:

Text-Based: 4/4

Inference: 1/3

Critical Response: 0/3

Total Comprehension %: 50%

Autumn Leaves: 447 words

Reader's copy on p. 32 of the Reader's Passages. Note: This passage was used to assess listening comprehension.

Introductory Statement: Would you read this passage about a basketball player to yourself? When you are finished, I'll take the passage away. Then I'll ask you to tell me about what you read and what you think of it. After that, I'll ask you some questions about the passage."

Story

Rasheed was excited to be playing on his first basketball team. He hadn't played much basketball but he had always been big and fast and a good athlete. But this time things were different. The first time he had the ball, Rasheed dribbled it off his foot and out of bounds. The next two times, a quicker player stole it away from him. Finally Rasheed had his first chance to shoot the ball but he missed everything, even the backboard. Soon his teammates stopped passing the ball to him, even when he was open under the basket. His team lost the game badly and Rasheed went home angry with his team and angry with basketball.

That night, Rasheed went to his father and told him that he wanted to quit the basketball team. "I'm no good at basketball and the team is no good either," he said.

"Well, if you want to quit, that's your decision," said Mr. Singer. "But I think if you really want to, you can become a whole lot better and so can your team. Maybe you shouldn't just do things that are easy for you." Rasheed had to think this one over. Rasheed knew that whenever his father said, "It's your decision, but . . ." he really meant that he'd like Rasheed to think it over very carefully. Down deep, he knew that his father would be disappointed if he never even tried to become a better player.

Rasheed knew that his father wouldn't be much help at teaching him basketball but he had heard stories about their new neighbor, Mr. Armstrong, being named to the all-state team in high school. When Rasheed asked Mr. Armstrong if he could teach him basketball, Mr. Armstrong's eyes lit up. He said, "You stick with me, kid, and you'll be the best basketball player ever!" Rasheed laughed as the two of them took turns shooting baskets in Mr. Armstrong's back yard. But soon Rasheed was sweating and breathing hard as his new teacher put him through one basketball drill after another. Finally, Mr. Armstrong said, "Time to call it a day! But be here same time tomorrow and we'll do it again." Rasheed worked hard and even after just a few days, he could feel himself becoming more confident in his ability. When it was time for the next game, Rasheed scored eight points, grabbed five rebounds, and didn't lose the ball once. His team still lost the game but his teammates couldn't believe how much better he had become.

After the game, Mr. Singer put his arm around his son and said, "I'm really proud of the decision you made, Rasheed. You worked awfully hard and it really showed."

"Thanks, Dad. Thanks for not letting me quit the team."

"Who told you that you couldn't quit? It wasn't me!"

Rasheed just smiled. (473 words)

Retelling

Examiner: "Tell me about what you just read and what you thought about it."

Rasheed didn't do good playing basketball and he thought he was good but he wasn't. So he asked his neighbor to help him get better and he did and his dad was really proud that he was a good player now.

If there is no spontaneous response, repeat the request, "Tell me what you thought about the passage."

It shows that Rasheed's Dad was proud that he was a good player.

NOTE: Use the Retelling Rubric on the next page to assess the child's retelling performance.

Retelling Rubric

Story Structure:

1. **Key Characters and Setting:** Rasheed, his father, and Mr. Armstrong, in basketball league.	0
2. **Character's Problem or Goal:** Rasheed wants to quit the basketball team because he isn't very good.	0
3. **Problem-Solving or Goal-Meeting Process:**	
• Rasheed tries to play basketball and fails.	+1
• He wants to quit the team but his father wants him to think about it.	0
• Rasheed asks Mr. Armstrong to help him.	+1
• Mr. Armstrong and Rasheed work hard and he improves.	+½
• Rasheed plays better and his father is proud of his work.	+1
4. **Personal response:** Any well-supported positive or negative response to the characters or events in the story; any reaction to the humor or sadness in the story; any well-supported positive or negative reaction to the story as a whole.	0

Rubric:

4 = Complete retelling includes characters, problem/goal, all five steps in the problem-solving process, and a well-supported personal response.

3 = Retelling includes characters, problem/goal, and all five steps in the problem-solving process, but has no critical response.

2 = Retelling includes characters, problem/goal, and three or four steps in the problem-solving process; some key factual errors or omissions. Add ½ point for well-supported personal response.

1 = Retelling omits either characters or problem; includes one or two steps in the problem-solving process, but the account is disjointed and includes factual errors or serious omissions. Add ½ point for well-supported personal response.

0 = Provides a title or topic statement but shows no real awareness of the character's problem and how the problem is worked out.

Retelling Score: 1.0

Comprehension Questions

1. Why was Rasheed angry after his first game with the basketball team? (Must identify one.)

   Text-based: His teammates wouldn't pass the ball to him; he played badly; he was embarrassed. (Must identify one.)

   He didn't play very good.

   +10

2. How do you know that Mr. Armstrong really wanted to help Rasheed become a better player? (Must identify one.)

   Text-based: His eyes lit up when Rasheed asked him; he worked with Rasheed night after night.

   He practiced with him and he told him to come tomorrow so they could work again and again.

   +10

3. What kind of player was Rasheed expecting to be when he first started to play basketball? Why?

   Inference: A good player; was always a good athlete and expected basketball to be easy.

   He thought he'd be very good.

   +10

4. How do you think Rasheed knew that his father wouldn't be able to help him with basketball?

   Inference: He knew his father wasn't very good at basketball; his father may have been too busy.

   I don't think he asked his father.

   +0 points (missed relationship required of question)

5. Why would Rasheed's father think he should stay on the team, even if he wasn't very good?

   Critical Response: His son shouldn't just quit and walk away; knew his son could be better if he tried; wanted him to learn about how to stick with something and learn.

   He really wanted to be proud of his son.

   +0 points (again missed relationship that was the focus of question)

6. Why didn't Rasheed quit when Mr. Armstrong made him work so hard on basketball drills?

   Text-based: He had fun; they laughed together, and Mr. Armstrong told basketball stories.

   He was having fun laughing with him so he liked it.

   +10

7. Why do you think that Mr. Armstrong would spend so much time and energy on a neighbor's son?

Inference: Liked to share his knowledge of basketball; enjoyed spending time with Rasheed.

He was having fun playing basketball with Rasheed.

+10

8. How did Rasheed's teammates react to him after the second game?

Text-based: Surprised at his improvement.

They couldn't believe that he was that good now.

+10

9. Do you think Mr. Singer should let his son make his own decision even if he thought it was the wrong one? Explain.

Critical Response: Yes, he must learn to make his own decisions and accept consequences; will help him to become more mature and responsible.
No, he should give him some guidance and try to persuade him that he is making a mistake; stakes are too high to let kids make the wrong decision; kids really want guidance and advice.

No, you shouldn't let kids make important decisions. ?(Examiner's probe: Could you explain that a little more?) *They might make a wrong decision*

+0 (no relationship made to characters)

10. Do you think it would have been wrong if Rasheed had quit the team? Why or why not?

Critical Response: Yes, he really had not tried to improve; he would have disappointed his father.
No, he was not getting better; his teammates did not help him; his teammates ignored him and the team played badly anyway.

Yes, he wouldn't know that he could be a good player and now he knows and so does his father.

+10

Comprehension Analysis:

Text-Based: __4/4__
Inference: __2/3__
Critical Response: __1/3__

Total Comprehension %: __70%__

The Player: 473 words

Critical Reading Inventory—Recapitulation Record—Narrative Passages

Name **Tamika** Grade **5th** C.A. **10-4** Date of Testing **11/25** Examiner **M. Examiner**

Word List / Comprehending and Responding to Text

Level	Word List: Flash	Word List: Untimed	Context: RAI	Context: MMI	Oral: Comp. %	Oral: Retelling Score	Oral: Text-based	Oral: Inference	Oral: Critical	Silent: Comp. %	Silent: Retelling Score	Silent: Text-based	Silent: Inference	Silent: Critical	Average Oral & Silent	Listening Comp. %
Pre-Primer							/3	/3	/2			/3	/3	/2		
Primer							/3	/3	/2			/3	/3	/2		
First							/3	/3	/2			/3	/3	/2		
Second		100	100	100	100	3.0	4/4	3/3	3/3	80	2.5	4/4	2/3	1/3	90	
Third	100	100	100	100	80	2.5	4/4	2/3	2/3	60	1.0	4/4	0/3	2/3	70	
Fourth	95	100	100	100	55	2.0	4/4	1/3	.5/3	50	1.5	4/4	1/3	0/3	53	
Fifth / Listening	95	100				1.0	4/4	2/3	1/3			/4	/3	/3		70
Sixth	95	100					/4	/3	/3			/4	/3	/3		
Jr. High	80	95					/4	/3	/3			/4	/3	/3		
Sr. High																

Level One Interpretation

Level:

Highest Independent Level **2nd grade** Highest Instructional Level **3rd grade** Frustration Level **4th grade**

Word List and Miscue Analysis:

	Independent (2nd)	Instructional (3rd)	Frustration (4th)
Flash	—	100	95
MM	—	—	—
RAI	100	100	100
MV	—	—	—
MMI	100	100	100
Non-words	—	—	—

Comprehension and Retelling Scores:

	Independent — Comp. %	Independent — Retelling	Instructional — Comp. %	Instructional — Retelling	Frustration — Comp. %	Frustration — Retelling
Oral	100	3.0	80	2.5	55	2.0
Silent	80	2.5	60	1.0	50	1.5
Average	90	2.8	70	1.8	53	1.8

Oral Comprehension, Fluency, and MMI:

- Independent: Oral comp. % 100 MMI 100
- Instructional: Oral comp. % 80 MMI 100 Fluency 4.0
- Frustration: Oral comp. % 55 MMI 100

Question Type:

	Independent — Oral	Independent — Silent	Instructional — Oral	Instructional — Silent	Frustration — Oral	Frustration — Silent
Text-based	4/4	4/4	4/4	4/4	4/4	4/4
Inference	3/3	3/3	2/3	0/3	1/3	1/3
Critical	3/3	1/3	2/3	2/3	.5/3	0/3

Discussion of Case Study 1: Tamika

Tamika is 10 years and 4 months old and is currently in fifth grade in public school. She is considered by her teachers to be a very good student but her performance in state reading assessments has raised questions, particularly for her parents.

Preparing for the Interpretation of Data

All test materials gathered in the assessment of reading for both of the case studies included in this section have already been scored and the Recapitulation Record has been completed. But when you administer the CRI yourself, you will at this point have:

- scored the word lists.
- evaluated all miscues on the Miscue Analysis Worksheet (if necessary).
- calculated both the Reading Accuracy Index (RAI) and the Meaning Maintenance Index (MMI).
- scored all of your reader's responses to the comprehension questions.
- calculated overall comprehension score as well as subscores for all three question types.
- calculated the student's retelling scores for all passages administered.
- calculated the student's oral Reading Fluency Score at the highest instructional level.

Now, you will be ready to transcribe all of the relevant information onto the Recapitulation Record. In this section, all of the scoring and transcribing has been done for you in both case studies. Our focus will be on drawing conclusions about the child's reading on the basis of the data available to us.

Level One: Numerical Interpretation

We are now ready to begin the numerical interpretation (Level One Interpretation) of Tamika's reading performance on the CRI. The first step is to examine the reading level data recorded on the Recapitulation Record (see page 81). At the second grade level we note that Tamika has an RAI (and MMI) score of 100% and an Average Comprehension score of 90%. Her strength in word recognition and comprehension would lead us to conclude that Tamika can read independently at the second grade level. At the third grade level we find an RAI (and MMI) of 100% and an Average Comprehension score of 70%. Since it appears that she has some need for help in comprehension at this level, we conclude that Tamika's instructional level is third grade. When we move to the fourth grade level, we note that while Tamika's word recognition continues at very high levels of proficiency, her Average Comprehension has fallen so low that she barely comprehends half of what she reads. Thus we estimate that fourth grade material is likely to be too difficult for Tamika. She has reached her frustration level and there is just one step remaining in her reading test. Because Tamika is currently in a fifth-grade classroom, we want to see how she can handle materials at her current grade level that are read to her. Tamika scored 70% in Listening Comprehension with a weak retelling at her grade level, and for her the test is over. But our work as diagnosticians has just begun.

Now we are ready to move to the Level One Interpretation section immediately below the table on the Recapitulation Record. We will use these summary columns as a means of systematically reviewing test results. You will find that you will be rerecording the numerical data but in such a way that you will be structuring a clear breakdown of Tamika's scores at the three different reading levels, independent, instructional, and frustration. At each level, we would like to consider four comparisons of data that should shed considerable light on Tamika's overall reading performance. The first of these is the comparison of Flash (sight vocabulary) performance on the Word Lists with performance in oral reading (RAI and MMI). Next we will compare Tamika's oral and silent comprehension, along with her retellings. Then, we will complete a comparison of Tamika's overall word recognition (including her fluency) with her comprehension following oral reading. Finally, we will break down Tamika's comprehension performance into the three different question types that characterize the CRI.

Word Lists and Miscue Analysis.   We will begin at the independent level, grade 2, and note the score of 100% on the flash presentation, linked with 100% for both the RAI and the MMI. Normally, we would move directly to the Miscue Analysis Worksheet to try to gain some insight into the nature and source of Tamika's miscues, but since Tamika obtained a perfect score, there are no miscues to analyze. When we glance up at the data table under Word Lists, we find that Tamika's performance reflects a very strong sight vocabulary. She obtained a score of 100% on Flash at the third grade level and 95% through the sixth grade level and could be considered as having an adequate sight vocabulary through the junior high school level. This strength suggests several possible explanations, two of which are very salient: either Tamika has acquired this sight vocabulary by engaging in consistent reading of challenging materials or she has a particular proficiency in learning words.

When given more time to correct words that she missed in flash presentation, Tamika corrected the one word she missed at the fourth through sixth grade levels and three of the four words she missed at the junior high level, suggesting that she has solid word analysis skills as well. Both strengths were borne out in Tamika's oral reading miscue record, both at third and fourth grade levels. Despite the fact that Tamika read no passages at her current fifth grade level, she seems to have very few instructional needs, relative to her grade level, in the area of word recognition.

Comprehension and Retelling Scores.   At the independent level (second grade), Tamika obtained a score of 100% on the questions and a very good score of 3 on the retelling following oral reading. Following silent reading, she obtained a score of 80% on the questions and 2.5 on the retelling. This is a solid performance that clearly reflects independence in reading. While there is no drastic distinction between her comprehension and retelling scores following the oral and silent reading, the numbers suggest that Tamika is experiencing an easier time with comprehension of materials that she has read aloud. Of course, we would not conclude this based on a single set of scores but we will want to determine if a pattern emerges. When we move to the instructional level (third grade), we see that this pattern did indeed continue. Tamika obtained a score of 80% in the questions and a 2.5 in the retelling following oral reading, but only 60% and a retelling score of 1.0 following silent reading. We can still see this same pattern holding in both questions and retellings done at Tamika's frustration level (fourth grade). This consistent 15 to 20 point discrepancy between average oral and silent reading comprehension suggests that Tamika may actually be listening to her oral reading as a kind of support for her comprehension. When that support is removed in the silent reading, both her retellings and her comprehension responses seem to suffer.

Oral Comprehension, Fluency, and MMI.   We might expect Tamika's comprehension after oral reading to be very solid, given her excellent word recognition skills. And in fact at the second grade level, her comprehension is 100%. Her excellent fluency (scored at 4.0 on the Oral Reading Fluency Rubric at her instructional level) is nearly matched by a solid comprehension score of 80%. However, her comprehension drops quickly to 55% after oral reading at the fourth grade level. Given her fifth grade level placement at school, this is a serious discrepancy. When the examiner read a fifth grade level passage to Tamika, her score on Listening Comprehension was 70%. This suggests that Tamika still has instructional needs at her grade level, even when she has the opportunity to focus solely on her comprehension of ideas.

Question Types.   Tamika's performance at the independent level following both oral and silent reading suggests that she is very strong in responding to text-based questions. Her responses following oral reading result in perfect scores for inferential and critical responses; she missed only one each of the inferential and critical questions after silent reading at the second grade level. When we examine the instructional and frustration scores, however, we see a clear discrepancy between Tamika's text-based comprehension and her ability to think about that text. Her responses to inferential and critical response items were consistently weaker than her responses to text-based items. These results suggest a possible view of reading as consisting of literal recall of the information in the passage.

Conclusions Based on Level One Interpretation

Based solely upon numerical analysis, it seems reasonable to draw several conclusions about Tamika's reading performance:

1. Tamika demonstrates a strong sight vocabulary at her current grade level and beyond.
2. Tamika's oral reading is strong through fourth grade with very few miscues and none that could be considered serious.
3. Tamika's comprehension difficulties lead to frustration even a grade level below her current placement, despite her strong word recognition skills.
4. Tamika's comprehension (on both open-ended questions and retelling) is significantly stronger with text-based tasks than it is with inference or critical response tasks.
5. Tamika's comprehension seems to be consistently weaker following silent reading compared to her comprehension following oral reading.
6. Tamika's reading levels appear to be: independent at second grade, instructional at third grade, and frustration at fourth grade.

A more detailed analysis of Tamika's responses may call any of these interpretations into question, but for the time being we have a fairly reliable overview of her reading performance, one that may enable us to begin a solid if rather general program of instruction. But because an analysis of Tamika's responses may lead us to a much more detailed and useful interpretation of her reading profile, seldom would we stop at the level of pure numerical analysis. There is simply too much more there to ignore.

Level Two: Analytical Interpretation

Level Two analysis calls for a much closer look at Tamika's reading performance and an interpretation of the underlying strengths and weaknesses in reading revealed in her responses to questions and in her retellings. Once again, we will use the four categories listed under the table on the Recapitulation Record as a guideline for our analysis.

It is clear that Tamika's major strength is that of word recognition; she has scores of 100% through the fifth grade on the Flash word lists; in addition she obtained an MMI of 100% on all three passages she read orally. But the discrepancy between Tamika's word recognition abilities and her comprehension of text reveals a potentially serious problem, with her greatest difficulty linked to inferential thinking.

Consequently, we need to analyze Tamika's responses to inferential and critical response items in turn to see if there are patterns that can help us instruct her more effectively. At the second grade level following silent reading, Tamika responded incorrectly to two critical response questions. Her response to the first of these items, "Do you think it was right for Jessie to get back on the ride after she promised never to ride again?" was, "Yes, by the end she had changed her mind and wasn't afraid." Tamika misses the point that the item calls for a critique of the character's actions. She responds with only a brief retelling of the literal events in the story. Her answer to the critical response item ("Would the story end the same way if Jessie had taken the ride with her mother?") once again reflects her reliance upon the text and her failure to recognize the relationship required by the question. Her response: "*No, her mother wouldn't go on the ride*" was again followed by a probe question which emphasized the *if* in the question. Tamika seemed unable to connect background information to the text and hypothesize about the end result of the mother's fear.

At the third grade oral level, Tamika missed one inferential question and one critical response question. This time her response to the inferential item ("Do you think that David ever got to ride the horses that week?") appears to be based on speculation without use of related textual information. She responded: "*Yes, his grandmother wanted him to ride them.*" This response ignores the relevant text information that is needed to address the question. For example, she ignores the fact that David has already accepted the responsibility to continue working in spite of his grandmother's attempts to have him reconsider. The examiner, therefore, asked Tamika a probing question as to whether she could explain what she meant. Her response to the probe was: "*I don't remember if it said that.*" Her reaction to the critical response item ("Was Grandpa fair to expect David to do so much work that first week? Why?") again reflects her inability to select the relevant information from the text that would support a needed conclusion. Her response was: "*I don't know; the story didn't say anything about that.*" But here her response raises the possibility that Tamika's view of reading may be based on the expectation that answers to questions are clearly stated in the text.

Tamika's performance following silent reading at the third grade level reflects even greater difficulty with inferential responses. She responded incorrectly to all three inferential questions. Her response to question three ("Do you think that Jill and her teammates were good friends or not? Why?") seems to rely heavily upon background information. She responded: "*Yes, they played a lot of games together.*" This response is clearly insufficient and reflects her inability to identify the information from the text that is needed to make and support a judgment. Consequently, the examiner does not make use of a probing question. Her response to question four ("How important to Jill was winning the championship game?") is linked with a detail from the text that does not match the relationship required by the question. She stated: "*Real important; the national anthem made her think of being a pro.*" Here she ignores the many different ways in which Jill's attention is directed to her own performance and the excuses she makes for it while paying almost no attention to the team's effort. Again, no probing was necessary. Finally, her answer to question 7 ("Was Jill good at predicting how well her teammates would play?") reflects this same type of surface response linked with a story detail that has no connection to the relationship required in the question. She said: "*Yes, she saw the players making mistakes.*" Both of these questions require the ability to select specific textual information linked with a high-level interpretation to complete a logical relationship.

Tamika also missed one of the three critical response questions. Her response to question 9 ("Do you think that Jill needs help from her coach?") again emphasizes her background knowledge. She responded: "*Yes, coaches can help everybody.*" Again we see her inability to select the relevant information from the story that is needed in making a connection between Jill's actions and the coach's role; her response relies solely on the coach's role. She ignores Jill's excuse-making and her lack of team commitment, dimensions of a player that would be very important to a coach. The examiner seemed concerned about this response and attempted to trigger Jill's attention to the use of the story to support her response. Tamika responded: "*Not any more than anybody else*" suggesting that she could not use the probe to think differently about the question. Her view of reading does not seem to consider her responsibility to draw conclusions or make judgments about situations.

While we do have a clear indication of Tamika's difficulty with inferential and critical thinking, we should nonetheless make a quick check as to how she handled these areas at the fourth grade level when she clearly frustrated. At this level, Tamika missed two inferential and two and one half critical response items after oral reading. Again, her responses seemed to be connected to a difficulty selecting and connecting textual information that could be used to support a thoughtful conclusion. She tends to be comfortable getting sufficient textual information to make an inference but she is unable to connect relevant textual information that could serve as the basis of that inference. This same pattern is reflected following silent reading. She missed two of the inferential items, and missed all three critical response items. All in all, Tamika's difficulties with inferences and critical responses appear to be coming from one of two sources: (a) the use of vague general statements, which she is unable to support through details in the story, or (b) the use of details from the text that have little or no logical link to the question.

But no analysis of comprehension is complete without an examination of the retellings. Tamika provided solid retellings following oral reading at the second and third grade levels. But even at her independent level (second grade), Tamika's retelling after silent reading suggests a listing of factual information without the logical flow that the cause–effect relationships in the passage provide. After silent reading at the third grade level,

Tamika's retelling is even more disjointed, with omission of three of the five steps that led to the resolution of the character's problem. Not surprisingly, Tamika's retellings at the fourth grade level were both weak, with a focus on factual information and a seeming inability to enhance her memory for details by relating ideas one to another in a logical flow.

Our conclusions at the end of our Level Two Interpretation suggest that Tamika is a student who has a strong sight vocabulary and very solid literal comprehending skills. However, she has considerable difficulty with inferential and critical thinking that requires her to draw conclusions or make inferences that are clearly linked with textual information. In response to questions that call for higher levels of thinking, Tamika responds in one of two ways. She either looks for literal information in the text or draws upon pure background with no link at all to the ideas in the text. Because the items call for a combination of textual information with logical thinking drawn from experience, Tamika's responses are frequently inadequate. Furthermore, Tamika seems unable to respond to the text that she reads. She never offers a spontaneous reaction to the stories she reads. When she is prompted again to tell the examiner what she thought of what she has read, Tamika invariably responds with additional textual information from the passage. It may be that Tamika does not understand her need to think about what she reads.

Level Three: Comprehensive Interpretation

While we have gained some considerable insights into Tamika's reading based upon the time we spent with her and the time we spent analyzing the data we gathered, the picture is still far from complete. The purpose that will drive the comprehensive level of interpretation is our need to gain insights from as many sources as possible into those factors that are contributing to Tamika's reading problems. We begin with the interview with Tamika's current fifth grade teacher. Her teacher was initially shocked by Tamika's scores when she received the results of the latest state testing. She had expected that Tamika would receive relatively high scores in reading. Tamika's score on the multiple-choice section of the test fell into the average range and her score on a reader response task placed her in the below average range. Tamika's teacher characterized her performance on the tests as a quirk due to a poor testing day. However, she decided that she would talk with Tamika's fourth grade teacher. The fourth grade teacher reported that Tamika's score on the district assessment measure had been slightly lower than it had been in the third grade. However, she ignored this data because she believed that Tamika's classroom work was consistently above average and she felt that day-to-day performance should take precedence over the results of a one-time testing situation.

The Parent Interview revealed that Tamika's mother, when she received the results of the state assessment, requested a special conference with the teacher. She reported that she was very concerned and upset with Tamika's test results, particularly because she considers Tamika to be an extremely conscientious student. She reported that Tamika consistently "walks in the house and immediately does her homework" without any pressure from either parent. She has always regarded this behavior as a reflection of the fact that Tamika enjoyed school and reading. She did recall her conference with the fourth grade teacher after the drop in performance on the district test. She agreed with the teacher that because Tamika's daily schoolwork contradicted the testing data, it would be better to focus on daily performance. However, she reported that she has waited long enough and that in light of the current results, she wanted Tamika to be tested by the reading specialist.

The reading specialist initiated the testing by conducting the Student Interview. Tamika reported that she was "good at reading" and that reading was "not hard" for her. Nonetheless, there are several of Tamika's responses that are crucial to the picture that is emerging. First of all, Tamika reported that she had no favorite book or author. The books she reads at home are those that she needs to do her homework. The books she gets at the library are those that she can use to get good grades on her school projects and reports. She did mention that she read several books over the summer, in conjunction with the summer reading program sponsored by the school district. Tamika reported that she selected the first three books from the list that she could find at the library and that she completed the assignment as quickly as possible so that she could enjoy the rest of her vacation.

After completing the interview, the reading specialist administered the CRI and we have just reviewed the results she found. Now we can see how the information from the teacher, the parent, and the student can shed much light on Tamika's performance. Despite the fact that Tamika is conscientious and disciplined, reading seems to be a chore or responsibility to her. She readily accepts the responsibility associated with her schoolwork, but there appears to be little motivation to go beyond the minimum of what is required by academic tasks.

Tamika seems to enjoy the fruits of these efforts as reflected in good grades and positive feedback from parents and teachers. These external rewards seem to contribute to the internal motivation that enables her to maintain her high level of commitment and responsibility to academic success. However, the type of connection that is required of inferential and critical thinking is missing. Nonetheless, given an effective program of intervention, the prognosis for Tamika is very good.

Conclusions Based on Level Three Interpretation

1. Tamika's view of the nature of reading seems to center on recall of information directly from the text.
2. Tamika's attitude toward reading seems to be that reading is a chore with little enjoyment or challenge related to it.
3. Tamika appears highly motivated to achieve good grades and praise, but less so to think and respond to text.
4. Tamika appears to have solid parental support.
5. Tamika's teacher appears to focus her instruction on text-based issues and word recognition and does not appear to ask students for higher level responses.

Planning Diagnostic Instruction

In this case, the reading specialist plans to meet with Tamika's teacher to discuss the CRI results. Her hope is that when she and the classroom teacher study the type of questions that Tamika consistently missed, they will also review the types of questions used in the classroom. The reading specialist expects to discover that the teacher rarely asks questions that would require the thinking reflected in the inferential and critical questions. The best-case scenario would be a joint plan of instruction, with lessons jointly planned but demonstrated by the reading specialist, that would require a balance in text-based, inferential, and critical thinking.

The reading specialist will help the classroom teacher focus on prereading discussions with literature that fosters the learners' connection to characters. It will be very helpful if those discussions are clearly linked with themes embedded in the literature selections. The discussion should help children to identify character traits and discuss the ways in which those traits foster different actions. In this way, Tamika and others will begin to develop an orientation to literature that fosters a personal connection with the lives of the characters. Instruction needs to emphasize the importance of personal reactions to the story so that students have the opportunity to see the different ways that their classmates respond to the same story. The atmosphere of the classroom needs to encourage acceptance of different reactions to the characters and their actions. Reading in that classroom should become an invitation to children to share in the experiences and ideas of a writer as well as the ideas that many readers link to the text.

Student Interview
Fifth Grade–Senior High

Name: _____John_____ **Date:** _____11/15_____

1. What kinds of things do you like to do when you're not in school?
   I ride bikes with my friends, I play video games and I surf the Web to find out all about the Eagles, the Phillies, and the Flyers.

2. How about reading? (If reader does not volunteer the information, probe for how often, what kinds of materials, topics of interest, where materials are obtained, etc.).
   I don't like to read schoolbooks but I am good reading on the Web.

3. How do you think you do with reading in school? What about writing?
   I'm not good. I go to reading class. I'm not good (at writing).

4. What have you read recently for enjoyment? For school? Did you find them enjoyable? Were they easy for you to understand?
   Just on the Web and the newspapers about sports. I don't like to read books. I have to read what the teacher gives as homework.

5. What is the hardest part about reading?
   The big words are hard.

6. What are the best and worst things about school?
   I don't really like school.

7. Is writing hard or easy for you? What do you think makes it that way?
   It's hard. I can't spell a lot of the words.

8. Are you on any clubs or teams at school? Do have any hobbies? Do you have a job?
   We play after school; I'm a good first baseman and I'm good at hockey.

9. How are your grades in school? Do you have any concerns with any subjects?
   Not good.

10. Have you ever thought about what kind of job you'd like to have when you're older?
    I'd really like to be like my Dad but he had to go to college to be an accountant; I don't think I want to go to college.

11. Is there anything else that you'd like to share about yourself?
    No.

Parent/Guardian Interview

Name: _____John_____   Date: ___11/15_____

1. What made you think that it would be a good idea for ____John____ (student's name) to be tested at this time?
   When we found out that he had acted out in class; it's not like him.

2. How is ____John____ doing in school, particularly in reading?
   He has always had trouble with reading. We didn't expect that because when he was younger, we couldn't read enough to him. He loved books.

3. What kind of reading does ____John____ do at home?
   Really none . . . only what we do with him for school.

4. How would you characterize ____John____'s:
   a. **Ability**—*He's very quick figuring out how things work; he's also very insightful in sports games. The only problem area has been academics.*
   b. **Attitude**—*It's not been good because he's had difficulty reading, right from the start.*
   c. **Interests**—*He loves sports, video games, and TV.*
   d. **Needs**—*That's primarily reading; what's amazing is that he has great success finding out all about sports in magazines and on the computer.*
   e. **Behavior**—*Up until this past month, he's never been a problem. The concerns we've heard were in reference to his lack of motivation.*

5. What would you say is the major reason for ____John____'s school performance?
   He's always had a difficult time reading, specifically sounding words out.

6. How long has he/she had this difficulty?
   Right from the first grade on.

7. What kinds of help has he/she gotten so far?
   He's worked with the reading teacher all through school.

8. What are you currently doing at home to help ____John____?
   We do homework with him and we help him read the books he has to do for homework. They are the only books he reads now. It's sad, both my husband and I love to read and I think that's how he started loving books.

9. Is there anything else you think might be helpful for you to do?
   I used to ask whether John could have more stories to read. But I guess he can't do comprehension until he learns how to read all the words.

10. What is the school or the teacher doing this year to help ___John___?
The same as always, working with the reading teacher.

11. What else do you think it would be helpful for the school or teacher to do?
I'm getting worried that he is starting to get frustrated with failure, he's always gotten along with his classmates. We can't figure out what triggered this recent outburst. We do want to get to the bottom of it so we can help him.

Teacher Interview
(Special reading teacher)

Name: _____John_____   Date: __11/15_____

1. What would you say are the greatest needs in reading of the class you have this year?
    John's group works primarily with word recognition skills.

2. Could you describe for me a typical reading/language arts period in your classroom (this should include time spent, materials used, methods, grouping techniques)?
    We only have 30 to 35 minutes for our group and I have the list of words his classroom teacher gives me and we work on those first. Then we use the skills book for practice applying phonics and syllabication rules.

3. How does _____John_____ (student's name) generally react to your instruction?
    He's pretty good with taking turns; my only concern is that he seems to have no desire to learn.

4. In your comprehension instruction and assessment, do you tend to emphasize recall of information, student response to the text, or both equally?
    His teacher has him in a group and they have to focus on the details; you can't do all the inferencing questions until they have the story down.

5. How would you characterize _____John_____'s:
    a. **Ability**—*I have no idea about his real ability; he doesn't seem like a dull student. He just has real problems with reading and writing.*
    b. **Attitude**—*He seems to have no desire to read or write.*
    c. **Interests**—*He loves sports and he's a very good athlete.*
    d. **Needs**—*His word recognition abilities.*
    e. **Behavior**—*In reading group, he's been good. It wasn't like him to get involved in that fight.*

6. What kinds of activities or strategies have you tried specifically with _____John_____? What seems to work best? What doesn't seem to be working?
    As I said, I use words that his classroom teacher gives me and I use skills books. That usually takes up the time we have.

7. What do you know about the type of support _____John_____ gets at home?
    His parents are extremely supportive; they have supported us since we started working with him in first grade.

8. If there were one thing that you could recommend that you think would help _____John_____, what would it be?
    I would love to help him succeed but we haven't been successful.

Word Lists: Examiner's Copy

First Grade

	Flash	Untimed
1. family	_____	_____
2. hear	_____	_____
3. school	_____	_____
4. happy	_____	_____
5. feet	_____	_____
6. together	_____	_____
7. fish	_____	_____
8. pet	_____	_____
9. blue	_____	_____
10. before	_____	_____
11. children	_____	_____
12. where	_____	_____
13. farm	_____	_____
14. surprise	_____	_____
15. friend	_____	_____
16. drop	_____	_____
17. will	_____	_____
18. made	_____	_____
19. bike	_____	_____
20. game	_____	_____
Score	__/20__	__/20__
	__%__	__%__

Second Grade

	Flash	Untimed
1. teacher	+	_____
2. clean	+	_____
3. remember	+	_____
4. horse	+	_____
5. anyone	+	_____
6. birthday	+	_____
7. garden	+	_____
8. street	+	_____
9. guess	+	_____
10. pretty	+	_____
11. always	+	_____
12. walking	+	_____
13. pull	+	_____
14. fast	+	_____
15. have	+	_____
16. spring	+	_____
17. when	+	_____
18. help	+	_____
19. know	+	_____
20. brother	+	_____
Score	**20/20**	**20/20**
	100%	**100%**

Word Lists: Examiner's Copy

Third Grade

	Flash	Untimed
1. enter	*either*	+
2. change	+	
3. lesson	+	
4. think	+	
5. music	+	
6. trust	+	
7. human	+	
8. pencil	+	
9. mail	+	
10. phone	+	
11. fright	*fight*	+
12. unusual	*un-a-sal*	*un-a-sal*
13. they'll	+	
14. bread	+	
15. forest	+	
16. early	+	
17. hurt	+	
18. water	+	
19. because	+	
20. hour	+	
Score	**17/20**	**19/20**
	85%	**95%**

Fourth Grade

	Flash	Untimed
1. doesn't	+	
2. concern	+	
3. sample	*sam-ble*	+
4. official	*off*	*off-fic-al*
5. given	+	
6. present	+	
7. decorate	*de-sore*	*de-sore-ate*
8. windshield	*win-win*	+
9. exercise	*ex-*	+
10. finish	+	
11. enjoyable	+	
12. wrong	+	
13. daughter	*dou-gr*	*dou-gou-ter*
14. quiet	+	
15. morning	+	
16. huge	*hug-e*	*hu-ja*
17. covered	+	
18. thought	+	
19. creature	*cee-tra*	*cee-tra*
20. people	+	
Score	**12/20**	**15/20**
	60%	**75%**

Second Grade Oral: The Race

Reader's copy on p. 24 of the Reader's Passages.

Introductory Statement: "Would you read this passage about two cats who race each other out loud for me? When you are finished, I'll take the passage away. Then I'll ask you to tell me about what you read and what you think of it. After that, I'll ask you some questions about the passage."

Story

TP
(Spencer) was the fastest animal in the jungle. All of the other animals knew it. Spencer made sure of that. He would say, "No one can beat me! You are all too afraid to
x✔ race!" It was true. No one wanted to race *again*/against
x✔ Spencer. He always won. Then he would brag even more.

One day another family of cats moved in. Spencer
x✔ ran up *and* to the new family. He said, "I'm the fastest ani-
x✔ mal in the jungle. Do you want to race?" The father
x said, "No, thank you. But maybe our *dou*/ daughter Annie will race with you." Annie smiled and said, "Yes. I'd
x✔ love to race. Soon the two cats were running for/the finish line.

SC ✔SC
Spencer was winning as always. But Annie was very fast. She raced past him and/crossed the finish line first.

The other animals /cheered in surprise. But
SC Spencer cried, "I want another/chance!" They raced *chose* ✔SC
x✔ again and again. But the result was still the same. There *And* was a new/champion in the jungle and her name was Annie.

All the animals came over to talk to Annie. But Spencer went away angry. Annie was a little sad. She hoped that Spencer would be her friend. "Well, at least we won't have to listen to him brag again," said the fox. The next day Spencer was back. The first thing he said was, "I can jump higher than anybody in the jungle! No
x✔ one can beat me!" The other animals/groaned and *growled*

rolled their eyes. Nothing had changed after all. (256 words)

Miscues

___7___ N of miscues that maintained meaning (checked). This is the MM.

___1___ N of miscues that violated meaning (unchecked). This is the MV.

Reading Accuracy Index: __97__ %
(N of words – N of miscues, checked and unchecked)/ N of words

Meaning Maintenance Index: __100__ %
(N of words – N of meaning-violating miscues, unchecked only)/N of words

The Race: 256 words

Miscue Chart

Miscues	%	Miscues	%	Miscues	%
1	100	13	95	25	90
2	99	14	95	26	90
3	99	15	94	27	89
4	98	16	94	28	89
5	98	17	93	29	89
6	98	18	93	30	88
7	97	19	93	31	88
8	97	20	92	32	88
9	96	21	92	33	87
10	96	22	91	34	87
11	96	23	91	35	86
12	95	24	91	36	86

Retelling

Examiner: "Tell me about what you just read and what you thought about it."

The animals didn't like Spencer because he was always wanting to race them because he knew he'd win. That's why they didn't like him. Then when he wants to race the new family he thought he'd win again but Annie beat him. They thought he'd stop bragging but then he said, "I can jump higher than everyone." Everybody rolled their eyes. I liked that story because Annie beat him!

If there is no spontaneous response, repeat the request, "Tell me what you thought about the passage."

I liked it when Annie beat Spencer because he was always bragging and nobody could ever beat him. That's why he was always bragging. Then Annie beats him and he should have learned his lesson but he didn't.

NOTE: Use the Retelling Rubric on the next page to assess the child's retelling performance.

Retelling Rubric

Story Structure:

1. **Key Characters and Setting:** Spencer, other animals, and Annie who moved into jungle. `+1`
2. **Character's Problem or Goal:** Spencer wants to be the fastest runner in the jungle and to brag about it. `+1`
3. **Problem-Solving or Goal-Meeting Process:**
   - Spencer brags and gets others to race with him so that he can brag more. `+1`
   - Annie moves in and Spencer races with her. `+1`
   - Spencer loses the race. `+1` `0`
   - Spencer walks away angrily and Annie is sad because she had wanted a friend. `+1`
   - Spencer returns the next day and brags about jumping.
4. **Personal Response:** Any well-supported positive or negative response to the characters or events in the story; any reaction to the humor or sadness in the story; any well-supported positive or negative reaction to the story as a whole. `+1`

Rubric:

4 = Complete retelling includes characters, problem/goal, all five steps in the problem-solving process, and a well-supported personal response.

3 = Retelling includes characters, problem/goal, and all five steps in the problem solving process, but has no personal response.

2 = Retelling includes characters, problem/goal, and three or four steps in the problem-solving process; some key factual errors or omissions. Add ½ point for well-supported personal response.

1 = Retelling omits either characters or problem; includes one or two steps in the problem-solving process, but the account is disjointed and includes factual errors or serious omissions. Add ½ point for well-supported personal response.

0 = Provides a title or topic statement but shows no real awareness of the character's problem and how the problem is worked out.

Retelling Score: __3.5__

Comprehension Questions

1. Why didn't any of the animals want to race against Spencer?

   Text-based: He always won and he bragged afterwards.

   He won every race and bragged about it.

   +10

2. What did the animals do when Annie won the race? (Must identify one.)

   Text-based: Cheered; talked with her.

   She surprised them. ?(Examiner's probe: What did they do?) *They cheered for her.*

   +10

3. Why would Spencer want to race against Annie again?

   Inference: He couldn't accept the fact that someone was faster; thought he could win.

   He thought he could win the next time.

   +10

4. Why did Annie agree to race against Spencer when no one else would?

   Inference: She knew she was very fast; she probably knew she could beat him.

   She thought she'd win but he was winning first.

   +10

5. What would have been the best thing for Spencer to do after Annie beat him? Why?

   Critical Response: Be a good loser and admit that she was faster; try to be her friend since he didn't have any friends; stop bragging about himself to the other animals.

   Just tell her that she was faster than him.

   +10

6. What did Spencer do when he came back the next day?

   Text-based: Started bragging about something else; bragged that he could jump higher than anyone else.

   He said he could jump higher than everybody.

   +10

7. Do you think that this was the first time Annie had ever raced against anyone? Why or why not?

Inference: No, she smiled when Spencer challenged her; she probably knew she could beat him.

No, her parents must have saw her win so they told her to race.

+10

8. What did the other animals hope would happen after Spencer lost the race?

Text-based: That Spencer would stop bragging.

That he'd stop bragging.

+10

9. If another new family moved into the jungle, do you think Spencer would ask them to race or not?

Critical Response: Yes, he did not seem to have learned anything; still bragged even after he lost. No, he has lost once; he may still brag but he didn't like to lose and he may not be as confident as he was once.

No, this time he'd tell them he can jump higher than they can and want a jumping race.

+10

10. If Spencer stopped bragging, do you think he would be a good friend for Annie or would he still have to change?

Critical Response: Yes, he wouldn't annoy people; others would give him a chance; others would like him better. No, has to be a better loser; shouldn't be so selfish; must admit she is a better runner.

Probably because that's why they don't like him—he wants to brag about himself. So if he wasn't like that, she'd like him.

+10

Comprehension Analysis:

Text-Based: __4/4__
Inference: __3/3__
Critical Response: __3/3__

Total Comprehension %: __100%__

Second Grade Silent: The Roller Coaster Ride

Reader's copy on p. 25 of the Reader's Passages.

Introductory Statement: "Would you read this passage about a ride on the roller coaster to yourself? When you are finished, I'll take the passage away. Then I'll ask you to tell me about what you read and what you think of it. After that, I'll ask you some questions about the passage."

Story

Today it was finally Jessie's birthday. She jumped out of bed and called to her mom, "Mom, can you come here and see how tall I am?" She ran to the wall and waited. Mother marked the spot where Jessie had grown since her last birthday. "I made it!" shouted Jessie. "I'm tall enough to ride the roller coaster now!" On Saturday, Jessie, her mom, and Aunt Jane would go to the park. Then she could take her first ride!

Mom was too afraid to ride so Aunt Jane took Jessie to the line to wait their turn. Jessie and Aunt Jane jumped into a car and pulled the bar over their heads. Then they waited for the ride to start. "Let's get going," thought Jessie. Soon the ride started and Jessie was really excited. She felt very grown up. Then the car climbed higher and higher. It came down and went faster and faster. Jessie was so afraid that she thought she was going to die.

Jessie held Aunt Jane's arm. She covered her face and screamed. Jessie prayed that the ride would end. "Don't let me die," she prayed, "and I'll never ride a roller coaster again." Aunt Jane hugged Jessie. Jessie opened her eyes and she saw people laughing and screaming. Aunt Jane was laughing too. They were all having fun.

The car slowed and then stopped. The ride was finally over. "Aunt Jane," said Jessie, "Can we do it again?" (244 words)

Retelling

Examiner: "Tell me about what you just read and what you thought about it."

When Jessie asked her Mom to measure her she found out she could ride the roller coaster but she had to do it with her aunt because her Mother was afraid. But Jessie was afraid too; at the start of the ride she was screaming and praying but then she wanted to take another ride. But she wanted her aunt to go with her. I think she was still too scared to ride by herself.

If there is no spontaneous response, repeat the request, "Tell me what you thought about the passage."

I liked that Jessie stopped being real scared and now she's just a little scared to ride alone so she still wants her aunt with her but she probably won't be holding on and screaming so much on the next ride.

NOTE: Use the Retelling Rubric on p. 98 to assess the child's retelling performance.

Retelling Rubric

Story Structure:

1. **Key Characters and Setting:** Jessie, Aunt Jane, and Mom at amusement park.   +1
2. **Character's Problem or Goal:** Jessie wants to finally be big enough to ride the roller-coaster.   +1
3. **Problem-Solving or Goal-Meeting Process:**
   - Jessie is finally tall enough to ride the roller coaster.   +1
   - Aunt Jane goes with her on the ride.   +1
   - Jessie becomes frightened.   +1
   - She promises she will never ride again.   0
   - She realizes that the ride is safe and fun.   +1
   - She decides to go on the ride again.   +1
4. **Personal Response:** Any well-supported positive or negative response to the characters or events in the story; any reaction to the humor or sadness in the story; any well-supported positive or negative reaction to the story as a whole.   +1

Rubric:

4 = Complete retelling includes characters, problem/goal, all six steps in the problem-solving process, and a well-supported personal response.

3 = Retelling includes characters, problem/goal, and five or six steps in the problem solving process, but has no personal response.

2 = Retelling includes characters, problem/goal, and three or four steps in the problem solving process; some key factual errors or omissions. Add ½ point for well-supported personal response.

1 = Retelling omits either characters or problem; includes two or three steps in the problem solving process, but the account is disjointed and includes factual errors or serious omissions. Add ½ point for well-supported personal response.

0 = Provides a title or topic statement but shows no real awareness of the character's problem and how the problem is worked out.

Retelling Score: 3.5

Comprehension Questions

1. Why did Jessie want her mother to see how tall she was?

   Text-based: Wanted to see if she was tall enough to ride the roller coaster.

   That's how she'd know if she got big enough to ride.

   +10

2. Why didn't Mom want to ride on the roller coaster with Jessie?

   Text-based: She was afraid of roller coasters.

   Her Mom was afraid to ride.

   +10

3. Do you think that Jessie had ever been to an amusement park before? Why?

   Inference: Yes, she knew that she had to be a certain height to go on certain rides; may have seen a roller coaster at an amusement park before.

   Yes, she probably stood by the marker and couldn't reach the line so they didn't let her on.

   +10

4. Why would Jessie want so much to ride the roller coaster?

   Inference: Sign that she was growing up; was something she wasn't allowed to do before; she thought it would be fun.

   She saw all the other kids riding—the kids bigger than she was—and they just kept getting back in line again.

   +10

5. How do you think Mom felt about Jessie taking her first roller coaster ride? Why?

   Critical Response: Proud that she had grown up; afraid she might be hurt; happy that Aunt Jane would be with her.

   She probably knew she'd be scared—maybe she wished she wasn't scared of them.

   +10

6. How did Aunt Jane help Jessie during the ride?

   Text-based: Hugged her; held her close.

   She hugged her.

   +10

7. Why did Jessie decide to ride the roller coaster again?

Inference: She wanted to have more fun; may have wanted to prove to herself that she wasn't afraid; made her feel grown-up; she ended up liking it.

She was scared but she still made it so she knew she'd make it again but she still wanted her aunt with her.

+10

8. What did Jessie do during the ride to help herself stop being afraid? (Must identify one.)

Text-based: Hugged Aunt Jane; saw others having fun; prayed; screamed out loud.

She prayed.

+10

9. Do you think it was right for Jessie to get back on the ride after she promised never to ride again?

Critical Response: Yes, she didn't really mean what she had said. No, she gave her word and probably shouldn't break it.

Yes, because she did make it so she knew she could make it again.

+0 (missed point of promise)

10. Do you think the story would end the same way if Jessie took the ride with her mother instead of Aunt Jane? Explain.

Critical Response: No, her mother might have been afraid too and neither one would ever ride again. Yes, her mother probably would hide her fear for Jessie's sake.

Yes because they would have made it too but the Mother probably knew that but she was still afraid anyway.

+10

Comprehension Analysis:

Text-Based: _4/4_
Inference: _3/3_
Critical Response: _2/3_

Total Comprehension%: _90%_

The Roller Coaster Ride: 244 Words

Third Grade Oral: The Farm Vacation

Reader's copy on p. 26 of the Reader's Passages.

Introductory Statement: "Would you read this passage about a boy's visit to a farm out loud for me? When you are finished, I'll take the passage away. Then I'll ask you to tell me about what you read and what you think of it. After that, I'll ask you some questions about the passage."

Story

✗✔ It was five o'clock in the morning when David heard *(hears)* his grandfather call. David never got up this/early before but ✗ he didn't mind at all! He was visiting *(vĭs-ĭtĭng)* his grandfather's ✗ farm for the first time and he/was excited *(ĕz-cītĕd)*. He had always ✗✔ wanted to be a farmer and now he would have his *(a)* ✗✔ ✗✔ chance. Besides, Grandpa, had, horses too. and David *(he the)* ✗✔ looked /forward to learning how to ride.

When David ran into the kitchen, Grandfather said, "Eat a good breakfast, Dave. We've got a lot to do this morning. We'll start with the hay."

✗ "Don't/rush him!" *(rŭ-sh)* said Grandma. "Are you sure you want to work with Grandpa all day?" she asked David.

✗✔ "Sure am!" said David. He/gulped *(jū-lăpt)* down his ✗ *(I)* breakfast and /dashed out to help load the hay wagon. He never knew hay was so heavy.

✗✔ "You finish up here while I get *(go)* the tractor. We've got some work to do in the garden," said Grandpa.

SC David walked over to the garden and/ climbed *(clī-bĕd)* ✔SC on to the tractor. Up and down they drove, row after ✗ row,/turning *(touring)* up the soil as they went. "Lunch time," said Grandpa when the sun was /overhead.

"When do the horses get fed?" David asked Grandma as he walked into the kitchen.

"Do you want to do that after lunch? You've worked so much already," said Grandma.

"Don't forget, the honey," said Grandpa, "We've got ✗✔ lots to do. That's how life is on the farm."

"That's OK," said David. "Maybe I better stay and help Grandpa."

After lunch, David worked under the hot sun, helping Grandpa/dig postholes *(pŏ-stŏ-lĕs)* for a new fence. Then ✗ David and Grandpa picked corn and brought it to their roadside stand. David was/trudging *(trū-dȳing)* slowly back toward *(to)* ✗✔ the house when Grandma called, "Do you want to feed the horses?"

David ran to the barn and helped her to feed the ✗✔ *(her)* horses. "I wish I could ride you," he said to each one/as he rubbed *(rŭb-bĕd)* ✔SC its nose. "Maybe Grandpa will teach me!" SC David fell asleep (immediately) *(TP)* that night but when ✗ the sun rose the next morning, he was not/so eager *(early)* to get up. He had the feeling that today would be ✗✔ another day just like yesterday. As it turned out, he was right.

"Do you still want to be a farmer?" asked Grandfather at the end of the week. "I'm not so sure," *(too)* ✗✔ David/replied *(rĕp-lied)*. "If the sun rose at ten o'clock and there ✗ wasn't so much hard work, then maybe farming would be more fun." (417 words)

Miscues

__12__ N of miscues that maintained meaning (checked). This is the MM.

__9__ N of miscues that violated meaning (unchecked). This is the MV.

Reading Accuracy Index: __95__ %
(N of words – N of miscues, checked and unchecked)/ N of words

Meaning Maintenance Index: __98__ %
(N of words – N of meaning-violating miscues, unchecked only)/N of words

The Farm Vacation: 417 Words

Miscue Chart

Miscues	%	Miscues	%	Miscues	%
1	100	12	97	23	94
2	100	13	97	24	94
3	99	14	97	25	94
4	99	15	96	26	94
5	99	16	96	27	94
6	99	17	96	28	93
7	98	18	96	29	93
8	98	19	95	30	93
9	98	20	95	31	93
10	98	21	95	32	92
11	97	22	95	33	92

Retelling

Examiner: "Tell me about what you just read and what you thought about it."

David wanted to be like his grandfather so he stayed with him at the farm. His best thing was the horses and he wanted his grandfather to teach him how to ride.

If there is no spontaneous response, repeat the request, "Tell me what you thought about the passage."

I liked how David liked horses.

Retelling Rubric

Story Structure

1. **Key Characters and Setting:** David and his Grandparents on the farm. +1
2. **Character's Problem or Goal:** David visits farm to learn about farming and to learn to ride horses. +½
3. **Problem-Solving or Goal-Meeting Process:** +½
   - David wants to learn about farming and to ride horses. 0
   - Grandpa has him working hard but Grandma wants him to enjoy himself. 0
   - David decides to keep working with Grandpa. 0
   - David never gets chance to ride the horses. 0
   - David reconsiders his choice. 0
4. **Personal Response:** Any well-supported positive or negative response to the characters or events in the story; any reaction to the humor or sadness in the story; any well-supported positive or negative reaction to the story as a whole. 0

Rubric:

4 = Complete retelling includes characters, problem/goal, all five steps in the problem-solving process, and a well-supported personal response.

3 = Retelling includes characters, problem/goal, and all five steps in the problem-solving process, but has no personal response

2 = Retelling includes characters, problem/goal, and three or four steps in the problem-solving process; some key factual errors or omissions. Add ½ point for well-supported personal response.

1 = Retelling omits either characters or problem; includes one or two steps in the problem-solving process, but the account is disjointed and includes factual errors or serious omissions. Add ½ point for well-supported personal response.

0 = Provides a title or topic statement but shows no real awareness of the character's problem and how the problem is worked out.

Retelling Score: 1.0

Comprehension Questions

1. Why was David excited about visiting the farm?

    Text-based: He always wanted to be a farmer.

    He always wanted to learn how to ride the horses.

    +10

2. How did David feel about farming *at the end* of the week?

    Text-based: He wasn't sure about it; he had changed his mind.

    He still wanted to learn how to ride. ?(Examiner's probe: But how did he feel about farming?) *I don't remember.*

    +0

3. Do you think that David lived near his grandfather? Explain.

    Inference: Probably not, he was visiting the farm for the first time.

    He probably did; a lot of kids live near their grandfathers. ?(Examiner's probe: Was there anything in the story to help you think that?) *I don't remember.*

    +0

4. Do you think that Grandma was happy about how David's first week at the farm was going?

    Inference: Probably not, He was working very hard and having no fun; he should have been riding the horses.

    She probably wanted him to be a farmer too so she was glad he was getting the chance.

    +0 (missed point of Grandma's concern)

5. Do you think that Grandpa really wanted David to become a farmer? Why or why not?

    Critical Response: Probably not, made him work very hard, possibly because he wanted David to understand how difficult farming was. Probably so, wanted him to understand everything about farming, including the hard work.

    He probably did because he's a farmer so that's why he showed him how to learn to be a farmer and he'd probably be glad his grandson was like him.

    +10

6. What did David want most from Grandpa?

    Text-based: To learn how to ride the horses.

    To teach him how to ride the horses.

    +10

7. Do you think that David ever got to ride the horses that week? Why?

    Inference: Probably not; seemed that there was little time for play, and Grandpa didn't appear too interested in seeing David ride the horses.

    Yes, he probably did because he wanted to do that and his grandfather probably knew how so he'd teach him.

    +0 (relies on prior knowledge and speculation)

8. Why did David change his mind at the end of the week? (Must identify one.)

    Text-based: Had to get up too early and there was too much hard work.

    No, he still wanted to ride the horses.

    +0 (ignores power of question clue)

9. Do you think David and his grandfather had a close relationship? Why or why not?

    Critical Response: Yes, David cared for the grandfather; always helped him work even when he would rather ride the horses. No, seemed that they did not talk very much; Grandfather unaware that David wanted to ride the horses; didn't talk very much about farming.

    Yes, because he wanted to be just like him so he must know him really good.

    +10

10. Was Grandpa fair to expect David to do so much work that first week? Why?

    Critical Response: No, he seemed to have one task right after another with no rest. Yes, David wanted to learn about the farming life; it would be dishonest to present it in any other way.

    Yes, he wanted him to grow up to be like him so he had to know how to be a good farmer and that's what farmers do.

    +10

Comprehension Analysis:

Text-Based: _2/4_
Inference: _0/3_
Critical Response: _3/3_

Total Comprehension %: _50%_

Third Grade Silent: The Championship Game

Reader's copy on p. 28 of the Reader's Passages.

Introductory Statement: "Would you read this passage about an important baseball game to yourself? When you are finished, I'll take the passage away. Then I'll ask you to tell me about what you read and what you think of it. After that, I'll ask you some questions about the passage."

Story

At the end of a long softball season, Jill's team made it to the championship game. They would play against the top team in the league, the Ramblers. Before the game, the teams had batting and fielding practice. Jill watched her teammates. She knew that they would have a hard time winning. Their shortstop kept 'dropping the ball during fielding practice. Their starting pitcher was as wild as she had ever been. Jill thought that if her team was going to win, she would have to be the one to step forward. Soon the coach called the players in to sing the national anthem. Jill thought to herself, "This is just like it will be when I get to the pros." She knew the other players were nervous but not her! She couldn't wait to start the game.

Early in the game, Jill's team took a 1–0 lead. Jill came up to bat with a runner on second. But the umpire called her out on strikes. She couldn't believe that he called such a terrible pitch a strike! She really wanted to say to him, "You just called out Jill, the best player on the team." By the third inning, the lead was 3–0. Things were looking good for the team. But Jill still didn't have a hit. Her next time up, she hit a long fly to left. When the ball was caught, she blamed a gust of wind for taking away her home run.

Then the Ramblers scored four runs in their half of the inning. Now Jill had her chance to be the star. There were runners on second and third. With two strikes she got the pitch she was looking for. She swung with all her might. She couldn't believe that she missed it. Jill sat down, angry that the sun had gotten in her eyes at the wrong time. She just couldn't see the ball. Then the shortstop lined a double to left field and scored the two runs that the team needed. The pitcher struck out their last batter and Jill's team won 5–4. The team went wild, but Jill didn't feel like celebrating. Even after the team picture, Jill felt terrible. It was her worst game all season and it was the biggest game of the season, too. She wished that she had done better in front of all those people. (399 words)

Retelling

Examiner: "Tell me about what you just read and what you thought about it."

> It's the story of how they won the championship game. Like in the game it was really a ball and they said it was a strike and the wind made the ball go out of bounds and that's why she felt bad. But they still won the game.

If there is no spontaneous response, repeat the request, "Tell me what you thought about the passage."

> Just what I said.

NOTE: Use the Retelling Rubric on p. 104 to assess the child's retelling performance.

Retelling Rubric		**Comprehension Questions**

Retelling Rubric

Story Structure

1. **Key Characters and Setting:** Jill and her team playing in the championship game.
2. **Character's Problem or Goal:** Be the star of the game.
3. **Problem-Solving or Goal-Meeting Process:**
   - Jill has no confidence that her team can win the game.
   - Jill thinks she is better than the other players.
   - She plays badly but makes excuses for it.
   - Jill's team wins the championship.
   - Even though her team wins, Jill is unhappy about her play.
4. **Personal Response:** Any well-supported positive or negative response to the characters or events in the story; any reaction to the humor or sadness in the story; any well-supported positive or negative reaction to the story as a whole.

Score column:
- +1
- 0
- 0
- 0
- 0
- +1
- 0
- 0

Rubric:

4 = Complete retelling includes characters, problem/goal, all five steps in the problem-solving process, and a well-supported personal response.

3 = Retelling includes characters, problem/goal, and all five steps in the problem-solving process, but has no critical response.

2 = Retelling includes characters, problem/goal, and three or four steps in the problem-solving process; some key factual errors or omissions. Add ½ point for well-supported personal response

1 = Retelling omits either characters or problem; includes one or two steps in the problem-solving process, but the account is disjointed and includes factual errors or serious omissions. Add ½ point for well-supported personal response

0 = Provides a title or topic statement but shows no real awareness of the character's problem and how the problem is worked out.

Retelling Score: __1.0__

Comprehension Questions

1. Why didn't Jill think that her team was going to win the game?

   Text-based: Practice was going badly; shortstop dropped the ball often, and pitcher was wild.

   Because the other team was so good. ?(Examiner's probe: Do you remember anything about her team?) *I don't remember.*

   +0

2. Did the other players on the team feel the same way that Jill did about winning the championship? How do you know?

   Text-based: No, they were happy to win while Jill was disappointed in herself.

   Yes, they all wanted to win but they knew the other team was good.

   +0

3. Do you think that Jill and her teammates were good friends or not? Why?

   Inference: Probably not, she didn't seem to know their names. She didn't care too much about the team; said that they wouldn't play well.

   Yes, they were on the same team.

   +0 (missed focus of relationship)

4. How important to Jill was winning the championship game? What made you think that?

   Inference: Not very important. She was more concerned that she didn't have a hit. When her team was losing she thought about herself, not winning the game.

   Real important; she wanted to go to the pros when she grows up.

   +0 (missed focus of specific game)

5. Do you think that Jill has a chance of becoming a professional player? Why or why not?

   Critical Response: Probably not, won't work hard if she thinks everyone else is responsible when she doesn't play well; not a team player. Yes, she is the best player on the team; everyone can have a bad game; she has the confidence she needs.

   Yes, girls are starting to have professional sports too. ?(Examiner's probe: What about Jill?) *She's the best player of all so if she keeps up her talent she might make it.*

   +10

6. What reasons did Jill give for playing poorly in the game? (Must identify two.)

   Text-based: Blamed umpire; blamed the wind; blamed the sun.

   The umpire called the ball a strike, and the sun got in her eyes.

   +10

7. Was Jill good at predicting how well her teammates would play? Explain.

   Inference: Not very good; both players that she thought would do poorly played well.

   Yes, she thought they'd win and they did.

   +0 (missed textual link with Jill's expectation)

8. Why was Jill upset at the end of the game?

   Text-based: She played badly; she was embarrassed in front of the people; she wished she had played better.

   She didn't have a good game and she felt bad.

   +10

9. Do you think that Jill needs help from her coach? Why or why not?

   Critical Response: Yes, she may not be as good as she thinks she is; she needs to stop making excuses and practice more; she needs to be more of a team player. No, she is already the best player on the team.

   Yes, if she wants to be a pro she'll need the coach to help her get better so she has better games.

   +10

10. Why do you think that Jill didn't play as well as she thought she would in the big game?

    Critical Response: May have been overconfident; big crowd may have bothered her; may have tried too hard to be the star; made excuses instead of trying harder.

    She couldn't help it; the ball was called a strike and then the wind made her hit go out of bounds.

    +0

Comprehension Analysis:

Text-Based: __2/4__
Inference: __0/3__
Critical Response: __2/3__

Total Comprehension %: __40%__

The Championship Game: 399 words

Reader's copy on p. 32 of the Reader's Passages. Note: This passage was used to assess listening comprehension.

Introductory Statement: "Would you read this passage about a basketball player to yourself? When you are finished, I'll take the passage away. Then I'll ask you to tell me about what you read and what you think of it. After that, I'll ask you some questions about the passage."

Story

Rasheed was excited to be playing on his first basketball team. He hadn't played much basketball but he had always been big and fast and a good athlete. But this time things were different. The first time he had the ball, Rasheed dribbled it off his foot and out of bounds. The next two times, a quicker player stole it away from him. Finally Rasheed had his first chance to shoot the ball but he missed everything, even the backboard. Soon his teammates stopped passing the ball to him, even when he was open under the basket. His team lost the game badly and Rasheed went home angry with his team and angry with basketball.

That night, Rasheed went to his father and told him that he wanted to quit the basketball team. "I'm no good at basketball and the team is no good either," he said.

"Well, if you want to quit, that's your decision," said Mr. Singer. "But I think if you really want to, you can become a whole lot better and so can your team. Maybe you shouldn't just do things that are easy for you." Rasheed had to think this one over. Rasheed knew that whenever his father said, "It's your decision, but . . ." he really meant that he'd like Rasheed to think it over very carefully. Down deep, he knew that his father would be disappointed if he never even tried to become a better player.

Rasheed knew that his father wouldn't be much help at teaching him basketball but he had heard stories about their new neighbor, Mr. Armstrong, being named to the all-state team in high school. When Rasheed asked Mr. Armstrong if he could teach him basketball, Mr. Armstrong's eyes lit up. He said, "You stick with me, kid, and you'll be the best basketball player ever!" Rasheed laughed as the two of them took turns shooting baskets in Mr. Armstrong's back yard. But soon Rasheed was sweating and breathing hard as his new teacher put him through one basketball drill after another. Finally, Mr. Armstrong said, "Time to call it a day! But be here same time tomorrow and we'll do it again." Rasheed worked hard and even after just a few days, he could feel himself becoming more confident in his ability. When it was time for the next game, Rasheed scored eight points, grabbed five rebounds, and didn't lose the ball once. His team still lost the game but his teammates couldn't believe how much better he had become.

After the game, Mr. Singer put his arm around his son and said, "I'm really proud of the decision you made, Rasheed. You worked awfully hard and it really showed."

"Thanks, Dad. Thanks for not letting me quit the team."

"Who told you that you couldn't quit? It wasn't me!"

Rasheed just smiled. (473 words)

Retelling

Examiner: "Tell me about what you just read and what you thought about it."

Rasheed was in his first basketball game and he had a real bad game but he thought he'd have a good game so he thought he'd stop playing but his dad didn't think that was a good idea. So Rasheed asked his neighbor who was Mr. Armstrong if he'd help him and they played real hard but they had lots of fun. Then when

Rasheed played the next game he was really good and his dad was proud of him because he didn't quit. Rasheed told his dad that he helped him not quit and his dad and Rasheed smiled because they were really both proud.

If there is no spontaneous response, repeat the request, "Tell me what you thought about the passage."

I liked the part that Rasheed's neighbor helped him learn to play better even though it wasn't his son and they had so much fun. It was like practice turned out to be a lot of fun and staying with the team was something he and his dad were proud about.

Retelling Rubric

Story Structure	
1. **Key Characters and Setting:** Rasheed, his father, and Mr. Armstrong, in basketball league.	+1
2. **Character's Problem or Goal:** Rasheed wants to quit the basketball team because he isn't very good.	+1
3. **Problem-Solving or Goal-Meeting Process:**	
• Rasheed tries to play basketball and fails.	+1
• He wants to quit the team but his father wants him to think about it.	+1
• Rasheed asks Mr. Armstrong to help him.	+1
• Mr. Armstrong and Rasheed work hard and he improves.	+1
• Rasheed plays better and his father is proud of his work.	+1
4. **Personal Response:** Any well-supported positive or negative response to the characters or events in the story; any reaction to the humor or sadness in the story; any well-supported positive or negative reaction to the story as a whole.	+1

Rubric:

4 = Complete retelling includes characters, problem/goal, all five steps in the problem-solving process, and a well-supported personal response.

3 = Retelling includes characters, problem/goal, and all five steps in the problem solving process, but has no critical response.

2 = Retelling includes characters, problem/goal, and three or four steps in the problem-solving process; some key factual errors or omissions. Add ½ point for well-supported personal response.

1 = Retelling omits either characters or problem; includes one or two steps in the problem-solving process, but the account is disjointed and includes factual errors or serious omissions. Add ½ point for well-supported personal response.

0 = Provides a title or topic statement but shows no real awareness of the character's problem and how the problem is worked out.

Retelling Score: _4.0_

Comprehension Questions

1. Why was Rasheed angry after his first game with the basketball team? (Must identify one.)

   Text-based: His teammates wouldn't pass the ball to him; he played badly; he was embarrassed.

   He thought he'd play really good but he wasn't good.

   +10

2. How do you know that Mr. Armstrong really wanted to help Rasheed become a better player? (Must identify one.)

   Text-based: His eyes lit up when Rasheed asked him; he worked with Rasheed night after night.

   He practiced with him even though he wasn't his son and they had a lot of fun practicing.

   +10

3. What kind of player was Rasheed expecting to be when he first started to play basketball? Why?

   Inference: A good player; was always a good athlete and expected basketball to be easy.

   He thought he'd be very good. ?(Examiner's probe: Why?) *'Cause he was good at all sports*

   +10

4. How do you think Rasheed knew that his father wouldn't be able to help him with basketball?

   Inference: He knew his father wasn't very good at basketball; his father may have been too busy.

   Maybe his dad worked late so that's why he asked Mr. Armstrong instead.

   +10

5. Why would Rasheed's father think he should stay on the team, even if he wasn't very good?

   Critical Response: His son shouldn't just quit and walk away; knew his son could be better if he tried; wanted him to learn about how to stick with something and learn.

   He probably knew that if he was willing to practice more and have somebody older help him that he'd be as good as he thought.

   +10

6. Why didn't Rasheed quit when Mr. Armstrong made him work so hard on basketball drills?

   Text-based: He had fun; they laughed together and Mr. Armstrong told basketball stories.

   He was laughing with Mr. Armstrong— they had a lot of fun practicing.

   +10

7. Why do you think that Mr. Armstrong would spend so much time and energy on a neighbor's son?

   Inference: May not have had children himself; liked to share his knowledge of basketball; enjoyed spending time with Rasheed; enjoyed playing basketball.

   He must have known him a lot before and he knew he liked him and would have fun with him.

   +10

8. How did Rasheed's teammates react to him after the second game?

   Text-based: Surprised at his improvement.

   They saw he played good this time when he was real bad last time.

   +10

9. Do you think Mr. Singer should let his son make his own decision even if he thought it was the wrong one? Explain.

   Critical Response: Yes, must learn to make his own decisions and accept consequences; will help him to become more mature and responsible. No, he should give him some guidance and try to persuade him that he is making a mistake; stakes are too high to let kids make the wrong decision; kids really want guidance and advice.

   Yes, they seemed like they talked a lot about a lot of things and he knew that he'd make a good decision and he did and he was proud of him.

   +10

10. Do you think it would have been wrong if Rasheed had quit the team? Why or why not?

    Critical Response: Yes, he really had not tried to improve; he would have disappointed his father. No, he was not getting better; his teammates did not help him; his teammates ignored him and the team played badly anyway.

    Yes, he would be thinking he's a bad basketball player when he really was a good one and he would have missed all the fun he had with Mr. Armstrong and his Dad wouldn't be saying he's proud of him.

    +10

Comprehension Analysis:

Text-Based: _4/4_
Inference: _3/3_
Critical Response: _3/3_

Total Comprehension %: _100%_

The Player: 473 words

Critical Reading Inventory—Recapitulation Record—Narrative Passages

Name __John__ Grade __5th__ C.A. __10-8__ Date of Testing __11/25__ Examiner __M. Examiner__

Comprehending and Responding to Text

Level	Word List Flash	Word List Untimed	Context RAI	Context MMI	Oral Comp. %	Oral Retelling Score	Oral Text-based	Oral Inference	Oral Critical	Silent Comp. %	Silent Retelling Score	Silent Text-based	Silent Inference	Silent Critical	Average Oral & Silent	Listening Comp. %
Pre-Primer																
Primer							/3	/3	/2			/3	/3	/2		
First							/3	/3	/2			/3	/3	/2		
Second	100	100	97	100	100	3.5	4/4	3/3	3/3	90	3.5	4/4	3/3	2/3	95	
Third	85	95	95	98	50	1.0	2/4	0/3	3/3	40	1.0	2/4	0/3	2/3	45	
Fourth	60	75					/4	/3	/3			/4	/3	/3		
Fifth																
Listening							4/4	3/3	3/3		4.0	/4	/3	/3		100
Sixth							/4	/3	/3			/4	/3	/3		
Jr. High							/4	/3	/3			/4	/3	/3		
Sr. High																

Level One Interpretation

Level:	Highest Independent Level __2nd grade__	Highest Instructional Level ____	Frustration Level __3rd grade__
Word List and Miscue Analysis:	Flash __100__ MM __7__ RAI __97__ MV __1__ MMI __100__ Non-words __1__	Flash ____ MM ____ RAI ____ MV ____ MMI ____ Non-words ____	Flash __95__ MM __12__ RAI __95__ MV __9__ MMI __98__ Non-words __7__
Comprehension and Retelling Scores:	Comp. % / Retelling Oral: __100__ / __3.5__ Silent: __90__ / __3.5__ Average: __95__ / __3.5__	Comp. % / Retelling Oral: ____ / ____ Silent: ____ / ____ Average: ____ / ____	Comp. % / Retelling Oral: __50__ / __1.0__ Silent: __40__ / __1.0__ Average: __45__ / __1.0__
Oral Comprehension, and Fluency, and MMI:	Oral comp. % __100__ MMI __100__	Oral comp. % ____ MMI ____ Fluency ____	Oral comp. % __50__ MMI __98__
Question Type:	Oral / Silent Text-based: __4/4__ / __4/4__ Inference: __3/3__ / __3/3__ Critical: __3/3__ / __2/3__	Oral / Silent Text-based: ____ / ____ Inference: ____ / ____ Critical: ____ / ____	Oral / Silent Text-based: __2/4__ / __2/4__ Inference: __0/3__ / __0/3__ Critical: __3/3__ / __2/3__

Miscue Analysis Worksheet

Student __John__ Grade __5th__ Age __10.8__

Highest Independent Level __2nd__ Highest Instructional Level __N/A__ Frustration Level __3rd__

Highest Independent Level — 2nd

Miscue	Text	MM	MV	Non-words
again	against	X	-	-
-	He	X	-	-
-	up	X	-	-
and	-	X	-	-
dau-	daughter	X	X	X
-	race	X	-	-
and	but	X	-	-
growled	groaned	X	-	-
Totals		**7**	**1**	**1**

RAI __96%__ MMI __100%__

Highest Instructional Level — N/A

Miscue	Text	MM	MV	Non-words

RAI ____ MMI ____

Frustration Level — 3rd

Miscue	Text	MM	MV	Non-words
hears	heard	X	-	-
vis-iting	visiting	-	X	X
ez-cited	excited	-	X	X
a	his	X	-	-
he	-	X	-	-
the	-	X	-	-
-	and	X	-	-
ru-sh	rush	-	X	X
I	-	X	-	-
ju-laipt	gulped	-	X	X
go	-	X	-	-
touring	turning	-	X	-
the	-	X	-	-
po-sto-les	postholes	-	X	X
tru-dy-ing	trudging	-	X	X
to	toward	X	-	-
-	to	X	-	-
her	immediately	-	X	-
early	eager	X	-	-
too	so	X	-	-
rep-lied	replied	-	X	X
Totals		**12**	**9**	**7**

RAI __95%__ MMI __98%__

RAI: Count the number of scoreable miscues from Column 1 and use the Miscue Chart for that passage to obtain the RAI.
MMI: Count the number of meaning-violating miscues and use the Miscue Chart for that passage to obtain the MMI.
Non: The number of meaning-violating miscues that were Non-words.
MM: Miscue that represents an attempt to maintain the sense of the text.
MV: Miscue that violated the sense of the text.

110

Discussion of Case Study 2: John

John is 10 years and 8 months old and is currently in the fifth grade in a suburban school. He has been having academic problems since the second grade and since that time he has participated in a "pull-out" reading support program in which he leaves the regular classroom for special instruction in reading.

Level One: Numerical Interpretation

Our first step would normally be to transcribe the scores from all of our measures to the Recapitulation Record. In this case, the transcribing has been done for you and the results can be seen on page 109. Because John has demonstrated problems with the Word Lists, we will want to complete a Miscue Analysis Worksheet. This worksheet will facilitate the comparison of his word recognition in isolation to his word recognition in the actual task of reading (see p. 110).

We need to estimate tentative reading levels so that we can begin to examine John's performance in light of the four categories listed in the table on the Recapitulation Record under Level One Interpretation. As always, we will rely primarily on the comprehension scores and the RAI in identifying these levels. With a comprehension average of 95% and an RAI of 97%, it is clear that John can read independently at the second grade level. Despite the somewhat low RAI, John's MMI of 100% tells us at a glance that few of his miscues were serious ones. However, at the third grade level, in spite of the 95% RAI, John has an average comprehension score of only 45%. If this figure is an accurate estimate, we have clearly reached John's frustration level. It is somewhat unusual that in John's case, we can estimate no clear instructional level. Numerical interpretation should help us to identify problem areas that we can shed more light on during the analytic and comprehensive interpretations of the test data.

Word List and Miscue Analysis.   John scored 100% on the Flash Word Lists at the second grade level and this served as the basis for the decision to begin his oral reading at this level. During his oral reading, John scored 97% for his RAI and 100% for his MMI. Only one of his miscues could be regarded as failing to maintain meaning. John had no significant word recognition problems at the second grade level.

His performance at the third and fourth grade levels was a different matter. At these levels, John scored 85% and 60% respectively on the Flash presentation and 95% and 75% respectively on the Untimed presentation. When we contrast this with his oral reading of third grade materials, we find an RAI score of 95% and an MMI score of 98%. John made a total of 21 miscues, 9 of which violated the intended meaning. More importantly, 7 of these 9 serious miscues were non-words. This can be quite significant in that it may be indicative of a very distorted view of the nature of reading. The five self-corrections that John made in his oral reading are encouraging, but in both the analytic and comprehensive interpretations of his performance we will need to be mindful of other signs that may be indicative of an inaccurate view of reading. In light of his comprehension and current fifth grade level, John appears to be a struggling reader.

Comprehension Scores and Retelling Scores.   When we compare John's oral and silent comprehension, we find no appreciable differences between the two. John scored 100% following oral reading and 90% following silent reading at his independent level with identical retelling scores of 3.5. We find the same kind of consistency at the third grade level, though of a more unfortunate kind. John scored 50% in the comprehension questions after oral reading and 40% after silent reading, with identical retelling scores of 1.0.

Oral Comprehension, Fluency, and MMI.   Our comparison of these scores reveals a strong balance at the second grade level with an MMI of 100% and a score of 100% on comprehension questions following oral reading. This performance reflects the type of stability that characterizes an independent level. However, when we move to the third grade level, we find an MMI of 98% and an oral comprehension score of 50%. This is a major discrepancy between word recognition and comprehension. Note that fluency was not assessed because no instructional level was obtained.

Question Types.   At the second grade level, John was successful with all three item types: text-based, inferential, and critical response. But at the third grade level, our concern is less with question type and more with comprehension across the board. John correctly responded to only four of eight text-based items and zero of six inference items. However, he responded successfully to five of six critical response items, suggesting a solid ability to link his experiences with ideas from the text to address thought-provoking questions.

Reading Performance Overview.   We need to exercise some caution in our numerical interpretation when we discuss any student's performance at the frustration level. John's sight vocabulary at the third grade level (85% Flash) is adequate and he seems to have some word analysis skills at this level as suggested by two corrections in the Untimed setting. His oral reading performance is better when he is reading actual text (RAI of 95% and MMI of 98%), but his oral reading includes all-too-frequent violations of meaning. But in the final analysis, it is an average comprehension of 45% at the third grade level that is John's undoing. John had serious difficulties with text-based and inference items, but a fairly strong performance on critical response items.

At this point we can feel comfortable with the tentative levels we estimated: independent at second grade, no instructional level, and frustration at third grade level. These levels are based on numbers that are fairly unambiguous and fall clearly within guidelines for the various reading levels. Based on an examination of John's overall performance as reflected on the Recapitulation Record, we can draw several conclusions. First of all, John's sight vocabulary tends to be a major weakness contributing to his reading comprehension problem. John's sight vocabulary is not adequate at the fourth grade level and he is currently in fifth grade. Also, his steep drop in overall comprehension from 95% at the second grade level to 45% at the third grade level is a serious concern.

A second observation centers on his strong retellings following both oral and silent reading at the second grade level. Unfortunately, his retellings broke down dramatically when the passages became more complex and challenging. However, John's performance on the Listening Comprehension portion of the test is encouraging. When he was relieved of the burden of word recognition and the passage was read to him, John showed a solid ability to grasp concepts at the fifth grade level, scoring 100% in his overall comprehension and a perfect 4.0 in his retelling. This result suggests that John's problem may not center around thinking ability or concepts.

Conclusions Based on Level One Interpretation

Based solely upon numerical interpretation, it seems reasonable to draw several conclusions about John's reading performance:

1. John's sight vocabulary is weak, relative to his current grade level placement.
2. John's oral reading at third grade level is characterized by numerous meaning-altering miscues and the use of non-words.
3. John's comprehension at third grade level is weak in text-based and inference items but strong in critical response items.
4. Without considerable support, John is likely to experience significant frustration in reading at his current grade level placement.
5. John's comprehension at his current fifth grade level is excellent when he is relieved of the task of recognizing words.

Level Two: Analytical Interpretation

In the analytical interpretation we take a closer look at the student's actual responses to determine any underlying strengths and weaknesses. We can use the same issues we examined in the Level One Numerical Interpretation as a framework for our analysis. We will pay particularly close attention to patterns in John's performance that may shed light on his view of reading and the way in which that view may be contributing to his strengths and weaknesses.

Word List and Miscue Analysis.   The key data to consider here are John's use of non-words, such as his first uncorrected miscue: "*un-a-sal*" for *unusual*. Our concern is that John's view of reading may be making him comfortable with the use of nonsense words. We see the same pattern on the Flash presentation at the fourth grade level. For three of the eight words that John missed during the Flash presentation, he simply pronounced the first syllable; he appeared to have little faith in his ability to deal with unfamiliar multisyllabic words. All of the five other errors he made were also nonsense words. It would seem that John does not have an internal checking system based on the expectation that the words he reads are very much like the words that he uses when he listens and speaks; that is, they are supposed to make sense.

When we examine John's oral reading performance at the third grade level, we find a total of 21 miscues; of those 21 miscues there were 5 insertions and 1 omission that did not alter the meaning of the text. In addition to a single teacher-provided miscue, there were a total of 14 substitutions, only 6 of which fit the meaning of the text. The 8 substitutions that altered the meaning of the text tended once again to reflect John's weak sight vocabulary and word analysis skills. His sole approach to word analysis seems to be related to his attempts to "sound out" words, with little reference to the meaning of the text. Consequently, 7 of the 8 meaning-violating substitutions he made were nonsense words, such as "*jŭ-Lăpt*" for *gulped*, and "*pō-stō-les*" for *postholes*. Despite the context clues available to him in the meaningful text, John showed no tendency to use the clues and no discomfort with the use of non-words. While the substitutions that were based on non-words clearly reflect his difficulty with medial vowels in words of two or more syllables, instruction geared toward more effective "sounding out" of words may not be effective. Instead, it appears that John would benefit from an emphasis on comprehension monitoring and using the context along with print-to-speech matching to be sure that reading makes sense.

One other observation about John's reading deserves mention. John's request for a teacher-provided word seems to be a positive sign in that it signals John's emerging perspective on reading as a meaningful activity. John was nearing the end of the story and had read, "*David fell asleep . . . i-me-di-*." In what appeared to be a need for making some sense of the reading, he asked the examiner, "*What's that word?*" and was told "*immediately.*" He continued reading and made only three more miscues, two of which did not violate the sense of the passage. Prior to that point in the text, John had made 11 of his 14 substitutions, only 4 of which fit the sense of the story. His performance may be suggesting that as he was creating more and more sense out of the story, he made fewer nonsense word substitutions.

Comprehension Scores and Retelling Scores.   John's specific responses to questions following oral reading at his independent level shed some light on the way in which John sometimes identifies with and connects with characters. John demonstrates his ability to link his prior knowledge to the story in a very positive way. For example, in the story *The Race*, John responded to the question ("Do you think that this was the first time Annie had ever raced against anyone?") with, "*No, her parents must have saw her win so they told her to race.*" This response reflects sensitivity to a parent's sense of pride in a child's accomplishment. In addition, John's answers to two of the critical response questions include a similar insight into the characters. In one case, John notes that Spencer should admit that Annie is faster, but should stop bragging. In another case he was able to see that other characters might react differently to Spencer if he stopped bragging. The fact that John can respond at this level is very encouraging.

John's responses also include clear examples of his imprecision in language. When he was asked "*What did the animals do when Annie won the race?*", he answered, "*She surprised them.*" Because there is an element of correctness in that response, the examiner felt the need to probe for more specific information. Then John responded more precisely with: "*They cheered for her.*" John's response to question 4 ("Why did Annie agree to race against Spencer?") also revealed some confusion and imprecision: "*She thought she'd win but he was winning first.*" John switches from hypothesizing about Annie's motivation to the reality of the actual race as described in the story.

In his responses to the silent reading selection, *The Roller Coaster Ride*, John again seemed to connect to characters. He appreciates the mother's fears for her daughter in his responses to questions 5 and 10. John suggested that the mother regretted her own fear of the roller coaster but that she would probably still be afraid even if she were with her daughter. John's willingness to put himself into the shoes of the characters in a story is a powerful strength that suggests much promise for the eventual restructuring of John's view of reading. In his response to question 3 ("Do you think Jessie had been to an amusement park before?"), John clearly uses his own experiences at amusement parks. He stated, "*Yes, she probably stood by the marker and couldn't reach the line so they didn't let her on.*" This same type of connection is reflected in his response to question 4 ("Why would Jessie want so much to ride the roller coaster?"). He responded, "*She saw all the other kids riding—the kids bigger than she was—and they just kept getting back in line again.*" His answer to question 7 ("Why did Jessie decide to ride the roller coaster again?") reflects this same type of connection. He responded, "*She was scared but she still made it so she knew she'd make it again.*" These responses suggest positive elements of clear thinking that can become points of focus in John's program of instruction.

On the less positive side of the ledger, John demonstrated some lack of sensitivity to the types of thinking called for by various question types. For example, when he was asked question 9 ("Do you think it was right for Jessie to get back on the ride after she promised never to ride again?"), he responded, "*Yes, because she did make it so she knew she could make it again but she still wanted her aunt with her.*" It seems that John completely ignored the judgment that is required of the question; instead he focused solely on the safety of returning to a second ride. In the same vein, John's response to his third grade silent reading did not reflect the same level of character involvement as his previous responses had. Instead he seemed to approach the passage as more of a literal reading task and thus he failed to make several important logical connections. For example, John failed to focus at all on the character's tendency to make excuses for her poor performance.

Further insight into a reader's lack of precision is often provided by an analysis of retellings. Following oral reading at his independent level, John produced the following retelling: "*The animals didn't like Spencer because he was always wanting to race them because he knew he'd win. That's why they didn't like him. Then when he wants to race the new family he thought he'd win again but Annie beat him. They thought he'd stop bragging but then he said, 'I can jump higher than everyone.' Everybody rolled their eyes. I liked that story because Annie beat him*!" Because he did not effectively support his reason for liking the story, the examiner asked him the follow-up question provided. John concludes that Spencer's experiences should have taught him a lesson, a well-supported personal response to the story. John clearly enjoyed the story, and was irritated with Spencer's nature and delighted with Annie's win. But his retelling includes very imprecise linguistic structures and an incomplete linking of the causal relationships between ideas in the story. The same pattern is observed in the retelling following silent reading and in some of his responses to the second grade oral reading items: an ability to connect with characters and their situations but imprecision and omissions in the links between ideas. What remains to be determined is whether John's imprecision is a result of immature language facility or immature thinking.

As might be expected, John's retellings at third grade level were even less complete. While we need to be cautious as to how much emphasis we place on a student's reading at frustration level, John's retellings consistently omit key ideas. His retelling of *The Farm Vacation* was: "*Dave wanted to be like his grandfather so he stayed with him at the farm. His best thing was the horses and he wanted his grandfather to teach him how to ride.*" Here we see large gaps in his retelling. He has missed the key elements that this is David's first visit to the farm and that David wants to be a farmer and learn about farming. Also, he made no reference to Grandmother's role in the story. In addition, we see none of the emotional connection to characters that typified his retellings at the second grade level. A quick review of his retelling following silent reading reflects similar omissions of story elements needed to connect with the characters.

Oral Comprehension, Fluency, and MMI. We have noted the positive balance reflected by John's performance at second grade level reading. However, when we analyze his performance at the third grade level, it is clear that his word recognition difficulties, particularly his comfort with using non-words, are a hindrance to his reading comprehension. But John also failed to focus on several key ideas in the text which hindered his comprehension.

In *The Farm Vacation*, for example, John transforms David's desire to learn how to ride horses into the sole reason for his visit. He failed to note that this was David's first visit to his grandfather's farm. Nonetheless, several of his responses are based on the assumption that he has been there before and that David's desire to be a farmer is also a desire to follow in his grandfather's footsteps.

We also see a pattern emerging in which John relies solely upon his background knowledge, ignoring any restrictions to that background required by the text. For example, when asked if he thought that David lived near his grandfather (question 3), he responded "*He probably did; a lot of kids live near their grandfathers.*" Another example is provided in his response to question 7 ("Do you think that David ever got to ride the horses that week?"): "*He probably did because he wanted to do that and his grandfather probably knew how so he'd teach him.*" Again, John focuses on his assumption based on background knowledge, but fails to see the variety of clues in the story that could easily challenge his assumption.

Question Types. We have noted that, at his independent level, John was very successful responding to all but one of the comprehension questions following oral and silent reading. John's comprehension at this level seemed to be thorough and deep, as evidenced by his positive connections to the characters in the stories. While his responses often included run-on sentences, imprecision in pronoun references, and imprecise relational elements, they are generally thorough and well developed.

It would seem that even when John was reading at frustration level, he made an emotional connection and created in his mind a close relationship between David and his Grandfather in *The Farm Vacation*. An analysis of his responses does show that he is able to use his prior knowledge and thinking skills to answer five of the six critical response questions. David's comprehension strengths at his independent level reflect a solid balance with all types of thinking and his problems at the third grade level are reflected in difficulty with text-based and inferential items.

Conclusions Based on Level Two Interpretation

1. John appears to have a solid ability to think about stories and characters and link his own experiences to them, as evidenced by his strong performance in critical response items.
2. John demonstrates considerable imprecision in a number of his responses, either as a result of imprecise language or of fuzzy concepts.
3. John does not seem able to effectively make use of context clues as an aid to the construction of meaning. His use of non-words in oral reading suggests that he does not often expect that reading will make sense and that he does not regularly monitor his reading for comprehension.

Level Three: Comprehensive Interpretation

John's testing was initiated as a result of several angry outbursts on his part in both the playground and in the classroom. These incidents were completely inconsistent with his past conduct. John's parents were called to school for a special conference with John's teacher. The teacher reported that John had always been a very pleasant student, an assessment corroborated by his third and fourth grade teachers. She did not have a great deal of insight into John's reading problems because she was not his reading teacher; the school reading teacher provided the bulk of John's instruction in a pullout program. The only behavior of note that his teacher mentioned was John's tendency to daydream during class but she reiterated that, until recently, John had never disturbed the class.

John's mother reported that she was very frustrated with her inability to help her son overcome his long-standing reading problems. She reported that John had always experienced difficulty with reading; however, in the second grade he was formally assigned to a special reading teacher. Since that time, the majority of his reading instruction occurred in one-on-one or small group settings. She also mentioned that the reporting of John's difficulty was a shock to both her and her husband because John had loved books ever since he was a young child. His parents would take turns reading with him and his favorites tended to be the stories of Hans Christian Anderson and the Brothers Grimm. Both parents began participation in a library club while John was still a toddler. John started to have favorite authors and illustrators. When John was 3½ years old, the librarian, who had noticed his enjoyment with read alouds, suggested that his parents try reading a chapter book to John, a very successful activity. John was proud of his success with books and wanted to participate in "reading" to his newly born brother.

His parents reported that John always enjoyed discussing stories he read. The family continued this habit even after John started school; however, halfway into second grade, John told his parents that he was probably too big to have someone reading to him. They respected his wish and stopped reading to him. However, it was clear from his reading habits that John still loved stories.

John's parents reported that school and teacher conferences throughout the years centered on his problems with learning words. His reading teacher consistently sent home word lists that they were asked to help John master. In addition, John brought home worksheets that emphasized phonic rules and words to recognize through application of these rules. More recently, John was also working with worksheets that required the "finding of little words" that might be created with the letters of multisyllabic words. They also reported that John disliked having to go to a special reading class and said that he wished that he could be reading the stories that his friends were reading.

The reading teacher at that time reported that John was not motivated and that the pleasantness reported by his classroom teacher was never representative of his demeanor during special reading instruction. She mentioned that for several years the emphasis of instruction had been directed to word recognition since John did not have the type of sight vocabulary that would be needed to succeed with stories at his grade level. She believed that John's tendency to recognize words one day but fail with those same words several days later was a reflection of his lack of motivation and effort.

With these pictures in mind, the reading specialist met with John for testing. During the initial interview, John reported that he believed his biggest problem with reading was "hard words" and that he thought he should be getting better at "sounding out" words. He did not know why this was not happening. He mentioned that when he came to a hard word he would either try to sound it out or try to look for "little words inside the word" to help him sound it out.

John stated that he did not like having to leave the classroom to go to his special reading class. He also stated that he did not like reading at all but he did wish that he could be in the group with his friends who were reading *Hatchet* by Gary Paulsen. He mentioned that he periodically listened to what was happening in the story and he thought it would have been exciting to be flying in the plane but that it must have been terrible for Matt when the pilot died. The reading teacher later reported how surprised she was that John knew so much about the story. This incident provides additional confirmation of John's proficiency with listening comprehension at his current grade level.

After the interviews and the administration of the CRI which we have just reviewed, we have a much clearer picture of John's reading environment. The reading specialist then met with both John's classroom teacher and special reading teacher to review the results of the Level Two Interpretation of the CRI. When the two teachers saw the results of the testing, specifically the way in which John demonstrated his ability to connect with characters, they were eager to design a plan of instruction that would capitalize on John's obvious love of stories. The reading specialist volunteered to meet with them so that there could be a collaborative approach to instruction. They agreed to utilize high-interest books with John and develop prereading discussion. In these discussions, they would make use of activities to incorporate key vocabulary in a way that connected to the story and to John's experiences. In addition, John's special reading teacher agreed to help plan an instructional program that would build on the use of context as a significant aid to word recognition. She agreed that cloze activities would sharpen John's sensitivity to the use of context as an aid to word recognition. She also agreed that, for the time being, they would deemphasize sounding out words until John was more comfortable recognizing and using language clues as an aid to word recognition. John's teachers agreed with the suggestion that John needs to develop his self-monitoring so that he recognizes that random attempts at word recognition and the use of nonsense words contribute little or nothing to his reading.

The reading specialist also suggested that both of John's teachers engage him in guided reading activities where they could monitor his progress more closely and provide the instruction that he needs in order to develop confidence in his ability to handle reading materials at his grade level. A further suggestion was to involve John in literature circle activities where he could capitalize on his love of stories and develop his confidence in his ability to make positive contributions to group discussions. Activities that capitalize on John's strength in listening would make him capable of following stories on his grade level.

Conclusions Based on Level Three Interpretation

1. John's early love of stories and literature is a possible link that can be used in developing a plan of instruction for him.
2. Frustration with word recognition and overall failure in reading appears to be building in John and negatively impacting his behavior.
3. John's view of reading appears at this point to be centered upon decoding and needs to be expanded to include sense and meaning-making in response to text.
4. John's parents are likely to be a solid support for him and should be incorporated into any plan of action for his instruction.
5. The instructional focus of John's teachers, that is, work on word recognition in isolation from actual reading, has not worked. Their willingness to try different approaches is most encouraging.

Summary and Plan of Action

It is important to note that each level of interpretation added insights important to the total picture of John as a reader. Whether the user will need all of the detail that comprehensive interpretation or even analytical interpretation provides is a matter of professional judgment. However, with all of the insights we have gained into John's reading performance, we are ready to identify key elements of John's reading and develop a plan of action to address his needs.

Perhaps first and foremost, John's failure with reading is beginning to generalize to his entire outlook on school and has the potential to do long-term damage. The CRI user will want to prescribe heavy doses of success and to use two significant strengths as the cornerstones of the plan. First of all, based on John's performance with critical response items in the CRI, John has what appear to be solid thinking skills that enable him to enjoy literature. He still has a high level of motivation to read just as his friends are doing. Furthermore, he seems to have a history of enjoying stories even from his earliest years and has even exhibited considerable interest in the narrative book his classmates are reading. Any plan of action should include a great deal of reading in high-interest materials and discussion of ideas, with much emphasis on and positive reinforcement of any thinking and linking with past experience that John demonstrates. If at first he is not able to read along with his classmates, he could listen to a taped version so that he can participate in the discussion activities related to the text.

At the same time, we will need to focus on John's word recognition ability. At present, John appears to have fixated on decoding as his focal strategy when he encounters an unknown word. He also appears to have developed a view of reading as centered on pronunciation, as evidenced by his frequent use of nonsense words in his oral reading. John will need instruction in word recognition that will encourage him to expand his repertoire of skill to include the use of language and context clues, not as ends in themselves, but as additional means to approach the meaning-making task of reading. His weakness in sight vocabulary can be addressed through continued exposure to words in the actual context of his reading. The fact that John has been avoiding reading for a considerable number of years and has not fallen even further behind in his sight vocabulary suggests that he may experience a good measure of success in incidental learning of new words, so long as these are presented in the context of meaningful reading.

Any plan of action for John must also address his view of reading. John does not now appear to be consistently engaging in monitoring his reading for the purpose of comprehension. He will need to be consistently encouraged by his teachers and parents to stop and take steps to rectify the situation whenever his reading does not make sense. At the same time, his teachers will have to be willing to follow up any of John's imprecise responses with clarifying questions to help him to more clearly and precisely express his ideas related to his reading. A response journal related to his reading would appear to be an ideal means of addressing his needs and assessing his growth.

The optimum instructional program for John would also capitalize on his interest in sports and technology/games. *Sports Illustrated for Kids* and, for example, Matt Christopher books may help to rekindle an interest in reading. He could easily become a member of an expert group in the case of technology and games. But a program for John must also address the discrepancy that exists between his current reading level and his grade level. John will almost certainly experience long-term difficulties unless his program helps to close the gap between his reading level and grade level. A carefully monitored and coordinated program of tutoring would appear to be an essential part of any program for John.

John's performance on text-based and particularly inference items suggests that he is not consistently making logical connections between and among the ideas he is reading. He appears to be depending on pure memory as his primary comprehension strategy. Yet he has also demonstrated the ability to make logical connections in a number of his responses. Instruction that emphasizes the organizational structures of text, such as the story grammar, may prove to be most useful when coupled with the clarifying discussion questions noted above.

Many teachers who read this case study will raise the question of whether John has a reading or learning disability. This is a legitimate question, given John's overall profile of reading difficulties. However, we believe that it is most unwise to seek explanations for a child's difficulties before we have exhausted our repertoire of teaching techniques and diagnostic insights. Providing John with more intensive instruction of the same type he has been given will almost certainly lead to failure. Providing John with a program centered on a thoroughly different approach, one that focuses on meaningful relationships among ideas reflected in text and in his own experience, has the best chance of success. Rather than run the risk of labeling John as different, particularly since he wants so much to be just like his classmates, we believe that we must first maximize all of our pedagogical resources. This includes more coordination between the classroom teacher and the reading teacher, perhaps facilitated by the reading specialist. If John does not respond to this new program, then we are justified in seeking an explanation outside the teacher–student interaction and in seeking instructional support.

John's prognosis is good, given the strengths he brings to reading. The primary task of his teachers will be to build on those strengths and encourage John to recapture the love of reading and learning that he is now in danger of losing.

Part II

Section 7

Procedures/Forms/Records

Summary of Administration Procedures
for *The Critical Reading Inventory*

Rapport

- Establish rapport with the child; use the Child Interview form to assist in this activity.
- Explain the purpose and process of the assessment, answer any questions and address any concerns.

Word Lists

2 index cards
1 tape recorder

- Start at least two levels below grade level.
- Flash = 1-second exposure using two index cards; record child's exact (phonetic) response in case of a miscue; use "+" to indicate a correct response.
- Untimed = 10- to 15-second exposure to allow the child to "decode" or correct miscues from the flash portion.

6 wrong

- Discontinue once the child has scored 70% or less on the Flash portion.

Passages

- Start with oral reading at the highest level at which the child attained 100% on the Flash portion of the word lists.
- Introduce the process for the passages by reading the Introductory Statement on the Examiner's Copy of the CRI.
- Record the child's oral reading miscues on the Examiner's Copy, using the notation guidelines on the next page; later you will calculate the RAI and MMI for each oral reading passage that the child has completed.
- Remove the story from the child and ask the child to retell the story to you; record his or her retelling verbatim for scoring later. If the child does not do so in the course of the retelling, remind the child, "Tell me what you thought about the passage."
- Ask the comprehension questions and record the child's exact responses. Score as you go if you are an experienced user. Otherwise, estimate the level of the child's performance so that you do not exceed the child's Frustration Level.
- Follow the same procedures for the silent passage at each level (except, of course, for recording the oral reading performance).
- Estimate the average for the oral and the silent comprehension performance after each level is administered.
- Stop when either the oral reading performance RAI score is 90% or less *or* when the average (oral + silent reading comprehension/2) is 50% or less.
- Proceed to listening comprehension assessment if the child's Instructional Level is below the child's grade level or if you note that word recognition problems are seriously affecting comprehension.
- If you start with a level where the child does not obtain an "independent" score on oral reading performance and/or comprehension average, then go down a level until an independent level is established.

Estimating Levels

	Oral Reading Performance	Comprehension Average
Independent	98–100	90
Instructional	93–97	70–85
Frustration	92 or below	50 or less

Oral Reading Miscue Recording Procedures for
The Critical Reading Inventory

Scoreable Miscues	Coding System for Miscues
• Substitutions/mispronunciations	Write phonetic spelling over word
• Omissions	Cross out omitted word
• Insertions	Write inserted word in text
• Teacher Provided	Circle word/note with "TP"

Scoreable Miscues—Special Cases

- Same error repeated more than once, counts only as one miscue
  For example, says *robe* for *rode* three times in the story = 1 miscue
- Skips a whole line of print or several words in a line = 1 miscue
- Reversals = 1 miscue

Nonscoreable but Recorded Oral Reading Behaviors

• Self-corrections	Use check mark or "SC"
• Dialect mispronunciations/omissions	
For example, the child leaves off word	
endings in both speech and oral reading	Note phonetic spelling with "D"
• Proper name mispronunciation	Note phonetic spelling
• Inappropriate pauses or hesitations	Note with slash (/)
• Repetitions	Underline the text
• Finger-pointing	FP
• Head movement	HM
• Subvocalization during silent reading	SV
• Skipped punctuation	Circle punctuation mark
• Word-by-word reading	W×W
• Inappropriate pacing	Slow/Fast

Oral Reading Fluency Rubric

Name: _____ Grade: ____ Date: _____ Examiner: _____

Excellent (4 points)

- Reading is fluent, confident, and accurate.
- Intonations support meaning of the text.
- Natural use of and appreciation for punctuation.
- Pacing rapid but smooth and unexaggerated.

Good (3 points)

- Reading is fluent and accurate for the most part but reader occasionally falters or hesitates.
- Intonations are largely meaningful but may include exaggerations or inflections inappropriate for the text.
- Solid use of punctuation as an aid to intonation.
- Reading is well-paced with only occasional weakness in response to difficulties with the text.

Inconsistent (2 points)

- Reader lacks confidence at times and reading is characterized by frequent pauses, miscues, and hesitations.
- Intonation is characterized by some joining of words into meaningful phrases but this element often breaks down when the reader encounters difficulties.
- Reaction to punctuation marks results in pauses that are inappropriately long or short.
- Pacing is relatively slow and markedly slower (or markedly faster) when reader encounters difficult text.

Weak (1 point)

- Reader consistently lacks confidence and occasionally lapses into word-by-word reading with frequent meaning-violating miscues.
- Intonation is largely flat with lack of enthusiasm.
- Punctuation is occasionally ignored and meaning is distorted.
- Pacing is either very slow or inappropriately fast.

Poor (0 points)

- Largely word-by-word reading with little or no inflection, numerous meaning-violating miscues, some of which may be nonwords.
- Intonation is almost completely absent.
- Frequent ignoring of punctuation.
- Pacing is painfully slow and halting.

Note: Fluency should be assessed at the reader's instructional level. Fluency should not be interpreted apart from the reader's comprehension performance.

Student Interview
Kindergarten–Fourth Grade

Name: _____ **Grade:** _____ **Date:** _____ **Examiner:** _____

1. Do you have any brothers or sisters? Any best friends? What about pets?

2. What are some things that you like to do at home?

3. What makes these things fun?

4. Does anyone ever read to you at home? Who? When? What?

5. Do you like to read?

6. Do you have any favorite books or authors? What are they? Why do you like them?

7. Are you a good reader? Why or why not?

8. What do you think is the hardest part about reading? (If child answers "words," then follow up with item below).

9. What do you do when you come to a word that you don't know?

10. Where do you get the books you read at home? (Probe further if necessary: library, stores, gifts, etc.)

11. What do you like most about school?

12. What kinds of things do you do when you have reading at school?

13. What would you like to do when you are older?

14. Do you think reading will be important to you?

Student Interview

Fifth Grade–Senior High

Name: _____ Grade: _____ Date: _____ Examiner: _____

1. What kinds of things do you like to do when you're not in school?

2. How about reading? (If reader does not volunteer the information, probe for how often, what kinds of materials, topics of interest, where materials are obtained, etc.)

3. How do you think you do with reading in school? What about writing?

4. What have you read recently for enjoyment? For school? Did you find them enjoyable? Were they easy for you to understand?

5. What is the hardest part about reading?

6. What are the best and worst things about school?

7. Is writing hard or easy for you? What do you think makes it that way?

8. Are you on any clubs or teams at school? Do have any hobbies? Do you have a job?

9. How are your grades in school? Do you have any concerns with any subjects?

10. Have you ever thought about what kind of job you'd like to have when you're older?

11. Is there anything else that you'd like to share about yourself?

Parent/Guardian Interview

Name: _____ Grade: _____ Date: _____ Examiner: _____

1. What made you think that it would be a good idea for _____ (student's name) to be tested at this time?

2. How is _____ doing in school, particularly in reading?

3. What kind of reading does _____ do at home?

4. How would you characterize _____'s:

   a. ability

   b. attitude

   c. interests

   d. needs

   e. behavior

5. What would you say is the major reason for _____'s school performance?

6. How long has he/she had this difficulty?

7. What kinds of help has he/she gotten so far?

8. What are you currently doing at home to help _____?

9. Is there anything else you think might be helpful for you to do?

10. What is the school or the teacher doing this year to help _____?

11. What else do you think it would be helpful for the school or teacher to do?

Teacher Interview

Name: _____ Grade: _____ Date: _____ Examiner: _____

1. What would you say are the greatest needs in reading of the class you have this year?

2. Could you describe for me a typical reading/language arts period in your classroom (this should include time spent, materials used, methods, grouping techniques)?

3. How does _____ (student's name) generally react to your instruction?

4. What would you say is the greatest emphasis in your comprehension instruction and assessment? *If response is unclear, you may follow up with*: Do you tend to emphasize recall of information, student response to the text, or both equally?

5. How would you characterize _____'s:

   a. ability

   b. attitude

   c. interests

   d. needs

   e. behavior

6. What kinds of activities or strategies have you tried specifically with _____? What seems to work best? What doesn't seem to be working?

7. What do you know about the type of support _____ gets at home?

8. If there were one thing that you could recommend that you think would help _____, what would it be?

Critical Reading Inventory—Recapitulation Record—Narrative Passages

Name _____ Grade _____ C.A. _____ Date of Testing _____ Examiner _____

Word List / Comprehending and Responding to Text

Level	Flash	Untimed	Context RAI	Context MMI	Oral Comp. %	Retelling Score	Oral Text-based	Oral Inference	Oral Critical	Silent Comp. %	Retelling Score	Silent Text-based	Silent Inference	Silent Critical	Average Oral & Silent	Listening Comp. %
Pre-Primer							/3	/3	/2			/3	/3	/2		
Primer							/3	/3	/2			/3	/3	/2		
First							/3	/3	/2			/3	/3	/2		
Second							/4	/3	/3			/4	/3	/3		
Third							/4	/3	/3			/4	/3	/3		
Fourth							/4	/3	/3			/4	/3	/3		
Fifth							/4	/3	/3			/4	/3	/3		
Sixth							/4	/3	/3			/4	/3	/3		
Jr. High							/4	/3	/3			/4	/3	/3		
Sr. High							/4	/3	/3			/4	/3	/3		

Level One Interpretation

Level:	Highest Independent Level	Highest Instructional Level	Frustration Level
Word List and Miscue Analysis:	Flash ___ MM ___ RAI ___ MV ___ MMI ___ Non-words ___	Flash ___ MM ___ RAI ___ MV ___ MMI ___ Non-words ___	Flash ___ MM ___ RAI ___ MV ___ MMI ___ Non-words ___
Comprehension and Retelling Scores:	Comp. % ___ Retelling ___	Comp. % ___ Retelling ___	Comp. % ___ Retelling ___
	Oral: ___ Silent: ___ Average: ___	Oral: ___ Silent: ___ Average: ___	Oral: ___ Silent: ___ Average: ___
Oral Comprehension, Fluency, and MMI:	Oral comp.% ___ MMI ___ Oral ___ Silent ___	Oral comp.% ___ MMI ___ Fluency ___ Oral ___ Silent ___	Oral comp. % ___ MMI ___ Oral ___ Silent ___
Question Type:	Text-based: ___ Inference: ___ Critical: ___ Oral ___ Silent ___	Text-based: ___ Inference: ___ Critical: ___ Oral ___ Silent ___	Text-based: ___ Inference: ___ Critical: ___ Oral ___ Silent ___

Critical Reading Inventory—Recapitulation Record—Informational Passages

Name _____ Grade _____ C.A. _____ Date of Testing _____ Examiner _____

Word List / Comprehending and Responding to Text

	Word List		Context		Oral Comp. %	Retelling Score	Oral Text-based	Oral Inference	Oral Critical	Silent Comp. %	Retelling Score	Silent Text-based	Silent Inference	Silent Critical	Average Oral & Silent	Listening Comp. %
Level	Flash	Untimed	RAI	MMI												
Pre-Primer							/3	/3	/2			/3	/3	/2		
Primer							/3	/3	/2			/3	/3	/2		
First							/3	/3	/2			/3	/3	/2		
Second							/4	/4	/2			/4	/4	/2		
Third							/4	/4	/2			/4	/4	/2		
Fourth							/4	/4	/2			/4	/4	/2		
Fifth							/4	/4	/2			/4	/4	/2		
Sixth							/4	/4	/2			/4	/4	/2		
Jr. High							/4	/4	/2			/4	/4	/2		
Sr. High							/4	/4	/2			/4	/4	/2		

Level One Interpretation

	Highest Independent Level	Highest Instructional Level	Frustration Level
Level:			
Word List and Miscue Analysis:	Flash _____ RAI _____ MMI _____ MM _____ MV _____ Non-words _____	Flash _____ RAI _____ MMI _____ MM _____ MV _____ Non-words _____	Flash _____ RAI _____ MMI _____ MM _____ MV _____ Non-words _____
Comprehension and Retelling Scores:	Comp. % _____ Retelling _____ Oral: _____ Silent: _____ Average: _____	Comp. % _____ Retelling _____ Oral: _____ Silent: _____ Average: _____	Comp. % _____ Retelling _____ Oral: _____ Silent: _____ Average: _____
Oral Comprehension, Fluency and MMI:	Oral comp. % _____ MMI _____	Oral comp. % _____ MMI _____ Fluency _____	Oral comp. % _____ MMI _____
Question Type:	Oral _____ Silent _____ Text-based: _____ Inference: _____ Critical: _____	Oral _____ Silent _____ Text-based: _____ Inference: _____ Critical: _____	Oral _____ Silent _____ Text-based: _____ Inference: _____ Critical: _____

Miscue Analysis Worksheet

Student _____ Grade _____ Age _____

Highest Independent Level _____   Highest Instructional Level _____   Frustration Level _____

Miscue	Text	MM	MV	Non-words	Miscue	Text	MM	MV	Non-words	Miscue	Text	MM	MV	Non-words
Totals														

RAI _____   MMI _____   RAI _____   MMI _____   RAI _____   MMI _____

RAI: Count the number of scoreable miscues from Column 1 and use the Miscue Chart for that passage to obtain the RAI.
MMI: Count the number of meaning-violating miscues and use the Miscue Chart for that passage to obtain the MMI.
Non: The number of meaning-violating miscues that were Non-words.
MM: Miscue that represents an attempt to maintain the sense of the text.
MV: Miscue that violated the sense of the text.

Comprehension Percentage Charts

These charts are designed to act as a quick calculator for CRI users. Simply determine the number of comprehension items that the reader has answered correctly at each level tested. Then find the corresponding percentage in the adjoining box.

Pre-Primer to First Grade

N Correct	% Score	N Correct	% Score
0.5	6	4.5	56
1.0	13	5.0	63
1.5	19	5.5	69
2.0	25	6.0	75
2.5	31	6.5	81
3.0	38	7.0	88
3.5	44	7.5	94
4.0	50	8.0	100

Second Grade to Senior High

N Correct	% Score	N Correct	% Score
0.5	5	5.5	55
1.0	10	6.0	60
1.5	15	6.5	65
2.0	20	7.0	70
2.5	25	7.5	75
3.0	30	8.0	80
3.5	35	8.5	85
4.0	40	9.0	90
4.5	45	9.5	95
5.0	50	10.0	100

Section 8

Examiner's Copy of Word Lists

This section includes reproducible forms for recording students' performance on Flash and Untimed administration of the Word Lists.

Word Lists: Examiner's Copy

Pre-Primer

	Flash	Untimed
1. the	_____	_____
2. a	_____	_____
3. was	_____	_____
4. he	_____	_____
5. go	_____	_____
6. boy	_____	_____
7. stop	_____	_____
8. come	_____	_____
9. and	_____	_____
10. her	_____	_____
11. to	_____	_____
12. like	_____	_____
13. am	_____	_____
14. get	_____	_____
15. not	_____	_____
16. can	_____	_____
17. see	_____	_____
18. will	_____	_____
19. me	_____	_____
20. you	_____	_____
Score	_/20_	_/20_
	__%	__%

Primer

	Flash	Untimed
1. of	_____	_____
2. have	_____	_____
3. big	_____	_____
4. day	_____	_____
5. came	_____	_____
6. house	_____	_____
7. play	_____	_____
8. little	_____	_____
9. saw	_____	_____
10. thing	_____	_____
11. fly	_____	_____
12. jump	_____	_____
13. went	_____	_____
14. take	_____	_____
15. give	_____	_____
16. off	_____	_____
17. could	_____	_____
18. many	_____	_____
19. want	_____	_____
20. out	_____	_____
Score	_/20_	_/20_
	__%	__%

Word Lists: Examiner's Copy

First Grade	Flash	Untimed		Second Grade	Flash	Untimed
1. family	_____	_____		1. teacher	_____	_____
2. hear	_____	_____		2. clean	_____	_____
3. school	_____	_____		3. remember	_____	_____
4. happy	_____	_____		4. horse	_____	_____
5. feet	_____	_____		5. anyone	_____	_____
6. together	_____	_____		6. birthday	_____	_____
7. fish	_____	_____		7. garden	_____	_____
8. pet	_____	_____		8. street	_____	_____
9. blue	_____	_____		9. guess	_____	_____
10. before	_____	_____		10. pretty	_____	_____
11. children	_____	_____		11. always	_____	_____
12. where	_____	_____		12. walking	_____	_____
13. farm	_____	_____		13. pull	_____	_____
14. surprise	_____	_____		14. fast	_____	_____
15. friend	_____	_____		15. have	_____	_____
16. drop	_____	_____		16. spring	_____	_____
17. will	_____	_____		17. when	_____	_____
18. made	_____	_____		18. help	_____	_____
19. bike	_____	_____		19. know	_____	_____
20. game	_____	_____		20. brother	_____	_____

Score	/20	/20		Score	/20	/20
	___ %	___ %			___ %	___ %

Word Lists: Examiner's Copy

Third Grade		
	Flash	Untimed
1. enter	_____	_____
2. change	_____	_____
3. lesson	_____	_____
4. think	_____	_____
5. music	_____	_____
6. trust	_____	_____
7. human	_____	_____
8. pencil	_____	_____
9. mail	_____	_____
10. phone	_____	_____
11. fright	_____	_____
12. unusual	_____	_____
13. they'll	_____	_____
14. bread	_____	_____
15. forest	_____	_____
16. early	_____	_____
17. hurt	_____	_____
18. water	_____	_____
19. because	_____	_____
20. hour	_____	_____
Score	_/20_	_/20_
	___%	___%

Fourth Grade		
	Flash	Untimed
1. doesn't	_____	_____
2. concern	_____	_____
3. sample	_____	_____
4. official	_____	_____
5. given	_____	_____
6. present	_____	_____
7. decorate	_____	_____
8. windshield	_____	_____
9. exercise	_____	_____
10. finish	_____	_____
11. enjoyable	_____	_____
12. wrong	_____	_____
13. daughter	_____	_____
14. quiet	_____	_____
15. morning	_____	_____
16. huge	_____	_____
17. covered	_____	_____
18. thought	_____	_____
19. creature	_____	_____
20. people	_____	_____
Score	_/20_	_/20_
	___%	___%

Word Lists: Examiner's Copy

Fifth Grade

	Flash	Untimed
1. bravely	_____	_____
2. embarrass	_____	_____
3. important	_____	_____
4. guarantee	_____	_____
5. magical	_____	_____
6. prevent	_____	_____
7. typical	_____	_____
8. vision	_____	_____
9. handle	_____	_____
10. ledge	_____	_____
11. wounded	_____	_____
12. defend	_____	_____
13. jungle	_____	_____
14. seasonal	_____	_____
15. different	_____	_____
16. through	_____	_____
17. interesting	_____	_____
18. necessary	_____	_____
19. medicine	_____	_____
20. mysterious	_____	_____

Score   _/20_   _/20_

        _%_   _%_

Sixth Grade

	Flash	Untimed
1. athletic	_____	_____
2. psychology	_____	_____
3. realize	_____	_____
4. ridiculous	_____	_____
5. successful	_____	_____
6. reluctant	_____	_____
7. consideration	_____	_____
8. mountain	_____	_____
9. partial	_____	_____
10. graceful	_____	_____
11. applause	_____	_____
12. survival	_____	_____
13. materials	_____	_____
14. pressure	_____	_____
15. license	_____	_____
16. vehicle	_____	_____
17. definite	_____	_____
18. experience	_____	_____
19. predictable	_____	_____
20. conform	_____	_____

Score   _/20_   _/20_

        _%_   _%_

Word Lists: Examiner's Copy

Junior High

	Flash	Untimed
1. continuous		
2. uncertainty		
3. imperative		
4. precious		
5. appreciation		
6. regularity		
7. disregard		
8. encyclopedia		
9. computerized		
10. prognosis		
11. synthesize		
12. journalist		
13. opportunity		
14. participated		
15. employment		
16. nucleotide		
17. occurrence		
18. holocaust		
19. obsolete		
20. irony		

Score   /20   /20

          %   %

Senior High

	Flash	Untimed
1. acquiesce		
2. discrepancy		
3. figurative		
4. connotation		
5. reiterate		
6. vehement		
7. subsidiary		
8. innocuous		
9. mandatory		
10. tangential		
11. fathomable		
12. cursory		
13. impervious		
14. poignant		
15. exuberant		
16. ambidextrous		
17. suave		
18. officious		
19. ultimatum		
20. limpid		

Score   /20   /20

          %   %

Section 9

Examiner's Copy of Narrative Passages: Form A

Reader's copy on p. 11 of the Reader's Passages.

Introductory Statement: "Would you read this passage about a trip to the library out loud for me? When you are finished, I'll take the passage away. Then I'll ask you to tell me about what you read and what you think of it. After that, I'll ask you some questions about the passage."

Story

"I want a book.

I want a good book.

Please find a pet book for me."

"Here is a cat book. I can read you this cat book,"

   said Mom.

"No, I do not like that book."

"Here is a dog book. I can read you this dog book,"

   said Mom.

"No, I do not like that book."

"What pet would you like to have?" asked Mom.

"I would like to have a bird."

"That's a good pet," said Mom.

"Here is a bird book."

"Oh, I like that book.

Please read me that book!" (95 words)

Miscues

_____ N of miscues that maintained meaning
(checked). This is the MM.
_____ N of miscues that violated meaning
(unchecked). This is the MV.

Reading Accuracy Index: _____ %
   (N of words – N of miscues, checked and unchecked) /
   N of words

Meaning Maintenance Index: _____ %
   (N of words – N of meaning-violating miscues, unchecked
   only) / N of words

At the Library: 95 words

Miscue Chart

Miscues	%	Miscues	%
1	99	7	93
2	98	8	92
3	97	9	91
4	96	10	89
5	95	11	88
6	94	12	87

Retelling

Examiner: "Tell me about what you just read and what you thought about it."

   If there is no spontaneous response, repeat the request, "Tell me what you thought about the passage."

NOTE: Use the Retelling Rubric on the next page to assess the child's retelling performance.

Retelling Rubric

Story Structure:

1. **Key Characters and Setting:** Child and mother in library.
2. **Character's Problem or Goal:** Finding a book.
3. **Problem-Solving or Goal-Meeting Process:**
   - Child wants the mother to find a good book.
   - Mother's suggestions are rejected.
   - Mother asks child and child identifies his or her choice.
   - Mother finds the "right" book.
4. **Personal Response:** Any well-supported positive or negative response to the characters or events in the story; any reaction to the humor or sadness in the story; any well-supported positive or negative reaction to the story as a whole.

Rubric:

4 = Complete retelling includes characters, problem/goal, all four steps in the problem-solving process, and a well-supported personal response.

3 = Retelling includes characters, problem/goal, and all four steps in the problem-solving process, but has no personal response.

2 = Retelling includes characters, problem/goal, and three steps in the problem solving process; some key factual errors or omissions. Add ½ point for well-supported personal response.

1 = Retelling omits either characters or problem; includes two or three steps in the problem-solving process, but the account is disjointed and includes factual errors or serious omissions. Add ½ point for well-supported personal response.

0 = Provides a title or topic statement but shows no real awareness of the character's problem and how the problem is worked out.

Retelling Score: _____

Comprehension Questions

1. What was the first book about that Mom showed her child?

   Text-based: A cat book.

2. What did the child tell Mom about the cat book?

   Text-based: Didn't like it.

3. Do you think the child has a pet at home? Why or why not?

   Inference: No, Mom asked what kind of pet the child would like; child doesn't have a cat or dog at home.

4. Do you think Mom and her child started talking about pets *before* they went to the library? Why or why not?

   Critical Response: No, child had no idea what pet he or she would like to have. Yes, they must have if they are trying to find books about pets.

5. Why do you think Mom asked what pet the child would like to have?

   Inference: So she could find out what book the child might like to read.

6. What kind of pet did the child want?

   Text-based: A bird.

7. Why did Mom have to tell her child what the book was about?

Inference: Child could not read; child was too young.

8. What could Mom have done *before* they went to the library to help her child get a book?

Critical Response: Talk about the kind of book the child wanted; talk about having a pet to see if the child could get one and then get a book.

Comprehension Analysis:

Text-Based: __/3__
Inference: __/3__
Critical Response: __/2__

Total Comprehension %: _____

Pre-Primer Silent: The Baker

Reader's copy on p. 12 of the Reader's Passages.

Introductory Statement: "Would you read this passage about a bakery to yourself? When you are finished, I'll take the passage away. Then I'll ask you to tell me about what you read and what you think of it. After that, I'll ask you some questions about the passage."

Story

"Come in!" said the baker.

"I like to bake!

Look at the big cakes!

Look at the little cakes!"

"I want a big cake," said Jane.

"The cake is for my birthday party.

Four girls will come.

I will be four years old."

"I want a big cake," said Bill.

"The cake is for my birthday party.

Seven boys will come.

I will be seven years old."

"I want a big cake," said Mom.

"The cake is for my little girl.

She will be two years old.

We will have a party."

"I want the cake now," cried the little girl.

"I don't want a party."

"Look," said the baker.

"Here is a cupcake for you."

Thank you!" said Mom. (120 words)

Reading Accuracy Index: _____ %
(N of words – N of miscues, checked and unchecked) /
N of words

Meaning Maintenance Index: _____ %
(N of words – N of meaning-violating miscues, unchecked
only) / N of words

The Baker: 120 words

Miscue Chart (for optional use as oral passage)

Miscues	%	Miscues	%
1	99	8	93
2	98	9	93
3	98	10	92
4	97	11	91
5	96	12	90
6	95	13	89
7	94	14	88

Retelling

Examiner: "Tell me about what you just read and what you thought about it."

If there is no spontaneous response, repeat the request, "Tell me what you thought about the passage."

NOTE: Use the Retelling Rubric on p. 144 to assess the child's retelling performance.

Retelling Rubric

Story Structure:

1. **Key Characters and Setting:** Baker, children, and Mom in the bakery.
2. **Character's Problem or Goal:** Buy cake for birthday party.
3. **Problem-solving or Goal-Meeting Process:**
   - Children go to the bakery to get cake for a party.
   - Cake must be big enough for all the guests.
   - Mother wants cake for a party but the little girl doesn't want a party.
   - Baker gives girl a cupcake.
4. **Personal Response:** Any well-supported positive or negative response to the characters or events in the story; any reaction to the humor or sadness in the story; any well-supported positive or negative reaction to the story as a whole.

Rubric:

4 = Complete retelling includes characters, problem/goal, all four steps in the problem-solving process, and a well-supported personal response.

3 = Retelling includes characters, problem/goal, and all four steps in the problem-solving process, but has no personal response.

2 = Retelling includes characters, problem/goal, and three steps in the problem-solving process, some key factual errors or omissions. Add ½ point for well-supported personal response.

1 = Retelling omits either characters or problem; includes two or three steps in the problem-solving process, but the account is disjointed and includes factual errors or serious omissions. Add ½ point for well-supported personal response.

0 = Provides a title or topic statement but shows no real awareness of the character's problem and how the problem is worked out.

Retelling Score: _____

Comprehension Questions

1. Where does the story take place?

   Text-based: At a bakery.

2. Does the baker like his job? Explain.

   Text-based: Yes, he said that he likes to bake cakes.

3. Why did the baker in this story make big cakes and little cakes?

   Inference: Sometimes there are lots of people; sometimes there are just a few.

4. Should the baker have given the little girl a cupcake?

   Critical response: Yes, he was being nice to her; wanted to cheer her up. No, because she cried; she was not polite; shouldn't eat dessert before meals.

5. Who would need a bigger cake, Jane or Bill?

   Inference: Bill because he has seven guests at the party; Jane has only four guests.

6. Why does Mom need to buy a cake?

   Text-based: She wants to have a party for the little girl.

7. Do you think they will play the same games at all three birthday parties? Why or why not?

Inference: Probably not, children are different ages; games might be boring, too hard, or too easy.

8. Do you think Mom or the little girl should have thanked the baker for the cupcake? Explain.

Critical response: Mom—it is the polite thing to do; he gave her daughter a gift. Girl—she got the gift and should have thanked him; encourage the girl to learn manners.

Comprehension Analysis:

Text-Based: _/3__
Inference: _/3__
Critical Response: _/2__

Total Comprehension %: _____

Reader's copy on p. 15 of the Reader's Passages.

Introductory Statement: "Would you read this passage about a family of fish out loud for me? When you are finished, I'll take the passage away. Then I'll ask you to tell me about what you read and what you think of it. After that, I'll ask you some questions about the passage."

Story

"Come Blue! Come Red!" said Mother Fish.

"Come, let's eat dinner."

Blue went to eat dinner.

Red saw a big fish come by and she chased the big

fish away.

"Go away! This is our home!" said Red.

"What great food!" said Blue.

"Yes, this is good food," said Mother Fish.

"Come and eat, Red."

But Red would not eat because she did not want to

let the big fish come close.

"Come Blue! Come Red!" said Mother Fish.

"Come, let's look at our pretty world."

Blue looked and looked.

Red saw a little fish come by and she chased the little

fish away.

"Go away! This is our home!" said Red.

"Come and look, Red," said Mother.

But Red would not look because she did not want to

let the little fish come close.

"Come Blue! Come Red!" said Mother Fish.

"We will have work to do tomorrow and we need to

sleep."

Mother Fish fell asleep right away.

Blue fell asleep right away.

But Red could not sleep because she was still angry.

(175 words)

Miscues

_____ N of miscues that maintained meaning (checked). This is the MM.

_____ N of miscues that violated meaning (unchecked). This is the MV.

Reading Accuracy Index: _____ %
(N of words – N of miscues, checked and unchecked) / N of words

Meaning Maintenance Index: _____ %
(N of words – N of meaning-violating miscues, unchecked only) / N of words

The Little Fish: 175 Words

Miscue Chart

Miscues	%	Miscues	%	Miscues	%
1	100	11	94	21	89
2	99	12	94	22	88
3	99	13	93	23	87
4	98	14	93	24	87
5	98	15	92	25	86
6	97	16	91	26	86
7	97	17	92	27	85
8	96	18	90	28	85
9	95	19	90	29	84
10	95	20	89	30	83

Retelling

Examiner: "Tell me about what you just read and what you thought about it."

If there is no spontaneous response, repeat the request, "Tell me what you thought about the passage."

NOTE: Use the Retelling Rubric on the next page to assess the child's retelling performance.

Retelling Rubric

Story Structure:

1. **Key Characters and Setting:** Mother Fish, Blue, and Red in the ocean.
2. **Character's Problem or Goal:** Red's anger keeps her from being happy.
3. **Problem-Solving or Goal-Meeting Process:**
   - Mother asks Blue and Red to eat and explore.
   - Blue listens but Red does not.
   - Red is chasing other fish.
   - Red can't sleep because she is still angry.
4. **Personal Response:** Any well-supported positive or negative response to the characters or events in the story; any reaction to the humor or sadness in the story; any well-supported positive or negative reaction to the story as a whole.

Rubric:

4 = Complete retelling (includes characters, problem/goal, all four steps in the problem-solving process, and a well-supported personal response.

3 = Retelling includes characters, problem/goal, and all four steps in the problem-solving process, but has no personal response.

2 = Retelling includes characters, problem/goal, and three steps in the problem-solving process; some key factual errors or omissions. Add ½ point for well-supported personal response.

1 = Retelling omits either characters or problem; includes two or three steps in the problem-solving process, but the account is disjointed and includes factual errors or serious omissions. Add ½ point for well-supported personal response.

0 = Provides a title or topic statement but shows no real awareness of the character's problem and how the problem is worked out.

Retelling Score: _____

Comprehension Questions:

1. Why didn't Red want to eat when mother called her?

   Text-based: She was too busy chasing fish away; she was too angry; she didn't want other fish coming by.

2. Why was Red so angry with the other fish?

   Text-based: They were swimming too close by; she was afraid the fish would come into their home.

3. Why weren't Mother and Blue angry when other fish swam near their home?

   Inference: They did not think there was any danger; they were used to other fish swimming nearby.

4. Do you think it is a good idea for Red to chase other fish away from their home? Why or why not?

   Critical Response: No, they were doing no real harm; no one else seemed worried. Yes, they could be dangerous; may want to attack the smaller fish.

5. Why did Mother Fish and Blue fall asleep right away?

   Inference: Had a busy day; enjoyed what they were doing; were not angry or upset.

6. Why couldn't Red fall asleep?

   Text-based: She was too angry.

7. Who do you think will get more work done tomorrow, Red or Blue?

Inference: Blue, better rested; not as concerned with other things as Red is.

8. Do you think Red is brave or just a bully? Why?

Critical Response: Brave, swims at fish that are bigger than she is; defends her mother and sister. A bully, chases other fish for no reason.

Comprehension Analysis:

Text-Based: __/3__
Inference: __/3__
Critical Response: __/2__

Total Comprehension %: _____

Primer Silent: Learning to Fish

Reader's copy on p. 18 of the Reader's Passages.

Introductory Statement: "Would you read this passage about a fishing trip to yourself? When you are finished, I'll take the passage away. Then I'll ask you to tell me about what you read and what you think of it. After that, I'll ask you some questions about the passage."

Story

Pat said, "This is not fun!"

He was learning how to fish with his sister.

But the fish would not bite.

Pat jumped up. He shook the fishing rod.

He tried to get his bait closer to the fish.

"Don't move the rod or you will scare the fish away,"

    said Dad.

Pat looked at his sister.

She had caught three fish already.

Then Pat threw some stones into the water.

"You will scare the fish away," said Dad.

Pat was angry. He moved his rod and tried to make a

    fish take his bait.

This time Dad just watched.

Pat dropped his rod on the dock and walked away

    angry.

He sat on the shore and would not talk to his father

    or sister.

Just then a big fish took his bait.

Dad called, "Come quick! You've caught a fish!"

But Pat was not fast enough.

The fish pulled the whole rod into the deep water.

(157 words)

Reading Accuracy Index: _____ %
  (N of words – N of miscues, checked and unchecked) /
  N of words.

Meaning Maintenance Index: _____ %
  (N of words – N of meaning-violating miscues, unchecked
  only) / N of words

Learning to Fish: 157 Words

Miscue Chart (for optional use as oral passage)

Miscues	%	Miscues	%
1	99	11	93
2	99	12	92
3	98	13	92
4	97	14	91
5	97	15	90
6	96	16	90
7	96	17	89
8	95	18	89
9	94	19	88
10	94	20	87

Retelling

Examiner: "Tell me about what you just read and what you thought about it."

    If there is no spontaneous response, repeat the request, "Tell me what you thought about the passage."

NOTE: Use the Retelling Rubric on p. 150 to assess the child's retelling performance.

Retelling Rubric

Story Structure:

1. **Key Characters and Setting:** Pat, his father, and sister fishing.
2. **Character's Problem or Goal:** Father wants to help Pat learn to fish.
3. **Problem-Solving or Goal-Meeting Process:**
   - Pat is fishing in the wrong way.
   - Pat fails but his sister succeeds.
   - Father gives Pat advice.
   - Pat won't listen and gets angry at failure.
   - Pat misses his chance to catch a fish.
4. **Personal Response:** Any well-supported positive or negative response to the characters or events in the story; any reaction to the humor or sadness in the story; any well-supported positive or negative reaction to the story as a whole.

Rubric:

4 = Complete retelling includes characters, problem/goal, all five steps in the problem-solving process, and a well-supported personal response.

3 = Retelling includes characters, problem/goal, and all five steps in the problem-solving process, but has no personal response.

2 = Retelling includes characters, problem/goal, and three or four steps in the problem-solving process; some key factual errors or omissions. Add ½ point for well-supported personal response.

1 = Retelling omits either characters or problem; includes one or two steps in the problem-solving process, but the account is disjointed and includes factual errors or serious omissions. Add ½ point for well-supported personal response.

0 = Provides a title or topic statement but shows no real awareness of the character's problem and how the problem is worked out.

Retelling Score: _____

Comprehension Questions

1. Why didn't Pat have fun fishing?

   Text-based: He couldn't catch any fish.

2. What was one thing that Pat did to keep the fish from biting?

   Text-based: He shook the rod; scared fish away; threw stones into the water.

3. Why would Pat's sister be better at fishing than Pat?

   Inference: She had learned how to fish correctly; she listened to her father.

4. How well do you think Dad taught the children to fish? Explain.

   Critical Response: Good job—Pat's sister learned well; Pat's problems were his own fault. Poor job—let the kid make mistakes; didn't follow through.

5. Why would Pat be angry with his sister?

   Inference: She was successful and he was not; Pat was jealous of her success.

6. Why did Dad want Pat to stop throwing stones?

   Text-based: Didn't want him to scare the fish.

7. Why did the fish take the bait when Pat was on the shore but not when he was on the dock?

Inference: No one was moving the rod; no one was scaring the fish; no one was throwing stones into the water.

8. Do you think Dad will take Pat fishing again? Why or why not?

Critical Response: Yes, he can teach him better when he's older; he has learned his lesson now. No, he missed his chance; ruined the trip for everyone; the others will catch more if he isn't there.

Comprehension Analysis:

Text-Based: __/4__
Inference: __/4__
Critical Response: __/2__

Total Comprehension %: _____

First Grade Oral: Where Is the Dog?

Reader's copy on p. 19 of the Reader's Passages.

Introductory Statement: "Would you read this passage about a girl and her dog out loud for me? When you are finished, I'll take the passage away. Then I'll ask you to tell me about what you read and what you think of it. After that, I'll ask you some questions about the passage."

Story

Jan waited at the door. She was waiting for the car to come. Aunt Saru was coming for a visit and she was bringing Sally. Jan loved to play with Sally and she loved Aunt Saru, too.

"Here they are!" Jan called to Mother. Jan ran outside to meet Sally and Aunt Saru.

"Look what I have," said Sally. Sally showed Jan her little white puppy.

"Can I hold the puppy?" asked Jan.

"Oh, yes," said Sally.

Sally took the puppy into the house.

Jan and Sally played with the puppy. Then they read books and played games. They had fun.

Then Sally went to help her mother. Jan played with the puppy. After lunch, Sally looked for her puppy. She looked and looked but she could not find her.

Aunt Saru and Mother helped her look. They asked Jan to help find the puppy.

"She is outside," said Jan.

"How did she get out?" asked Mother.

"She wanted to go out," said Jan.

"So I let her go."

Aunt Saru and Mother ran outside. Everyone looked and looked for the puppy. Jan was afraid.

Then Sally saw the puppy sitting under a car.

Everyone was happy!

"You can not let the dog go out," said Aunt Saru.

"She is too young. She will get lost." (217 words)

Miscues

_____ N of miscues that maintained meaning (checked). This is the MM.

_____ N of miscues that violated meaning (unchecked). This is the MV.

Reading Accuracy Index: _____ %
(N of words – N of miscues, checked and unchecked) / N of words

Meaning Maintenance Index: _____ %
(N of words – N of meaning-violating miscues unchecked only) / N of words

Where Is the Dog?: 217 Words

Miscue Chart

Miscues	%	Miscues	%	Miscues	%
1	100	12	94	23	89
2	99	13	94	24	89
3	99	14	94	25	88
4	98	15	93	26	88
5	98	16	93	27	88
6	97	17	92	28	87
7	97	18	92	29	87
8	96	19	91	30	86
9	96	20	91	31	86
10	95	21	90	32	85
11	95	22	90	33	85

Retelling

Examiner: "Tell me about what you just read and what you thought about it."

If there is no spontaneous response, repeat the request, "Tell me what you thought about the passage."

Retelling Rubric

Story Structure:

1. **Key Characters and Setting:** Jan and Mother waiting for Sally and Aunt Saru to visit their home.
2. **Character's Problem or Goal:** Jan nearly loses a puppy.
3. **Problem-Solving or Goal-Meeting Process:**
   - Sally and Aunt Saru bring a new puppy for a visit.
   - Sally leaves the puppy with Jan.
   - Jan lets the puppy go outside.
   - The search for the puppy is successful.
   - Jan learns that the puppy is too young to go outside alone.
4. **Personal Response:** Any well-supported positive or negative response to the characters or events in the story; any reaction to the humor or sadness in the story; any well-supported positive or negative reaction to the story as a whole.

Rubric:

4 = Complete retelling includes characters, problem/goal, all five steps in the problem-solving process, and a well-supported personal response.

3 = Retelling includes characters, problem/goal, and all five steps in the problem-solving process, but has no personal response.

2 = Retelling includes characters, problem/goal, and three or four steps in the problem-solving process; some key factual errors or omissions. Add ½ point for well-supported personal response.

1 = Retelling omits either characters or problem; includes one or two steps in the problem-solving process, but the account is disjointed and includes factual errors or serious omissions. Add ½ point for well-supported personal response.

0 = Provides a title or topic statement but shows no real awareness of the character's problem and how the problem is worked out.

Retelling Score: _____

Comprehension Questions

1. How do you know that Jan was glad that her aunt and cousin were coming to visit her?

   Text-based: She was waiting at the door.

2. Why did Jan let the puppy go outside?

   Text-based: The puppy wanted to go out.

3. How did Aunt Saru and Mother feel when they heard that the puppy was outside?

   Inference: Worried because they ran outside and looked for the puppy; unhappy at Jan for letting the puppy out; afraid the puppy was lost.

4. Do you think that Jan *should* have been punished for letting the dog go outside?

   Critical Response: Yes, the dog could have been hurt; she should have asked someone; she was very careless. No, she did not really want to hurt the dog; she did not know that she was wrong.

5. Why was Jan afraid when she saw everyone looking for the puppy?

   Inference: Afraid she might get into trouble or punished; afraid that the dog may be lost or injured.

6. Where did they find the puppy?

   Text-based: Under the car outside.

7. What might have happened if no one found out that the puppy was gone?

   Inference: She might have been lost, injured, or killed.

8. Do you think that it would be good for Jan to have her own pet? Why or why not?

   Critical Response: Yes, she probably learned a lesson and would care for one if she knew what they needed. No, she was very foolish to do something without knowing how harmful it could be.

Comprehension Analysis:

Text-Based: __/3__
Inference: __/3__
Critical Response: __/2__

Total Comprehension %: _____

First Grade Silent: The Pigs Get a Job

Reader's copy on p. 21 of the Reader's Passages.

Introductory Statement: "Would you read this passage about two pigs who start a business to yourself? When you are finished, I'll take the passage away. Then I'll ask you to tell me about what you read and what you think of it. After that, I'll ask you some questions about the passage."

Story

Father Pig had a big apple farm.

He had two sons.

Their names were Pete and Jake.

They worked every day with Father.

Soon Pete and Jake got older.

They were ready to leave home.

Pete bought an apple farm.

He remembered working very hard with Father.

"I will find someone to work hard for me," he said.

He asked a little pig to work for him.

The little pig worked hard.

But Pete wanted more money.

He told the little pig to work harder.

The little pig came to work early.

He picked more apples.

But he was always tired.

He did not like his job.

Jake bought an apple farm too.

He remembered the fun he had working with Father.

"I will find someone to work with me," he said.

He asked a little pig to work with him.

Jake and the little pig worked together every day.

Jake said, "You can keep all the extra apples we pick."

The little pig came in early.

He worked longer every day.

But he was happy.

He sold his apples.

He made more money.

Soon Jake had to find more pigs to work with him.

(195 words)

Reading Accuracy Index: _____ %
  (N of words – N of miscues, checked and unchecked) / N of words

Meaning Maintenance Index: _____ %
  (N of words – N of meaning-violating miscues, unchecked only) / N of words

The Pigs Get a Job: 195 words

Miscue Chart (for optional use as oral passage)

Miscue	%	Miscue	%
1	99	13	94
2	99	14	94
3	98	15	93
4	98	16	93
5	97	17	92
6	97	18	92
7	96	19	91
8	96	20	91
9	95	21	90
10	95	22	90
11	95	23	89
12	95	24	89

Retelling

Examiner: "Tell me about what you just read and what you thought about it."

If there is no spontaneous response, repeat the request, "Tell me what you thought about the passage."

NOTE: Use the Retelling Rubric on p. 156 to assess the child's retelling performance.

Retelling Rubric

Story Structure:

1. **Key Characters and Setting:** Pete and Jake, their father, and their workers on apple farms.
2. **Character's Problem or Goal:** Pete and Jake start up farm to make a living for themselves.
3. **Problem-Solving or Goal-Meeting Process:**
   - Pete remembers working hard with his father and Jake remembers the fun of working with his father.
   - Pete hires a worker and expects him to work hard.
   - Jake hires a worker and works together with him.
   - Pete's worker works hard but does not like his job and Jake's worker works hard and likes his job.
4. **Personal Response:** Any well-supported positive or negative response to the characters or events in the story; any reaction to the humor or sadness in the story; any well-supported positive or negative reaction to the story as a whole.

Rubric:

4 = Complete retelling includes characters, problem/goal, all four steps in the problem-solving process, and a well-supported personal response.

3 = Retelling includes characters, problem/goal, and all four steps in the problem-solving process, but has no personal response.

2 = Retelling includes characters, problem/goal, and three steps in the problem-solving process; some key factual errors or omissions. Add ½ point for well-supported personal response.

1 = Retelling omits either characters or problem; includes two or three steps in the problem-solving process, but the account is disjointed and includes factual errors or serious omissions. Add ½ point for well-supported personal response.

0 = Provides a title or topic statement but shows no real awareness of the character's problem and how the problem is worked out.

Retelling Score: _____

Comprehension Questions

1. What did Father Pig do for a living?

   Text-based: Owned an apple farm.

2. After they left home, did Pete and Jake remember the same things about working with their father? How do you know?

   Text-based: No, Pete remembered working hard but Jake remembered having fun.

3. Why didn't the pig who worked for Pete like his job?

   Inference: Pete made him work very hard; Pete was selfish; Pete did not share anything with the little pig; Pete did not work with the pig.

4. Who do you think will make more money from his apple farm, Pete or Jake?

   Critical Response: Jake—treats his workers well, shares with them, needs another worker already. Pete—keeps more of his money, makes his employees work hard.

5. Do you think that Father would be more proud of Pete or Jake? Why?

   Inference: Jake because he is more likely to be successful; treated his workers well.

6. What did Pete do to get more money?

   Text-based: He asked the little pig to work harder.

7. Why didn't the pig who worked for Jake feel as tired as the pig who worked for Pete?

Inference: He was treated better; made extra money for his work; decided himself to work longer hours; he was working for himself too.

8. If someone wanted to make money from a business, how could this story help him?

Critical Response: Don't be too greedy; treat your workers well; people work better when they are happy.

Comprehension Analysis:

Text-Based: __/3__
Inference: __/3__
Critical Response: __/2__

Total Comprehension %: _____

Reader's copy on p. 24 of the Reader's Passages.

Introductory Statement: "Would you read this passage about two cats who race each other out loud for me? When you are finished, I'll take the passage away. Then I'll ask you to tell me about what you read and what you think of it. After that, I'll ask you some questions about the passage."

Story

Spencer was the fastest animal in the jungle. All of the other animals knew it. Spencer made sure of that. He would say, "No one can beat me! You are all too afraid to race!" It was true. No one wanted to race against Spencer. He always won. Then he would brag even more.

One day another family of cats moved in. Spencer ran up to the new family. He said, "I'm the fastest animal in the jungle. Do you want to race?" The father said, "No, thank you. But maybe our daughter Annie will race with you." Annie smiled and said, "Yes. I'd love to race." Soon the two cats were running for the finish line. Spencer was winning as always. But Annie was very fast. She raced past him and crossed the finish line first.

The other animals cheered in surprise. But Spencer cried, "I want another chance!" They raced again and again. But the result was still the same. There was a new champion in the jungle and her name was Annie.

All the animals came over to talk to Annie. But Spencer went away angry. Annie was a little sad. She hoped that Spencer would be her friend. "Well, at least we won't have to listen to him brag again," said the fox. The next day Spencer was back. The first thing he said was, "I can jump higher than anybody in the jun-

gle! No one can beat me!" The other animals groaned and rolled their eyes. Nothing had changed after all.

(256 words)

Miscues

_____ N of miscues that maintained meaning (checked). This is the MM.

_____ N of miscues that violated meaning (unchecked). This is the MV.

Reading Accuracy Index: _____ %
(N of words – N of miscues, checked and unchecked) / N of words

Meaning Maintenance Index: _____ %
(N of words – N of meaning-violating miscues, unchecked only) / N of words

The Race: 256 words

Miscue Chart

Miscues	%	Miscues	%	Miscues	%
1	100	13	95	25	90
2	99	14	95	26	90
3	99	15	94	27	89
4	98	16	94	28	89
5	98	17	93	29	89
6	98	18	93	30	88
7	97	19	93	31	88
8	97	20	92	32	88
9	96	21	92	33	87
10	96	22	91	34	87
11	96	23	91	35	86
12	95	24	91	36	86

Retelling

Examiner: "Tell me about what you just read and what you thought about it."

If there is no spontaneous response, repeat the request, "Tell me what you thought about the passage."

NOTE: Use the Retelling Rubric on the next page to assess the child's retelling performance.

Retelling Rubric

Story Structure:

1. **Key Characters and Setting:** Spencer, other animals, and Annie who moved into jungle.
2. **Character's Problem or Goal:** Spencer wants to be the fastest runner in the jungle and to brag about it.
3. **Problem-Solving or Goal-Meeting Process:**
   - Spencer brags and gets others to race with him so that he can brag more.
   - Annie moves in and Spencer races with her.
   - Spencer loses the race.
   - Spencer walks away angrily and Annie is sad because she had wanted a friend.
   - Spencer returns the next day and brags about jumping.
4. **Personal Response:** Any well-supported positive or negative response to the characters or events in the story; any reaction to the humor or sadness in the story; any well-supported positive or negative reaction to the story as a whole.

Rubric

4 = Complete retelling includes characters, problem/goal, all five steps in the problem-solving process, and a well-supported personal response.

3 = Retelling includes characters, problem/goal, and all five steps in the problem-solving process, but has no personal response.

2 = Retelling includes characters, problem/goal, and three or four steps in the problem-solving process; some key factual errors or omissions. Add ½ point for well-supported personal response.

1 = Retelling omits either characters or problem; includes one or two steps in the problem-solving process, but the account is disjointed and includes factual errors or serious omissions. Add ½ point for well-supported personal response.

0 = Provides a title or topic statement but shows no real awareness of the character's problem and how the problem is worked out.

Retelling Score: _____

Comprehension Questions

1. Why didn't any of the animals want to race against Spencer?

   Text-based: He always won and he bragged afterwards.

2. What did the animals do when Annie won the race? (Must identify one.)

   Text-based: They cheered; talked with her.

3. Why would Spencer want to race against Annie again?

   Inference: He couldn't accept the fact that someone was faster; thought he could win.

4. Why did Annie agree to race against Spencer when no one else would?

   Inference: She knew she was very fast; she probably knew she could beat him.

5. What would have been the best thing for Spencer to do after Annie beat him? Why?

   Critical Response: Be a good loser and admit that she was faster; try to be her friend since he didn't have any friends; stop bragging about himself to the other animals.

6. What did Spencer do when he came back the next day?

   Text-based: Started bragging about something else; bragged that he could jump higher than anyone else.

7. Do you think that this was the first time Annie had ever raced against anyone? Why or why not?

Inference: No, she smiled when Spencer challenged her; she probably knew she could beat him.

8. What did the other animals hope would happen after Spencer lost the race?

Text-based: That Spencer would stop bragging.

9. If another new family moved into the jungle, do you think Spencer would ask them to race or not?

Critical Response: Yes, he did not seem to have learned anything; still bragged even after he lost. No, he has lost once; he may still brag but he didn't like to lose and he may not be as confident as he was once.

10. If Spencer stopped bragging, do you think he would be a good friend for Annie or would he still have to change?

Critical Response: Yes, he wouldn't annoy people; others would give him a chance; others would like him better. No, has to be a better loser; shouldn't be so selfish; must admit she is a better runner.

Comprehension Analysis:

Text-Based: __/4__
Inference: __/3__
Critical Response: __/3__

Total Comprehension %: _____

Second Grade Silent: The Roller Coaster Ride

Reader's Copy on p. 25 of the Reader's Passages.

Introductory Statement: "Would you read this passage about a ride on the roller coaster to yourself? When you are finished, I'll take the passage away. Then I'll ask you to tell me about what you read and what you think of it. After that, I'll ask you some questions about the passage."

Story

Today it was finally Jessie's birthday. She jumped out of bed and called to her mom. "Mom, can you come here and see how tall I am?" She ran to the wall and waited. Mother marked the spot where Jessie had grown since her last birthday. "I made it!" shouted Jessie. "I'm tall enough to ride the roller coaster now!" On Saturday, Jessie, her mom, and Aunt Jane would go to the park. Then she could take her first ride!

Mom was too afraid to ride so Aunt Jane took Jessie to the line to wait their turn. Jessie and Aunt Jane jumped into a car and pulled the bar over their heads. Then they waited for the ride to start. "Let's get going," thought Jessie. Soon the ride started and Jessie was really excited. She felt very grown up. Then the car climbed higher and higher. It came down and went faster and faster. Jessie was so afraid that she thought she was going to die.

Jessie held Aunt Jane's arm. She covered her face and screamed. Jessie prayed that the ride would end. "Don't let me die," she prayed, "and I'll never ride a roller coaster again." Aunt Jane hugged Jessie. Jessie opened her eyes and she saw people laughing and screaming. Aunt Jane was laughing too. They were all having fun.

The car slowed and then stopped. The ride was finally over. "Aunt Jane," said Jessie, "Can we do it again?" (244 words)

Reading Accuracy Index: _____ %
    (N of words – N of miscues, checked and unchecked) / N of words

Meaning Maintenance Index: _____ %
    (N of words – N of meaning-violating miscues, unchecked only) / N of words

The Roller Coaster Ride: 244 Words

Miscues Chart (for optional use as oral passage)

Miscues	%	Miscues	%	Miscues	%
1	100	11	96	21	92
2	99	12	95	22	91
3	99	13	95	23	91
4	98	14	94	24	90
5	98	15	94	25	90
6	98	16	94	26	90
7	97	17	93	27	89
8	97	18	93	28	89
9	96	19	92	29	88
10	96	20	92	30	88

Retelling

Examiner: "Tell me about what you just read and what you thought about it."

If there is no spontaneous response, repeat the request, "Tell me what you thought about the passage."

NOTE: Use the Retelling Rubric on p. 162 to assess the child's retelling performance.

Retelling Rubric

Story Structure:

1. **Key Characters and Setting:** Jessie, Aunt Jane, and Mom at amusement park.
2. **Character's Problem or Goal:** Jessie wants to finally be big enough to ride the roller coaster.
3. **Problem-Solving or Goal-meeting Process:**
   - Jessie is finally tall enough to ride the roller coaster.
   - Aunt Jane goes with her on the ride.
   - Jessie becomes frightened.
   - She promises she will never ride again.
   - She realizes that the ride is safe and fun.
   - She decides to go on the ride again.
4. **Personal Response:** Any well-supported positive or negative response to the characters or events in the story; any reaction to the humor or sadness in the story; any well-supported positive or negative reaction to the story as a whole.

Rubric:

4 = Complete retelling includes characters, problem/goal, all six steps in the problem-solving process, and a well-supported personal response.

3 = Retelling includes characters, problem/goal, and five or six steps in the problem-solving process, but has no personal response.

2 = Retelling includes characters, problem/goal, and three or four steps in the problem-solving process; some key factual errors or omissions. Add ½ point for well-supported personal response.

1 = Retelling omits either characters or problem; includes two or three steps in the problem-solving process, but the account is disjointed and includes factual errors or serious omissions. Add ½ point for well-supported personal response.

0 = Provides a title or topic statement but shows no real awareness of the character's problem and how the problem is worked out.

Retelling Score: _____

Comprehension Questions

1. Why did Jessie want her mother to see how tall she was?

   Text-based: Wanted to see if she was tall enough to ride the roller coaster.

2. Why didn't Mom want to ride on the roller coaster with Jessie?

   Text-based: She was afraid of roller coasters.

3. Do you think that Jessie had ever been to an amusement park before? Why?

   Inference: Yes, she knew that she had to be a certain height to go on certain rides; may have seen a roller coaster at an amusement park before.

4. Why would Jessie want so much to ride the roller coaster?

   Inference: Sign that she was growing up; was something she wasn't allowed to do before; she thought it would be fun.

5. How do you think Mom felt about Jessie taking her first roller coaster ride? Why?

   Critical Response: Proud that she had grown up; afraid she might be hurt; happy that Aunt Jane would be with her.

6. How did Aunt Jane help Jessie during the ride?

   Text-based: Hugged her; held her close.

7. Why did Jessie decide to ride the roller coaster again?

Inference: She wanted to have more fun; may have wanted to prove to herself that she wasn't afraid; made her feel grown-up; she ended up liking it.

8. What did Jessie do during the ride to help herself stop being afraid? (Must identify one.)

Text-based: Hugged Aunt Jane; saw others having fun; prayed; screamed out loud.

9. Do you think it was right for Jessie to get back on the ride after she promised never to ride again?

Critical Response: Yes, she didn't really mean what she had said. No, she gave her word and probably shouldn't break it.

10. Do you think the story would end the same way if Jessie took the ride with her mother instead of Aunt Jane? Explain.

Critical Response: No, her mother might have been afraid too and neither one would ever ride again. Yes, her mother probably would hide her fear for Jessie's sake.

Comprehension Analysis:

Text-Based: __/4__
Inference: __/3__
Critical Response: __/3__

Total Comprehension %: _____

Third Grade Oral: The Farm Vacation

Reader's copy on p. 26 of the Reader's Passages.

Introductory Statement: "Would you read this passage about a boy's visit to a farm out loud for me? When you are finished, I'll take the passage away. Then I'll ask you to tell me about what you read and what you think of it. After that, I'll ask you some questions about the passage."

Story

It was five o'clock in the morning when David heard his grandfather call. David never got up this early before but he didn't mind at all! He was visiting his grandfather's farm for the first time and he was excited. He had always wanted to be a farmer and now he would have his chance. Besides, Grandpa had horses too and David looked forward to learning how to ride.

When David ran into the kitchen, Grandfather said, "Eat a good breakfast, Dave. We've got a lot to do this morning. We'll start with the hay."

"Don't rush him!" said Grandma. "Are you sure you want to work with Grandpa all day?" she asked David.

"Sure am!" said David. He gulped down his breakfast and dashed out to help load the hay wagon. He never knew hay was so heavy.

"You finish up here while I get the tractor. We've got some work to do in the garden," said Grandpa.

David walked over to the garden and climbed on to the tractor. Up and down they drove, row after row, turning up the soil as they went. "Lunch time," said Grandpa when the sun was overhead.

"When do the horses get fed?" David asked Grandma as he walked into the kitchen.

"Do you want to do that after lunch? You've worked so much already," said Grandma.

"Don't forget, honey," said Grandpa, "We've got lots to do. That's how life is on the farm."

"That's OK," said David. "Maybe I better stay and help Grandpa."

After lunch, David worked under the hot sun, helping Grandpa dig postholes for a new fence. Then David and Grandpa picked corn and brought it to their roadside stand. David was trudging slowly back toward the house when Grandma called, "Do you want to feed the horses?"

David ran to the barn and helped to feed the horses. "I wish I could ride you," he said to each one as he rubbed its nose. "Maybe Grandpa will teach me!" David fell asleep immediately that night but when the sun rose the next morning, he was not so eager to get up. He had the feeling that today would be another day just like yesterday. As it turned out, he was right.

"Do you still want to be a farmer?" asked Grandfather at the end of the week. "I'm not so sure," David replied. "If the sun rose at ten o'clock and there wasn't so much hard work, then maybe farming would be more fun." (417 words)

Miscues

_____ N of miscues that maintained meaning (checked). This is the MM.

_____ N of miscues that violated meaning (unchecked). This is the MV.

Reading Accuracy Index: _____ %
   (N of words – N of miscues, checked and unchecked) / N of words

Meaning Maintenance Index: _____ %
   (N of words – N of meaning-violating miscues, unchecked only) / N of words

The Farm Vacation: 417 Words

Miscue Chart

Miscues	%	Miscues	%	Miscues	%
1	100	12	97	23	94
2	100	13	97	24	94
3	99	14	97	25	94
4	99	15	96	26	94
5	99	16	96	27	94
6	99	17	96	28	93
7	98	18	96	29	93
8	98	19	95	30	93
9	98	20	95	31	93
10	98	21	95	32	92
11	97	22	95	33	92

Retelling

Examiner: "Tell me about what you just read and what you thought about it."

If there is no spontaneous response, repeat the request, "Tell me what you thought about the passage."

Retelling Rubric

Story Structure:

1. **Key Characters and Setting:** David and his grandparents on the farm.
2. **Character's Problem or Goal:** David visits farm to learn about farming and to learn to ride horses.
3. **Problem-Solving or Goal-Meeting Process:**
   - David wants to learn about farming and to ride horses.
   - Grandpa has him working hard but Grandma wants him to enjoy himself.
   - David decides to keep working with Grandpa.
   - David never gets chance to ride the horses.
   - David reconsiders his choice.
4. **Personal Response:** Any well-supported positive or negative response to the characters or events in the story; any reaction to the humor or sadness in the story; any well-supported positive or negative reaction to the story as a whole.

Rubric:

4 = Complete retelling includes characters, problem/goal, all five steps in the problem-solving process, and a well-supported personal response.

3 = Retelling includes characters, problem/goal, and all five steps in the problem-solving process, but has no personal response.

2 = Retelling includes characters, problem/goal, and three or four steps in the problem-solving process; some key factual errors or omissions. Add ½ point for well-supported personal response.

1 = Retelling omits either characters or problem; includes one or two steps in the problem-solving process, but the account is disjointed and includes factual errors or serious omissions. Add ½ point for well-supported personal response.

0 = Provides a title or topic statement but shows no real awareness of the character's problem and how the problem is worked out.

Retelling Score: _____

Comprehension Questions

1. Why was David excited about visiting the farm?

   Text-based: He always wanted to be a farmer.

2. How did David feel about farming *at the end* of the week?

   Text-based: He wasn't sure about it; he had changed his mind.

3. Do you think that David lived near his grandfather? Explain.

   Inference: Probably not, he was visiting the farm for the first time.

4. Do you think that Grandma was happy about how David's first week at the farm was going?

   Inference: Probably not, He was working very hard and having no fun; he should have been riding the horses.

5. Do you think that Grandpa really wanted David to become a farmer? Why or why not?

   Critical Response: Probably not, made him work very hard, possibly because he wanted David to understand how difficult farming was. Probably so, he wanted him to understand everything about farming, including the hard work.

6. What did David want most from Grandpa?

   Text-based: To learn how to ride the horses.

7. Do you think that David ever got to ride the horses that week? Why?

   Inference: Probably not; seemed that there was little time for play and Grandpa didn't appear too interested in seeing David ride the horses.

8. Why did David change his mind at the end of the week? (Must identify one.)

   Text-based: Had to get up too early and there was too much hard work.

9. Do you think David and his grandfather had a close relationship? Why or why not?

   Critical Response: Yes, David cared for the grandfather; always helped him work even when he would rather ride the horses. No, seemed that they did not talk very much; Grandfather unaware that David wanted to ride the horses; didn't talk very much about farming.

10. Was Grandpa fair to expect David to do so much work that first week? Why?

    Critical Response: No, he seemed to have one task right after another with no rest. Yes, David wanted to learn about the farming life; it would be dishonest to present it in any other way.

Comprehension Analysis:

Text-Based: __/4__
Inference: __/3__
Critical Response: __/3__

Total Comprehension %: _____

Third Grade Silent: The Championship Game

Reader's copy on p. 28 of the Reader's Passages.

Introductory Statement: "Would you read this passage about an important baseball game to yourself? When you are finished, I'll take the passage away. Then I'll ask you to tell me about what you read and what you think of it. After that, I'll ask you some questions about the passage."

Story

At the end of a long softball season, Jill's team made it to the championship game. They would play against the top team in the league, the Ramblers. Before the game, the teams had batting and fielding practice. Jill watched her teammates. She knew that they would have a hard time winning. Their shortstop kept dropping the ball during fielding practice. Their starting pitcher was as wild as she had ever been. Jill thought that if her team was going to win, she would have to be the one to step forward. Soon the coach called the players in to sing the national anthem. Jill thought to herself, "This is just like it will be when I get to the pros." She knew the other players were nervous but not her! She couldn't wait to start the game.

Early in the game, Jill's team took a 1–0 lead. Jill came up to bat with a runner on second. But the umpire called her out on strikes. She couldn't believe that he called such a terrible pitch a strike! She really wanted to say to him, "You just called out Jill, the best player on the team." By the third inning, the lead was 3–0. Things were looking good for the team. But Jill still didn't have a hit. Her next time up, she hit a long fly to left. When the ball was caught, she blamed a gust of wind for taking away her home run.

Then the Ramblers scored four runs in their half of the inning. Now Jill had her chance to be the star. There were runners on second and third. With two strikes she got the pitch she was looking for. She swung with all her might. She couldn't believe that she missed it. Jill sat down, angry that the sun had gotten in her eyes at the wrong time. She just couldn't see the ball. Then the shortstop lined a double to left field and scored the two runs that the team needed. The pitcher struck out their last batter and Jill's team won 5–4. The team went wild, but Jill didn't feel like celebrating. Even after the team picture, Jill felt terrible. It was her worst game all season and it was the biggest game of the season, too. She wished that she had done better in front of all those people. (399 words)

Reading Accuracy Index: _____ %
(N of words – N of miscues, checked and unchecked) / N of words

Meaning Maintenance Index: _____ %
(N of words – N of meaning-violating miscues, unchecked only) / N of words

The Championship Game: 399 words

Miscue Chart (for optional use as oral passage)

Miscues	%	Miscues	%	Miscues	%
1	100	13	97	25	94
2	99	14	96	26	93
3	99	15	96	27	93
4	99	16	96	28	93
5	99	17	96	29	93
6	98	18	95	30	92
7	98	19	95	31	92
8	98	20	95	32	92
9	98	21	95	33	92
10	97	22	94	34	91
11	97	23	94	35	91
12	97	24	94	36	91

Retelling

Examiner: "Tell me about what you just read and what you thought about it."

If there is no spontaneous response, repeat the request, "Tell me what you thought about the passage."

Retelling Rubric

Story Structure:

1. **Key Characters and Setting:** Jill and her team playing in the championship game.
2. **Character's Problem or Goal:** Be the star of the game.
3. **Problem-Solving or Goal-Meeting Process:**
   - Jill has no confidence that her team can win the game.
   - Jill thinks she is better than the other players.
   - She plays badly but makes excuses for it.
   - Jill's team wins the championship.
   - Even though her team wins, Jill is unhappy about her
4. **Personal Response:** Any well-supported positive or negative response to the characters or events in the story; any reaction to the humor or sadness in the story; any well-supported positive or negative reaction to the story as a whole.

Rubric:

4 = Complete retelling includes characters, problem/goal, all five steps in the problem-solving process, and a well-supported personal response.

3 = Retelling includes characters, problem/goal, and all five steps in the problem-solving process, but has no personal response.

2 = Retelling includes characters, problem/goal, and three or four steps in the problem-solving process; some key factual errors or omissions. Add ½ point for well-supported personal response

1 = Retelling omits either characters or problem; includes one or two steps in the problem-solving process, but the account is disjointed and includes factual errors or serious omissions. Add ½ point for well-supported personal response

0 = Provides a title or topic statement but shows no real awareness of the character's problem and how the problem is worked out.

Retelling Score: _____

Comprehension Questions

1. Why didn't Jill think that her team was going to win the game?

    Text-based: Practice was going badly; shortstop dropped the ball often, and pitcher was wild.

2. Did the other players on the team feel the same way that Jill did about winning the championship? How do you know?

    Text-based: No, they were happy to win while Jill was disappointed in herself.

3. Do you think that Jill and her teammates were good friends or not? Why?

    Inference: Probably not, she didn't seem to know their names. She didn't care too much about the team; said that they wouldn't play well.

4. How important to Jill was winning the championship game? What made you think that?

    Inference: Not very important, she was more concerned that she didn't have a hit. When her team was losing she thought about herself, not winning the game.

5. Do you think that Jill has a chance of becoming a professional player? Why or why not?

    Critical Response: Probably not, won't work hard if she thinks everyone else is responsible when she doesn't play well; not a team player. Yes, she is the best player on the team; everyone can have a bad game; she has the confidence she needs.

6. What reasons did Jill give for playing poorly in the game? (Must include two.)

    Text-based: Blamed umpire; blamed the wind; blamed the sun.

7. Was Jill good at predicting how well her teammates would play? Explain.

    Inference: Not very good; both players that she thought would do poorly played well.

8. Why was Jill upset at the end of the game?

    Text-based: She played badly; she was embarrassed in front of the people; she wished she had played better.

9. Do you think that Jill needs help from her coach? Why or why not?

    Critical Response: Yes, she may not be as good as she thinks she is; she needs to stop making excuses and practice more; she needs to be more of a team player. No, she is already the best player on the team.

10. Why do you think that Jill didn't play as well as she thought she would in the big game?

    Critical Response: May have been overconfident; big crowd may have bothered her; may have tried too hard to be the star; made excuses instead of trying harder.

Comprehension Analysis:

Text-Based: __/4__
Inference: __/3__
Critical Response: __/3__

Total Comprehension %: _____

Fourth Grade Oral: The Vacation

Reader's copy on p. 29 of the Reader's Passages.

Introductory Statement: "Would you read this passage about a family vacation out loud for me? When you are finished, I'll take the passage away. Then I'll ask you to tell me about what you read and what you think of it. After that, I'll ask you some questions about the passage."

Story

Juan burst into his sister's room. "Only eight more days!" he shouted.

"I started packing already!" said Maria. "I can't wait to see what Florida is like."

Juan and Maria had started every day for the last two weeks talking about their Florida vacation. Mom and Dad were just as eager as they were.

But that evening, Father walked into the house, looking like a ghost. "What's wrong?" Mother asked. "No more overtime for the rest of the year," he stammered. Mother knew that they were going to use the overtime money to pay for the hotel rooms and the plane tickets to Florida. This was their first family vacation!

Mr. Ruiz struggled as he told the children that they would have to cancel their vacation. Juan ran up to his room crying while Maria hugged her father and sobbed.

"Let me see what I can do," said Mrs. Ruiz as she left the room.

She was smiling from ear to ear when she returned. "I just spoke with my brother Sal and he said that we could use his van to drive to Florida and we can stay with his wife's sister!"

Maria was excited with the news but Juan was angry! That wasn't the fun vacation he had been dreaming of for weeks. He had never flown on an airplane and he had never stayed in a hotel.

During the trip, the family stopped to look at different sights along the way. But every time, Juan refused to leave the van. He was irritated with their jabbering about what they had seen at each stop. The following day, Juan again sat in the van while the others went out to see a nearby river. Suddenly, Maria came rushing back to the van. "Juan! Juan!" she called, "Hurry, there's an alligator!" Juan jumped out of the van and dashed the quarter mile to where his parents were standing.

"You missed it," said his father sadly. "It's gone!"

Maria, Mom, and Dad told Juan how they first saw the alligator sunning itself on the bank of the river. Maria had quietly run back to get Juan but a squawking bird startled the alligator and it dashed into the river. Everyone saw how disgusted Juan was and no one said a word for over twenty minutes.

"You know, Juan . . . " began Mother.

"I know, Mom," said Juan. "I've been missing one of the best chances I've ever had! But I won't do it again!" (412 words)

Miscues

_____ N of miscues that maintained meaning (checked). This is the MM.

_____ N of miscues that violated meaning (unchecked). This is the MV.

Reading Accuracy Index: _____ %
    (N of words – N of miscues, checked and unchecked) / N of words

Meaning Maintenance Index: _____ %
    (N of words – N of meaning-violating miscues, unchecked only) / N of words

The Vacation: 412 words

Miscue Chart

Miscues	%	Miscues	%	Miscues	%	Miscues	%
1	100	13	97	25	94	37	91
2	100	14	97	26	94	38	91
3	99	15	96	27	93	39	91
4	99	16	96	28	93	40	90
5	99	17	96	29	93	41	90
6	99	18	96	30	93	42	90
7	98	19	95	31	92	43	90
8	98	20	95	32	92	44	89
9	98	21	95	33	92	45	89
10	98	22	95	34	92	46	89
11	97	23	94	35	92	47	89
12	97	24	94	36	91	48	88

Retelling

Examiner: "Tell me about what you just read and what you thought about it."

If there is no spontaneous response, repeat the request, "Tell me what you thought about the passage."

Retelling Rubric

Story Structure:

1. **Key Characters and Setting:** Juan, Maria, his mother, father on family vacation.
2. **Character's Problem or Goal:** Juan is disappointed with a change in travel plans.
3. **Problem-Solving or Goal-Meeting Process:**
   - Juan's family plans a trip to Florida.
   - Trip must be cancelled because of money problems.
   - Mother makes arrangements so trip can take place.
   - Juan is disappointed that the trip is not everything he wanted.
   - Juan does not participate in the family's fun.
   - Juan misses seeing the alligator and realizes that he has been wrong.
4. **Personal Response:** Any well-supported positive or negative response to the characters or events in the story; any reaction to the humor or sadness in the story; any well-supported positive or negative reaction to the story as a whole.

Rubric:

4 = Complete retelling includes characters, problem/goal, all six steps in the problem-solving process, and a well-supported personal response.

3 = Retelling includes characters, problem/goal, and five or six steps in the problem-solving process, but has no personal response.

2 = Retelling includes characters, problem/goal, and three or four steps in the problem-solving process; some key factual errors or omissions. Add ½ point for well-supported personal response.

1 = Retelling omits either characters or problem; includes two or three steps in the problem-solving process, but the account is disjointed and includes factual errors or serious omissions. Add ½ point for well-supported personal response.

0 = Provides a title or topic statement but shows no real awareness of the character's problem and how the problem is worked out.

Retelling Score: _____

Comprehension Questions

1. Why was everyone in the family excited about the vacation in Florida?

   Text-based: It was their first family vacation; first trip to Florida.

2. Why did it seem that the family would have to cancel their vacation?

   Text-based: Mr. Ruiz could get no more overtime at work.

3. Why didn't Mrs. Ruiz ask her brother earlier if they could borrow his van?

   Inference: The family planned to fly to Florida.

4. What reason would Juan have for being upset when his family talked about what they had seen?

   Inference: Jealous of them; didn't want to be reminded of what he had missed; wanted everyone else to suffer along with him.

5. Who do you think was older, Juan or Maria? Why do you think so?

   Critical Response: Maria—seemed more concerned with her father's feelings; handled the disappointment better than Juan did; was willing to enjoy the vacation with her family. Juan— Maria was just the messenger when the family saw the alligator; she would have teased him if he were younger.

6. Why was Juan disappointed when he heard that the family would drive the van to Florida? (Must identify one.)

   Text-based: He was looking forward to flying and staying in a hotel for the first time.

7. How did the family show that they cared about Juan's feelings after he missed seeing the alligator?

   Inference: They didn't force him to go with them; they didn't preach to him; they stayed silent for 20 minutes after he missed seeing the alligator; they gave him some think time.

8. Why was the family still able to go to Florida without the extra overtime money?

   Text-based: Mrs. Ruiz got help from her brother; brother gave her his van and found a place for them to stay.

9. Do you think Juan's parents were right to let him sulk for so long?

   Critical Response: Yes, maybe they were trying to help him learn a lesson; you can't really force someone to have a good time; he learned something from the experience. No, he was trying to put a damper on everyone else's vacation; he had already made up his mind not to have a good time.

10. What lesson do you think Juan could learn from his experience?

    Critical Response: Don't sulk because you could miss some very good things; don't think the worst because sometimes things work out for the best; keep your mind on what is important in life.

> **Comprehension Analysis:**
>
> Text-Based: __/4__
> Inference: __/3__
> Critical Response: __/3__
>
> **Total Comprehension %:** _____

Reader's copy on p. 30 of the Reader's Passages.

Introductory Statement: "Would you read this passage about two sisters who have a job to do to yourself? When you are finished, I'll take the passage away. Then I'll ask you to tell me about what you read and what you think of it. After that, I'll ask you some questions about the passage."

Story

"Libby, come here quick," I called. "The leaves are all falling." It is fall and my little sister, Libby, and I will have to rake the leaves together every day. Mom said that Libby is finally old enough to help with the chores and that I have the job of showing her how to clean up the yard. If we don't rake up the leaves, they will clutter up the lawn, the sidewalks, and even the rainspouts. Mom says that falling leaves are messy and dangerous, especially when they are wet.

"Look at all the leaves, Sue!" shouted Libby. "I want to go out and play right now!" I told her that we couldn't play just then. "Mom wants us to rake the leaves up. If it rains, people walking by our house might slip and fall."

"Please, Sue. Let's just jump in them for a little while," she begged. So I told her that if she would help me clean up afterwards, we could pile them up into a big mound and jump in. She was so excited that she promised to help me.

We went out and raked the leaves into a big pile and then we shouted, "One, two, three, jump!" And we jumped on the pile of leaves again and again until the leaves were scattered over the entire yard. Then I told Libby that it was time to rake them up, but Libby just wanted to keep playing. While she played, I had to gather the leaves and put them in the trash bags myself.

Then I had to drag all of the bags out to the sidewalk for the trucks to come and pick up the next morning. I knew that more leaves would fall tomorrow but I wondered if Libby would help me clean them up then.

The next day, I had piano lessons so I didn't get home until late. I was surprised to find that Libby had gone outside and raked the leaves herself. But then she remembered the fun she had the day before and she jumped in them and they flew all over the yard. When I saw the mess I told Libby that she would have to clean up the leaves. I even offered to help her rake them up before Mom came home. But Libby ran away to play with her friend and I was left to do all of the work again. I really wanted to just leave everything there in the yard but I knew that Mom would be disappointed. Falling leaves can be fun for kids but grown-ups don't see it that way. I think I'm starting to see the reason. (447 words)

Reading Accuracy Index: _____ %
   (N of words – N of miscues, checked and unchecked) / N of words.

Meaning Maintenance Index: _____ %
   (N of words – N of meaning-violating miscues, unchecked only) / N of words

Autumn Leaves: 447 words

Miscue Chart (for optional use as oral passage)

Miscues	%	Miscues	%	Miscues	%
1	100	16	96	31	93
2	100	17	96	32	93
3	99	18	96	33	93
4	99	19	96	34	92
5	99	20	96	35	92
6	99	21	95	36	92
7	98	22	95	37	92
8	98	23	95	38	91
9	98	24	95	39	91
10	98	25	94	40	91
11	98	26	94	41	91
12	97	27	94	42	91
13	97	28	94	43	90
14	97	29	94	44	90
15	97	30	93	45	90

Retelling

Examiner: "Tell me about what you just read and what you thought about it."

If there is no spontaneous response, repeat the request, "Tell me what you thought about the passage."

Retelling Rubric

Story Structure:

1. **Key Characters and Setting:** Sue and younger sister (Libby) at home.
2. **Character's Problem or Goal:** Sue has difficulty getting her little sister to help her with the leaves.
3. **Problem-Solving or Goal-Meeting Process:**
   - Sue tells Libby about their job raking the leaves.
   - Libby wants to play and leaves Sue with the work.
   - The next day it happens again.
   - Sue does not know what to do about Libby.
   - Sue begins to understand why parents look at leaves differently.
4. **Personal Response:** Any well-supported positive or negative response to the characters or events in the story; any reaction to the humor or sadness in the story; any well-supported positive or negative reaction to the story as a whole.

Rubric:

4 = Complete retelling (includes characters, problem/goal, all five steps in the problem-solving process, and a well-supported personal response.

3 = Retelling includes characters, problem/goal, and all five steps in the problem-solving process, but has no personal response

2 = Retelling includes characters, problem/goal, and three or four steps in the problem-solving process; some key factual errors or omissions. Add ½ point for well-supported personal response.

1 = Retelling omits either characters or problem; includes one or two steps in the problem-solving process, but the account is disjointed and includes factual errors or serious omissions. Add ½ point for well-supported personal response.

0 = Provides a title or topic statement but shows no real awareness of the character's problem and how the problem is worked out.

Retelling Score: _____

Comprehension Questions

1. In what season does this story take place?

   Text-based: Fall.

2. What chore do the children have to do in the story?

   Text-based: Raking the leaves up.

3. How much older do you think Sue is than her sister Libby? Why do you think this?

   Inference: Must be several years; older one is responsible for the other; tells her what Mom wants her to do; decides if they can play in the leaves or not.

4. Do you think Libby might have a good reason for not wanting to work with Sue? Explain.

   Inference: Libby might think she is bossy; makes her do things she doesn't want to do; she might think her sister nags her about their jobs.

5. What do you think that Sue should do the next time Libby promises to help? Why?

   Critical Response: Should refuse to do it until Libby shows she can keep her promises; should talk to Libby about the importance of keeping her word.

6. Why couldn't the two girls work together on the next day?

   Text-based: Sue had piano lessons.

7. What do you think Sue meant when she said that she's beginning to see why adults don't see falling leaves as fun?

   Inference: They are a lot of work and responsibility; lot of work when no one helps.

8. Why wasn't Sue happy that Libby raked the leaves by herself while Sue was at her piano lesson?

   Text-based: She played in the leaves and scattered them all over the yard.

9. Do you think that Sue should have done Libby's work for her? Why or why not?

   Critical Response: No, she will only do the same thing again if she gets away with it. Yes, because if she didn't do it, someone might be hurt; she is being responsible.

10. Do you think that Sue should tell Mom that Libby did not help with the work? Why or why not?

    Critical Response: Yes, Libby is not being fair or responsible and will not listen to her sister. No, that would be tattling; she should refuse to let her play until she helps.

Comprehension Analysis:

Text-Based: __/4__
Inference: __/3__
Critical Response: __/3__

Total Comprehension %: _____

Reader's copy on p. 31 of the Reader's Passages.

Introductory Statement: "Would you read this passage about a girl who gets her wish out loud for me? When you are finished, I'll take the passage away. Then I'll ask you to tell me about what you read and what you think of it. After that, I'll ask you some questions about the passage."

Story

Many years ago a young woman named Winnie Yua lived in a small Chinese village where her family kept a few rice paddies. Winnie's family was very poor. Winnie was the oldest of five girls and she would help her father take the rice to the city and sell it on market days. Her parents had always hoped for a son who would be able to go to school and perhaps work in the city for better pay. They never had their son but their daughters were all good and kind and worked hard on the farm with their parents.

One day in the marketplace, Winnie heard news from the province that the emperor had announced a counting contest. The winner would get a valuable, secret prize but only boys were permitted to participate.

"Father, I wish I were a boy. I know that I can count very well. It isn't fair that only boys can join."

"Winnie, you really need to stop wishing you were a boy. Sometimes I think it is our fault that you feel that way. You are a good daughter and a great help to us. I know it isn't fair that the emperor is allowing only boys to participate but that is the way it is. Perhaps one day things will change but you must accept your fate for now."

Winnie honored and respected her father, but she still wanted a chance to win a valuable prize and help her family. Helping at the market had made her an excellent counter. She could calculate bills and change without an abacus. And she never made a mistake. So on the day of the competition, Winnie disguised herself as a young man and entered the contest. One by one the others failed but Winnie knew her numbers well. At the end of the contest, she was the only one left. She had achieved her goal!

Now the emperor's minister came forward to award the prize. Winnie's heart was pounding. It seemed as if everyone in the entire city was there to hear the announcement. She prayed that no one would recognize her. All she wanted was to take the money, go home to her own village, and surprise her family, especially her father. Then the minister spoke in a loud voice, "The emperor has decreed that the winner of this contest is the man who will marry his only daughter!"

(404 words)

Miscues

_____ N of miscues that maintained meaning (checked). This is the MM.
_____ N of miscues that violated meaning (unchecked). This is the MV.

Reading Accuracy Index: _____ %
    (N of words – N of miscues, checked and unchecked) / N of words
Meaning Maintenance Index: _____ %
    (N of words – N of meaning-violating miscues, unchecked only) / N of words
Getting What You Want: 404 words

Miscue Chart

Miscues	%	Miscues	%	Miscues	%	Miscues	%
1	100	13	97	25	94	37	91
2	100	14	97	26	94	38	91
3	99	15	96	27	93	39	90
4	99	16	96	28	93	40	90
5	99	17	96	29	93	41	90
6	99	18	96	30	93	42	90
7	98	19	95	31	92	43	89
8	98	20	95	32	92	44	89
9	98	21	95	33	92	45	89
10	98	22	95	34	92	46	89
11	97	23	94	35	91	47	88
12	97	24	94	36	91	48	88

Retelling

Examiner: "Tell me about what you just read and what you thought about it."

If there is no spontaneous response, repeat the request, "Tell me what you thought about the passage."

Retelling Rubric

Story Structure:

1. **Key Characters and Setting:** Winnie Yua, her family, and the emperor in a small Chinese village.
2. **Character's Problem or Goal:** Winnie wants a chance to win the counting contest for boys only.
3. **Problem-Solving or Goal-Meeting Process:**
   - Winnie hears about a counting contest with a valuable prize.
   - Winnie wants to enter but only boys are allowed.
   - Her father tells her to accept her fate as a girl.
   - Winnie disguises herself and enters anyway.
   - Winnie wins but finds that the prize is the emperor's daughter in marriage.
4. **Personal response:** Any well-supported positive or negative response to the characters or events in the story; any reaction to the humor or sadness in the story; any well-supported positive or negative reaction to the story as a whole.

Rubric:

4 = Complete retelling includes characters, problem/goal, all five steps in the problem-solving process, and a well-supported personal response.

3 = Retelling includes characters, problem/goal, and all five steps in the problem-solving process, but has no personal response.

2 = retelling includes characters, problem/goal, and three or four steps in the problem-solving process; some key factual errors or omissions. Add ½ point for well-supported personal response.

1 = Retelling omits either characters or problem; includes one or two steps in the problem-solving process, but the account is disjointed and includes factual errors or serious omissions. Add ½ point for well-supported personal response.

0 = Provides a title or topic statement, but shows no real awareness of the character's problem and how the problem is worked out.

Retelling Score: _____

Comprehension Questions

1. What skill did Winnie have that helped her father on market days?

   Text-based: Counting ability.

2. What did Winnie have to do to get into the counting contest?

   Text-based: Disguise herself as a boy.

3. Why would Winnie's father think it was his fault that his daughter wished she were a boy?

   Inference: He and his wife had hoped for a son; Winnie may have overheard them.

4. Was the emperor really unfair to allow only boys in *this* counting contest?

   Inference: No, he knew what the prize would be.

5. If Winnie had the chance to talk to the emperor, what do you think she should say?

   Critical Response: Try to explain her actions; try to convince him that girls could learn; try to convince him that it is unfair to exclude girls; girls can also contribute to the country.

6. What advice did Winnie's father give her when she said that she wished she were a boy?

   Text-based: Told her she should accept her fate and stop wishing she were a boy.

7. Why would Winnie be especially anxious to tell her father that she had won the contest?

   Inference: He advised her to accept her fate; told her to stop wishing that she were a boy.

8. Why did Winnie enter the contest?

   Text-based: Thought she could win a valuable prize; wanted to help the family.

9. Do you think it was it right for Winnie to disguise herself and break the rules of the contest?

   Critical Response: No, she broke the rules and now is in trouble; she was dishonest in disguising herself. Yes, it wasn't right that girls should be excluded; she should have been given a chance to prove herself.

10. What do you think Winnie should do now that she knows what the prize is?

    Critical Response: Apologize for disguising herself; go back to her family without claiming the prize and hope that no one recognized her.

Comprehension Analysis:

Text-Based: __/4__
Inference: __/3__
Critical Response: __/3__

Total Comprehension %: _____

Fifth Grade Silent: The Player

Reader's copy on p. 32 of the Reader's Passages.

Introductory Statement: "Would you read this passage about a basketball player to yourself? When you are finished, I'll take the passage away. Then I'll ask you to tell me about what you read and what you think of it. After that, I'll ask you some questions about the passage."

Story

Rasheed was excited to be playing on his first basketball team. He hadn't played much basketball but he had always been big and fast and a good athlete. But this time things were different. The first time he had the ball, Rasheed dribbled it off his foot and out of bounds. The next two times, a quicker player stole it away from him. Finally Rasheed had his first chance to shoot the ball but he missed everything, even the backboard. Soon his teammates stopped passing the ball to him, even when he was open under the basket. His team lost the game badly and Rasheed went home angry with his team and angry with basketball.

That night, Rasheed went to his father and told him that he wanted to quit the basketball team. "I'm no good at basketball and the team is no good either," he said.

"Well, if you want to quit, that's your decision," said Mr. Singer. "But I think if you really want to, you can become a whole lot better and so can your team. Maybe you shouldn't just do things that are easy for you." Rasheed had to think this one over. Rasheed knew that whenever his father said, "It's your decision, but . . . " he really meant that he'd like Rasheed to think it over very carefully. Down deep, he knew that his father would be disappointed if he never even tried to become a better player.

Rasheed knew that his father wouldn't be much help at teaching him basketball but he had heard stories about their new neighbor, Mr. Armstrong, being named to the all-state team in high school. When Rasheed asked Mr. Armstrong if he could teach him basketball, Mr. Armstrong's eyes lit up. He said, "You stick with me, kid, and you'll be the best basketball player ever!" Rasheed laughed as the two of them took turns shooting baskets in Mr. Armstrong's back yard. But soon Rasheed was sweating and breathing hard as his new teacher put him through one basketball drill after another. Finally, Mr. Armstrong said, "Time to call it a day! But be here same time tomorrow and we'll do it again." Rasheed worked hard and even after just a few days, he could feel himself becoming more confident in his ability. When it was time for the next game, Rasheed scored eight points, grabbed five rebounds, and didn't lose the ball once. His team still lost the game but his teammates couldn't believe how much better he had become.

After the game, Mr. Singer put his arm around his son and said, "I'm really proud of the decision you made, Rasheed. You worked awfully hard and it really showed."

"Thanks, Dad. Thanks for not letting me quit the team."

"Who told you that you couldn't quit? It wasn't me!"

Rasheed just smiled. (473 words)

Reading Accuracy Index: _____ %
(N of words – N of miscues, checked and unchecked) / N of words

Meaning Maintenance Index: _____ %
(N of words – N of meaning-violating miscues, unchecked only) / N of words

The Player: 473 Words

Miscue Chart (for optional use as oral passage)

Miscues	%	Miscues	%	Miscues	%
1	100	16	97	31	93
2	100	17	96	32	93
3	99	18	96	33	93
4	99	19	96	34	93
5	99	20	96	35	93
6	99	21	96	36	92
7	99	22	95	37	92
8	98	23	95	38	92
9	98	24	95	39	92
10	98	25	95	40	92
11	98	26	95	41	91
12	97	27	94	42	91
13	97	28	94	43	91
14	97	29	94	44	91
15	97	30	94	45	90

Retelling

Examiner: "Tell me about what you just read and what you thought about it."

If there is no spontaneous response, repeat the request, "Tell me what you thought about the passage."

Retelling Rubric

Story Structure:

1. **Key Characters and Setting:** Rasheed, his father, and Mr. Armstrong in basketball league.
2. **Character's Problem or Goal:** Rasheed wants to quit the basketball team because he isn't very good.
3. **Problem-Solving or Goal-Meeting Process:**
   - Rasheed tries to play basketball and fails.
   - He wants to quit the team but his father wants him to think about it.
   - Rasheed asks Mr. Armstrong to help him.
   - Mr. Armstrong and Rasheed work hard and he improves.
   - Rasheed plays better and his father is proud of his work.
4. **Personal response:** Any well-supported positive or negative response to the characters or events in the story; any reaction to the humor or sadness in the story; any well-supported positive or negative reaction to the story as a whole.

Rubric:

4 = Complete retelling includes characters, problem/goal, all five steps in the problem-solving process, and a well-supported personal response.

3 = Retelling includes characters, problem/goal, and all five steps in the problem-solving process, but has no personal response.

2 = Retelling includes characters, problem/goal, and three or four steps in the problem-solving process; some key factual errors or omissions. Add ½ point for well-supported personal response.

1 = Retelling omits either characters or problem; includes one or two steps in the problem-solving process, but the account is disjointed and includes factual errors or serious omissions. Add ½ point for well-supported personal response.

0 = Provides a title or topic statement, but shows no real awareness of the character's problem and how the problem is worked out.

Retelling Score: _____

Comprehension Questions

1. Why was Rasheed angry after his first game with the basketball team? (Must identify one.)

   Text-based: His teammates wouldn't pass the ball to him; he played badly; he was embarrassed.

2. How do you know that Mr. Armstrong really wanted to help Rasheed become a better player? (Must identify one.)

   Text-based: His eyes lit up when Rasheed asked him; he worked with Rasheed night after night.

3. What kind of player was Rasheed expecting to be when he first started to play basketball? Why?

   Inference: A good player; was always a good athlete and expected basketball to be easy.

4. How do you think Rasheed knew that his father wouldn't be able to help him with basketball?

   Inference: He knew his father wasn't very good at basketball; his father may have been too busy.

5. Why would Rasheed's father think he should stay on the team, even if he wasn't very good?

   Critical Response: His son shouldn't just quit and walk away; knew his son could be better if he tried; wanted him to learn about how to stick with something and learn.

6. Why didn't Rasheed quit when Mr. Armstrong made him work so hard on basketball drills?

   Text-based: He had fun; they laughed together and Mr. Armstrong told basketball stories.

7. Why do you think that Mr. Armstrong would spend so much time and energy on a neighbor's son?

   Inference: Liked to share his knowledge of basketball; enjoyed spending time with Rasheed.

8. How did Rasheed's teammates react to him after the second game?

   Text-based: Surprised at his improvement.

9. Do you think Mr. Singer should let his son make his own decision even if he thought it was the wrong one? Explain.

   Critical Response: Yes, must learn to make his own decisions and accept consequences; will help him to become more mature and responsible. No, he should give him some guidance and try to persuade him that he is making a mistake; stakes are too high to let kids make the wrong decision; kids really want guidance and advice.

10. Do you think it would have been wrong if Rasheed had quit the team? Why or why not?

    Critical Response: Yes, he really had not tried to improve; he would have disappointed his father. No, he was not getting better; his teammates did not help him; his teammates ignored him and the team played badly anyway.

Comprehension Analysis:

   Text-Based: __/4__
   Inference: __/3__
   Critical Response: __/3__

Total Comprehension %: _____

Sixth Grade Oral: The Motor Bike

Reader's copy on p. 34 of the Reader's Passages.

Introductory Statement: "Would you read this passage about two friends and their families out loud for me? When you are finished, I'll take the passage away. Then I'll ask you to tell me about what you read and what you think of it. After that, I'll ask you some questions about the passage."

Story

Vic sprinted down the street knowing that Jameer would be waiting for him. For the past several months they had been meeting with Mr. Hunter before school started to discuss the books they were reading. On the way, Vic's mind wandered back to his third grade teacher, Ms. Woodson, and how she had changed his way of thinking. She helped him see that reading and learning could help people improve their lives.

"Guess what?" hollered Jameer when Vic was still a distance away. "I'm getting that incredible motor for my bike that I've been telling you about. Everybody in the family gets something special for their sixteenth birthday and this is my special gift!" Vic was happy for his old friend but he couldn't help feeling just a little envious too. He really wished that he had something exceptional to look forward to on his birthday.

Mr. Hunter started class and the book discussion turned toward the influences and contributions of parents to the lives of authors. Vic realized with a growing sense of discomfort that he had absolutely nothing to add to the conversation. How could he tell them that he hardly ever saw his mother, that she had two jobs, and that he was the one who had to supervise his brothers and sisters? By the end of the class, his self-pity was overflowing. Mr. Hunter walked out with Vic at the end of class and said, "My wife and I would like you to spend next weekend with us. See if it's OK for you."

Vic spent the following weekend with the Hunter family. That Saturday evening, Mrs. Hunter sat with Vic after dinner and showed him photographs from her childhood. In her entire collection, she had only three photographs of her mother but when Mrs. Hunter got to the first one, her face softened. She told Vic how her mother had worked at two jobs from day to night to be sure that her children always had clothes and food. "This picture was taken shortly before she died," she said. "That was the first time I told her that I resented the fact that she had missed practically every important occasion in my life. That's when she showed me her album. She kept photos and clippings from every one of those events that she had missed because she couldn't take time off from her job. Some people can't express their love with words but they certainly can show it. We just have to have enough insight to read it."

Vic had a lot to mull over that weekend and the next day he said, "You know, Mrs. Hunter, I learned about reading from Ms. Woodson but she never taught me about the different kinds of reading; I guess we have to read things besides books. I think I'm going to try to get better at reading people. Maybe I've been getting special gifts, just like Jameer, but I never even knew it. Thanks." (497 words)

Miscues

_____ N of miscues that maintained meaning (checked). This is the MM.

_____ N of miscues that violated meaning (unchecked). This is the MV.

Reading Accuracy Index: _____ %
(N of words – N of miscues, checked and unchecked) / N of words

Meaning Maintenance Index: _____ %
(N of words – N of meaning-violating miscues, unchecked only) / N of words

The Motor Bike: 497 words

Miscue Chart

Miscues	%	Miscues	%	Miscues	%	Miscues	%
1	100	13	97	25	95	37	93
2	100	14	97	26	95	38	92
3	99	15	97	27	95	39	92
4	99	16	97	28	94	40	92
5	99	17	97	29	94	41	92
6	99	18	96	30	94	42	92
7	99	19	96	31	94	43	91
8	98	20	96	32	94	44	91
9	98	21	96	33	93	45	91
10	98	22	96	34	93	46	91
11	98	23	95	35	93	47	91
12	98	24	95	36	93	48	90

Retelling

Examiner: "Tell me about what you just read and what you thought about it."

If there is no spontaneous response, repeat the request, "Tell me what you thought about the passage."

Retelling Rubric

Story Structure:

1. **Key Characters and Setting:** Vic and his friend Jameer, their teacher and his wife, in school and at their home.
2. **Character's Problem or Goal:** Vic is jealous of his friend's family relationship.
3. **Problem-Solving or Goal-Meeting Process:**
   - Vic is jealous about his friend's family.
   - Mr. Hunter notices Vic's self-pity and invites him to his home.
   - Mrs. Hunter shares her experiences with Vic.
   - Vic changes his views about his own mother.
4. **Personal Response:** Any well-supported positive or negative response to the characters or events in the story; any re-action to the humor or sadness in the story; any well-supported positive or negative reaction to the story as a whole.

Rubric:

4 = Complete retelling includes characters, problem/goal, all four steps in the problem-solving process, and a well-supported personal response.

3 = Retelling includes characters, problem/goal, and all four steps in the problem-solving process, but has no personal response.

2 = Retelling includes characters, problem/goal, and three steps in the problem-solving process; some key factual errors or omissions. Add ½ point for well-supported personal response.

1 = Retelling omits either characters or problem; includes two or three steps in the problem-solving process, but the account is disjointed and includes factual errors or serious omissions. Add ½ point for well-supported personal response.

0 = Provides a title or topic statement, but shows no real awareness of the character's problem and how the problem is worked out.

Retelling Score: _____

Miscue Chart (for optional use as oral passage)

Miscues	%	Miscues	%	Miscues	%
1	100	17	97	33	93
2	100	18	96	34	93
3	99	19	96	35	93
4	99	20	96	36	93
5	99	21	96	37	93
6	99	22	96	38	92
7	99	23	95	39	92
8	98	24	95	40	92
9	98	25	95	41	92
10	98	26	95	42	92
11	98	27	95	43	91
12	98	28	94	44	91
13	97	29	94	45	91
14	97	30	94	46	91
15	97	31	94	47	91
16	97	32	94	48	90

Retelling

Examiner: "Tell me about what you just read and what you thought about it."

If there is no spontaneous response, repeat the request "Tell me what you thought about the passage."

Retelling Rubric

Story Structure:

1. **Key Characters and Setting:** Jack and young Carl, whom he tutors at school.
2. **Character's Problem or Goal:** Jack is afraid he will embarrass himself or the boy he will tutor.
3. **Problem-Solving or Goal-Meeting Process:**
   - Jack is uncomfortable being a tutor.
   - He remembers his own problems with reading.
   - Jack and Carl discuss a book and share ideas.
   - Both Carl and Jack connect the book to their own lives.
   - Jack looks forward to working with Carl again.
4. **Personal Response:** Any well-supported positive or negative response to the characters or events in the story; any reaction to the humor or sadness in the story; any well-supported positive or negative reaction to the story as a whole.

Rubric:

4 = Complete retelling includes characters, problem/goal, all five steps in the problem-solving process, and a well-supported personal response.

3 = Retelling includes characters, problem/goal, and all five steps in the problem-solving process, but has no personal response.

2 = Retelling includes characters, problem/goal, and three or four steps in the problem-solving process; some key factual errors or omissions. Add ½ point for well-supported personal response.

1 = Retelling omits either characters or problem; includes one or two steps in the problem-solving process, but the account is disjointed and includes factual errors or serious omissions. Add ½ point for well-supported personal response.

0 = Provides a title or topic statement, but shows no real awareness of the character's problem and how the problem is worked out.

Retelling Score: _____

Comprehension Questions

1. Why didn't Jack want to be part of the tutoring program at first?

   Text-based: He was not very good at reading; remembered being embarrassed.

2. Was the tutoring as bad as Jack expected it to be? Why or why not?

   Text-based: No, the story was easy to read; both of them liked the story and talked about it.

3. How did the story that they read together help Jack and Carl to be more comfortable with each other?

   Inference: Enabled them to talk about ideas and relate the ideas to their own feelings.

4. If they ever talk about their experiences with school, what could Jack say to help Carl?

   Inference: Should share the difficulties he had; show Carl that anyone can overcome problems with the right kind of help; shouldn't let anyone make you feel inferior.

5. What do you think Jack learned from his tutoring experience?

   Critical Response: Things aren't always as bad as you expect them to be; learning about yourself can be valuable; learning can come from a very unexpected source.

6. Why does Carl think that he's dumb? (Must identify one.)

   Text-based: Has difficulty reading; friend also makes him feel dumb.

7. Is Carl's reading problem more about saying words or about understanding ideas? Why?

   Inference: Pronouncing words—he is very much able to discuss the ideas in the book.

8. Does Carl think that Jack is the same kind of reader that he is? Why or why not?

   Text-based: No, thinks he has no problems because he is the tutor; Jack read the story with ease when Carl could not.

9. Aside from their reading problems they share, how could you explain why Jack and Carl got along so well?

   Critical Response: Both had a sense of humor related to the story; both were willing to share the connections with themselves and their lives that they saw in the story.

10. Who do you think will learn more from the experience in the story, Jack or Carl? Why?

    Critical Response: Jack—he might find that his problems aren't as bad as he thinks; might be able to conquer his doubts. Carl—may become convinced that he isn't dumb.

Comprehension Analysis:

Text-Based: __/4__
Inference: __/3__
Critical Response: __/3__

Total Comprehension %: _____

Reader's copy on p. 38 of the Reader's Passages.

Introductory Statement: "Would you read this passage about a magician out loud for me? When you are finished, I'll take the passage away. Then I'll ask you to tell me about what you read and what you think of it. After that, I'll ask you some questions about the passage."

Story

Soon after the death of his father, the court magician to the Austrian king, Petruccio was named by the king to assume the post and to follow in his father's footsteps. As the magician, Petruccio would be an important figure in the king's court. He would be expected to foretell future events by reading the stars. He was also supposed to ward off evil spirits who might bring harm to the kingdom. Petruccio's father had loved his son dearly and sent him to the finest university in the world. But his study of logic and science at the university left Petruccio ill-equipped to traffic in spirits and "read" the stars. Petruccio found himself a court magician who did not believe in superstition. Petruccio's beliefs, however, mattered little to the court officials. The king needed a magician and there was no point in arguing with the king.

But Petruccio was a swift learner. He quickly realized that the best way to survive was to make the fewest predictions possible. He also developed the skill of taking credit for whatever good befell the kingdom. When the king asked him to predict future events, Petruccio would make predictions for which he had the best chance of being correct. Once the king asked Petruccio to predict whether his soon-to-be-born child would be male or female. Petruccio noted that the king had three sons and one daughter. So he correctly predicted the birth of a son. But after several years of good fortune, Petruccio's luck ran out. When the king's fa-

vorite aunt fell ill with the fever, Petruccio was asked to predict her fate. He observed that more people who had contracted the disease had died than who had survived. Thus he predicted that the aunt would die.

Petruccio was correct but he had not anticipated that the king would blame him for the death of his beloved aunt. Having resolved to behead his court magician, the king called Petruccio before him. With an ironic smile, the king asked him to foretell the manner in which he, Petruccio, would die. But the quick-thinking young man recognized the danger. He said to the king, "Your Majesty, I will die exactly three days before you." The king was dumbfounded. Instead of ordering his execution, the king ordered his guard to place Petruccio under special protection. He even commanded that they take care to be sure that Petruccio's needs were met. And so Petruccio lived for many years in comfort under the watchful care of his king. (419 words)

Miscues

_____ N of miscues that maintained meaning (checked). This is the MM.

_____ N of miscues that violated meaning (uncheeked). This is the MV.

Reading Accuracy Index: _____ 100 _____ %
(N of words – N of miscues, checked and unchecked) / N of words

Meaning Maintenance Index: _____ 100 _____ %
(N of words – N of meaning-violating miscues, unchecked only) / N of words

The Magician: 419 words

Miscue Chart:

Miscues	%	Miscues	%	Miscues	%	Miscues	%
1	100	13	97	25	94	37	91
2	100	14	97	26	94	38	91
3	99	15	96	27	94	39	91
4	99	16	96	28	93	40	90
5	99	17	96	29	93	41	90
6	99	18	96	30	93	42	90
7	98	19	95	31	93	43	90
8	98	20	95	32	92	44	90
9	98	21	95	33	92	45	89
10	98	22	95	34	92	46	89
11	97	23	95	35	92	47	89
12	97	24	94	36	91	48	89

Retelling

Examiner: "Tell me about what you just read and what you thought about it."

If there is no spontaneous response, repeat the request, "Tell me what you thought about the passage."

Retelling Rubric

Story Structure:

1. **Key Characters and Setting:** Petruccio, the court magician, and the King in their kingdom.
2. **Character's Problem or Goal:** Petruccio has to be smart enough to save his own life.
3. **Problem-Solving or Goal-Meeting Process:**
   • Petruccio is named court magician.
   • He does not believe in magic.
   • He learns to survive by outsmarting everyone.
   • His luck runs out when the king's aunt dies.
   • Petruccio outsmarts the king by telling him about his death.
   • The king protects Petruccio for the rest of his life.
4. **Personal Response:** Any well-supported positive or negative response to the characters or events in the story; any reaction to the humor or sadness in the story; any well-supported positive or negative reaction to the story as a whole.

Rubric:

4 = Complete retelling (includes characters, problem/goal, all six steps in the problem-solving process, and a well-supported personal response.

3 = Retelling includes characters, problem/goal, and five or six steps in the problem-solving process, but has no personal response.

2 = Retelling includes characters, problem/goal, and three or four steps in the problem-solving process; some key factual errors or omissions. Add ½ point for well-supported personal response.

1 = Retelling omits either characters or problem, includes two or three steps in the problem-solving process, but the account is disjointed and includes factual errors or serious omissions. Add ½ point for well-supported personal response.

0 = Provides a title or topic statement, but shows no real awareness of the character's problem and how the problem is worked out.

Retelling Score: _____

Comprehension Questions

1. Why wasn't Petruccio likely to be a good court magician?

   Text-based: He didn't believe in magic; his studies contradicted magic and superstition.

2. Why did the king plan to kill Petruccio?

   Text-based: He predicted that the king's favorite aunt would die; the king blamed him for his aunt's death.

3. Why didn't Petruccio just predict that the king's aunt would live?

   Inference: If she died, he would risk being found out; the king may be even angrier; the odds were against it; the king may not trust his predictions anymore.

4. Do you think that the king had studied science or logic? Explain.

   Inference: No, he believed in the superstitions.

5. Do you think that Petruccio survived mainly because of luck or because of his learning? Explain.

   Critical Response: Luck—had to be lucky because he really did not know what he was doing. His learning—his learning enabled him to make better decisions and to save his life in the end.

6. Why did making fewer predictions increase the magician's chances for survival?

   Text-based: If you don't predict, you can't be wrong.

7. If the king didn't trust Petruccio anymore, why did he believe in Petruccio's prediction about his own death?

   Inference: Probably felt he couldn't take the risk that Petruccio was right this time; too much at stake.

8. What made Petruccio predict that the king would die three days after he did?

   Text-based: Sensed danger; noticed that the king was angry.

9. Who do you think was more powerful in the kingdom, the king or Petruccio? Why?

   Critical Response: Petruccio—he was able to control the king by outsmarting him. The King—he really had power over life and death.

10. Did Petruccio's education at the university help him in any way as court magician?

    Critical Response: Yes, he learned to outsmart people; learned to calculate probability; learned to be logical. No, he didn't believe in what he was doing; could not believe in superstition.

Comprehension Analysis:

   Text-Based: _/4_
   Inference: _/3_
   Critical Response: _/3_

Total Comprehension %: _____

Junior High Silent (Grades 7–9): The Friend

Reader's copy on p. 39 of the Reader's Passages.

Introductory Statement: "Would you read this passage about a good friend to yourself? When you are finished, I'll take the passage away. Then I'll ask you to tell me about what you read and what you think of it. After that, I'll ask you some questions about the passage."

Story

Alex came home from the hair salon and put on her best party dress. Tonight she would be dining at the most exclusive and expensive restaurant at the lake resort where her parents had a cabin. Her old friend Jaime, who had always liked Alex, had invited her to the dinner, but it was Jaime's visiting cousin Carlos that she was really interested in. The three of them had played tennis that afternoon and Alex couldn't wait to see the handsome and sophisticated Carlos again.

Alex had persuaded her father that she could handle the small motorboat by herself for the short trip to the restaurant dock. After all, she drove the boat more often than anyone else in the family did! Alex drove very slowly so that her hairdo would be perfect when she arrived. Soon she pulled up to the dock in her tiny boat amid all of the expensive yachts and powerboats and was glad to see that Jaime and Carlos were waiting for her. Both young men were dressed in their finest clothes but Alex had eyes only for Carlos.

Alex turned the motor off and let the boat drift closer to the dock. She stretched out with the rope to tie the boat up but nearly lost her balance. Fortunately, she was able to grab on to the end of the pier. To her horror, Alex realized that the boat was drifting further away from the dock with her feet clinging desperately to its rail. Jaime immediately jumped down to the lower dock to try to help but he was too late. Alex fell headlong into the murky water next to the dock. Alex was an excellent swimmer but swimming was the furthest thing from her mind. She didn't know how she could face all of the people who had gathered at the dock watching her. They were all very polite and sympathetic but Carlos could not hide his amusement. Jaime tried to coax Alex toward his outstretched hand, but Alex could not bear the thought of facing the growing crowd of people on the dock. For Alex the evening was ruined.

Suddenly Jaime called, "Hold on, Alex! I'm coming to save you!" She watched in disbelief as Jaime leaped into the water with a tremendous splash and surfaced next to her with a huge grin. Despite her distress, Alex couldn't help but smile and soon the two of them were hugging each other and laughing so hard that they couldn't stop. When Jaime helped Alex from the water, she didn't mind the crowd of now-smiling onlookers nearly as much as she thought she would. Jaime whispered to her, "Let's go home and change and then we'll go out and get a pizza." During the boat ride back to her house, Alex watched her old friend laugh and shiver and joke about their experience, trying very successfully to cheer her up. Alex had to admit to herself that, despite the embarrassment, she had learned a great deal that night about true friends. (507 words)

Reading Accuracy Index: _____ %
(N of words – N of miscues, checked and unchecked) / N of words

Meaning Maintenance Index: _____ %
(N of words – N of meaning-violating miscues, unchecked only) / N of words

The Friend: 507 words

Miscue Chart (for optional use as oral passage)

Miscues	%	Miscues	%	Miscues	%
1	100	19	96	37	93
2	100	20	96	38	93
3	99	21	96	39	92
4	99	22	96	40	92
5	99	23	95	41	92
6	99	24	95	42	92
7	99	25	95	43	92
8	98	26	95	44	91
9	98	27	95	45	91
10	98	28	94	46	91
11	98	29	94	47	91
12	98	30	94	48	91
13	97	31	94	49	90
14	97	32	94	50	90
15	97	33	93	51	90
16	97	34	93	52	90
17	97	35	93	53	90
18	96	36	93	54	89

Retelling

Examiner: "Tell me about what you just read and what you thought about it."

If there is no spontaneous response, repeat the request, "Tell me what you thought about the passage."

Retelling Rubric

Story Structure:

1. **Key Characters and Setting:** Alex, her friend Jaime, and his cousin at the lake.
2. **Character's Problem or Goal:** Alex tries to impress Jaime's cousin and embarrasses herself.
3. **Problem-Solving or Goal-Meeting Process:**
   - Alex dresses up for dinner to impress Carlos.
   - Alex takes the boat to the restaurant and falls into the water.
   - She is embarrassed and does not want to face the crowd.
   - Jaime jumps into the water to help her.
   - Alex realizes what a good friend she has in Jaime.
4. **Personal Response:** Any well-supported positive or negative response to the characters or events in the story; any reaction to the humor or sadness in the story; any well supported positive or negative reaction to the story as a whole.

Rubric:

4 = Complete retelling includes characters, problem/goal, all five steps in the problem-solving process, and a well-supported personal response.

3 = Retelling includes characters, problem/goal, and all five steps in the problem-solving process, but has no personal response.

2 = Retelling includes characters, problem/goal, and three or four steps in the problem-solving process; some key factual errors or omissions. Add ½ point for well-supported personal response.

1 = Retelling omits either characters or problem; includes one or two steps in the problem-solving process, but the account is disjointed and includes factual errors or serious omissions. Add ½ point for well-supported personal response.

0 = Provides a title or topic statement, but shows no real awareness of the character's problem and how the problem is worked out.

Retelling Score: _____

Comprehension Questions

1. Why did Alex want to impress Carlos instead of Jaime?

   Text-based: Carlos was handsome and sophisticated.

2. How did the accident at the dock happen?

   Text-based: Alex lost her balance; tried to tie up the boat but slipped into the water; couldn't stay on the boat.

3. How did Jaime demonstrate his friendship for Alex?

   Inference: He cheered her up; made her feel less embarrassed, left the restaurant with her and took her home; jumped into water with her.

4. Why did Jaime jump into the water?

   Inference: His friend was embarrassed and he did it to relieve her embarrassment.

5. How does the saying "Beauty is only skin deep" apply to this story?

   Critical Response: Yes, Alex had a good friend in Jaime, a person who liked her; Carlos was not what she needed; Carlos was not what he seemed to be; Carlos laughed at her when she fell.

6. Why wasn't Alex's father afraid to let Alex take the boat alone to the restaurant?

   Text-based: She was experienced; she drove the boat more than anyone in the family did.

7. Why was Alex so surprised to see Jaime jump into the water with her?

   Inference: He was dressed in his best clothes.

8. Why was Alex so embarrassed when she fell into the water? (Must identify one.)

   Text-based: There were many people watching at the dock; Carlos laughed at her; she ruined her hair and clothes.

9. Do you think Alex will change her thinking about boyfriends as a result of this experience? Explain.

   Critical Response: Yes, she will probably value her friendships more; may not choose her friends for superficial reasons in the future. No, friendship has little to do with choosing boyfriends.

10. What did Alex learn about friendship that night?

    Critical Response: It is about putting someone else first, making sacrifices for others; recognizing a friend's needs.

Comprehension Analysis:

Text-Based: /4
Inference: /3
Critical Response: /3

Total Comprehension %: _____

Reader's copy on p. 41 of the Reader's Passages.

Introductory Statement: "Would you read this passage about a person who felt she was different out loud for me? When you are finished, I'll take the passage away. Then I'll ask you to tell me about what you read and what you think of it. After that, I'll ask you some questions about the passage."

Story

Lin sat thinking in silence in the rear seat of the car as her parents drove out of the tree-lined main drive of the idyllic university campus and began the long ride home. But there was no reflection of the campus serenity in Lin's mind that morning. She was trying desperately to control her anger as she relived the events of the past few days, events that dragged her memories back to the days of her youth when she felt so much like an outsider. The cinema in her mind replayed the first time that Lin had met her best friends, Marilyn and Cindy. Lin was seven years old and her family had just moved into their new home when her mother called her to tell her that two girls had knocked at the front door and asked if they could play with Lin.

The three girls sat on the front porch as her new friends bombarded Lin with questions about her life in China. She had all but forgotten the feeling that came over her, like being a strange specimen captured in a bottle to be scrutinized by inquisitive students. "They don't want to be my friends," Lin blurted out to her mother late one afternoon, "they just want to show me how different I am. I don't want to play with them again." But Lin's mother simply said, "Are you talking about how they feel or how you feel?" And so Lin decided not to run away and soon she joined Marilyn and Cindy in their imaginary world in the nearby woods, reading stories of faraway lands. Within

months, the girls had become inseparable and they were still the best of friends at the end of their junior year at the university. But it was the memory of being seven years old and feeling so terribly and unalterably different that consumed Lin during the ride home and not the friendship or the happy ending.

"You're pretty quiet, Lin," Mother said, but Lin was slow to respond. It had been her mother's idea for Lin to become acquainted with the four Chinese exchange students who began their university studies that semester. At that time Lin thought that serving as their mentor and assisting them in making the transition to American life and customs would be a marvelous way to help the girls. But their initial meeting had not been as fruitful as Lin had hoped it would be. At first, the girls sat in rapt attention and laughed as Lin shared with them stories of how she and her friends had learned to navigate the sometimes rough waters of the often convoluted campus procedures and protocol. But when Lin began to ask about their customs and point out the sharp contrasts between Chinese and American ideas of propriety and manners, the girls lapsed into an uncomfortable silence. Soon they were chattering nervously among themselves about Chinese poets and literature, books that Lin could not even read. The meeting ended awkwardly, with everyone sensing the presence of bruised egos but no one quite sure of their source.

"They seemed to relish making me feel like an outsider and you know, Mother, I can't really comprehend how a working knowledge of Chinese poetry will help them get very far in America."

"Are you certain that is what they wanted you to feel, Lin?" her mother asked. "Perhaps it was awkward for them to seem so different from you and all of the other students."

"That's no excuse for being impolite," snapped Lin, "especially when I was going out of my way to try to help them."

Later that week, on the family's long-planned trip to Niagara Falls, Lin stood mesmerized by the swiftness and intensity of the river, all very familiar but yet always somehow new. She felt her mother slip her arm around her and heard her whisper,. "The river always knows where it is going, perhaps because it knows where it has been." Lin knew her mother too well to believe that this was mere idle chatter; she had learned long ago that it was worth the effort to think long and hard to uncover the sometimes arcane lesson embedded in her mother's words.

Lin woke the next morning filled with a fresh resolve for the upcoming semester at the university. She would help her new friends organize discussion groups to explore Chinese literature and culture and she knew exactly whom she could invite to participate. The groups would dedicate themselves to the celebration of diversity, differences, and friendship in the university community, for as her mother knew so well, it always helps to know where you've been. (782 words)

Miscues

_____ N of miscues that maintained meaning (checked). This is the MM.

_____ N of miscues that violated meaning (unchecked). This is the MV.

Reading Accuracy Index: _____ %
   (N of words – N of miscues, checked and unchecked) / N of words

Meaning Maintenance Index: _____ %
   (N of words – N of meaning-violating miscues, unchecked only) / N of words

Differences: 782 words

Miscue Chart

Miscues	%	Miscues	%	Miscues	%	Miscues	%
1	100	13	98	25	97	37	95
2	100	14	98	26	97	38	95
3	100	15	98	27	97	39	95
4	99	16	98	28	96	40	95
5	99	17	98	29	96	41	95
6	99	18	98	30	96	42	95
7	99	19	98	31	96	43	94
8	99	20	97	32	96	44	94
9	99	21	97	33	96	45	94
10	99	22	97	34	96	46	94
11	99	23	97	35	96	47	94
12	98	24	97	36	95	48	94

Retelling

Examiner: "Tell me about what you just read and what you thought of it."

If there is no spontaneous response, repeat the request, "Tell me what you thought about the passage."

NOTE: Use the Retelling Rubric on p. 196 to assess the child's retelling performance.

Retelling Rubric

Story Structure:

1. **Key Characters and Setting:** Lin, her mother, Cindy and Marilyn, and four Chinese students.
2. **Character's Problem or Goal:** Lin must deal with feelings of not belonging.
3. **Problem-Solving or Goal-Making Process:**
   - Lin is angry at how she is treated by the four Chinese students.
   - She remembers feeling like an outsider when she first met her best friends.
   - She recalls that the students felt uncomfortable when she talked about differences.
   - Her mother's words about remembering where you've been make her reconsider her anger.
4. **Personal Response:** Any well-supported positive or negative response to the characters or events in the story; any reaction to the humor or sadness in the story; any well-supported positive or negative reaction to the story as a whole.

Rubric:

4 = Complete retelling includes characters, problem/goal, all four steps in the problem-solving process, and a well-supported personal response.

3 = Retelling includes characters, problem/goal, and all four steps in the problem-solving process, but has no personal response.

2 = Retelling includes characters, problem/goal, and two or three steps in the problem-solving process; some key factual errors or omissions. Add ½ point for well-supported personal response.

1 = Retelling omits either characters or problem; includes one or two steps in the problem-solving process, but the account is disjointed and includes factual errors or serious omissions. Add ½ point for well-supported personal response.

0 = Provides a title or topic statement, but shows no real awareness of the character's problem and how the problem is worked out.

Retelling Score: _____

Comprehension Questions

1. Why did Lin have a difficult time making friends with Marilyn and Cindy?

   Text-based: She thought they didn't really want to be her friends; they wanted to show how different Lin was.

2. What made Lin think that the Chinese students she tried to help were rude?

   Text-based: They began to talk about Chinese poetry and literature.

3. Why *should* Lin have understood how the Chinese students felt?

   Inference: Same thing had happened to her when she was young; emphasis on differences had made her feel uncomfortable; she had become good friends with people she was once suspicious of.

4. What do you think was the source of the bruised egos after Lin's first meeting with the Chinese students?

   Inference: Lin thought they were ungrateful and they thought she was insensitive to their feelings.

5. Do you think that Lin really learned the lesson her mother intended? Why or why not?

   Critical Response: Yes, she plans to change her approach to the Chinese students; she wants to become friends with the students. No, she does not seem to remember her own experiences with friendship.

6. What plan did Lin create as a result of her thinking about her mother's words?

   Text-based: To start a discussion group focusing on Chinese literature.

7. Why did both Lin and the four Chinese students react so negatively to the "help" they were given?

   Inference: May have felt that the other was acting superior; may have felt the others were trying to make them feel bad about their differences.

8. In what way was Lin's mother influential in helping her to resolve problems both early in life and later in life?

   Text-based: She questions Lin's judgment about the motives of others; she makes her rethink the statements she has made.

9. Was the lesson Lin's mother was trying to teach her really difficult to understand? Why or why not?

   Critical Response: Yes, she did not explain what she really meant; lesson was too complicated; Lin hadn't learned the lesson when she was young. No, Lin should have known what it was like to be treated as if you were different; Lin was not sensitive enough to learn the lesson; Lin was too self-centered to learn.

10. Do you think that Lin had forgotten where she had been? Explain.

    Critical Response: Yes, she had forgotten her early suspicions about her young friends; she did not learn from her experiences with differences; she did the same thing to the students that she was angry about when she was young. No, she did recall her early experiences; her memories helped her to come to grips with her feelings.

Reader's copy on p. 43 of the Reader's Passages.

Introductory Statement: "Would you read this passage about a young man's injury to yourself? When you are finished, I'll take the passage away. Then I'll ask you to tell me about what you read and what you think of it. After that, I'll ask you some questions about the passage."

Story

It seemed that the entire town was trying to fit into the Franklin High School football stadium for the final game of the season. But the buzz in the crowd was all about the recruiters from big-name colleges who had come to scout Ron, their local football and baseball hero. It seemed that their small town was finally on the map and it was a fine athlete and a fine young man who had put them there. At the end of the evening few people at the game even remembered the final score. The images that seem engraved on the minds of everyone at the game were the hard tackle, the awkward fall, and the stretcher that carried Ron to the ambulance that waited outside the field for just such emergencies. The diagnosis was grim. A torn rotator cuff would need immediate surgical repair and months of rehabilitation and there were no guarantees that Ron would ever regain the athletic skills that had set him apart from every other player in the entire league.

On his way to the hospital, Ron thought about his father, who would be anxiously praying and waiting for him there. Ron knew that his father had taken on the extra part-time job to earn the money to cover the expenses for Ron's participation in sports. His father had always been proud of his son's athletic success but Ron suspected that he was most grateful for the full scholarship it would bring, a scholarship to a private university that the family could never have afforded.

With that scholarship now in jeopardy, Ron knew that he would have to face some thorny decisions with some far-reaching consequences. But unfortunate decisions and still more regrettable consequences were things that Ron and his father had talked about for as long as Ron could remember. His father had dropped out of football because he hadn't kept up his grades. Then he had to watch his best friend, a player whom everyone recognized was not his father's equal, go on to win a football scholarship to a top-grade university and to have a thoroughly successful college career. How many times had he heard his father speculate wistfully on what might have been if he had only stayed with football? After graduation and a tour of duty in Vietnam, his father had returned determined to go on to earn a college degree, but after several months in the local community college, he became jealous of the spending money that his working friends always seemed to have. He dropped out of college and took a full-time job but he still somehow never seemed to earn enough or succeed enough to match his aspirations. Whenever he could, Ron's father would make a point of identifying the consequences he had paid and still continued to pay because of the poor decisions he had made in his youth. Ron knew that his father would be deeply disappointed in him if he made the wrong decision.

After his surgery, Ron's physical therapy was more painful than anything he had ever experienced. He began to wonder whether he really wanted to risk reinjuring the shoulder by trying to rejoin the team. But without football, what could he do to afford college? He had always been an honor roll student, but he knew that he would never qualify for an academic scholarship. Ron began to wonder whether he should drop out of sports altogether. Then he would have more time to devote to his studies. But what about the regrets that were sure to come later? What about the consequences if he made the wrong decision?

His father accompanied Ron, as always, to the doctor's office at the end of Ron's physical therapy program. The doctor told them what Ron had suspected all along: he could return to football but another injury to the shoulder could leave him with permanent damage and pain. Ron and his father drove in silence to the coffee shop where they had spent countless hours over the years discussing life's choices and consequences.

Ron wanted desperately to ask his father what he should do, but he sensed that the time for letting others decide for him had long since passed. Instead, Ron turned to his father and said, "You've never told me which regret was greater, dropping out of football or out of college."

To Ron's surprise, his father replied, "I'm really beginning to wonder if I've wasted too much of my life regretting the things that I've done. If I had stayed in college and in football, I may never have been fortunate enough to meet your mother or to have had a son like you. I may never have been nearly as contented as I've been over the years. I'm beginning to think that maybe it isn't always the choices that you make but what you make of the choices that really matters." Ron nodded; he didn't quite understand yet what his father meant but he had the distinct feeling that he soon would. (843 words)

Reading Accuracy Index: _____ %
(N of words – N of miscues, checked and unchecked) / N of words

Meaning Maintenance Index: _____ %
(N of words – N of meaning-violating miscues, unchecked only) / N of words

The Injury: 843 words

Miscue Chart (for optional use as oral passage)

Miscues	%	Miscues	%	Miscues	%
1	100	25	97	49	94
2	100	26	97	50	94
3	100	27	97	51	94
4	100	28	97	52	94
5	99	29	97	53	94
6	99	30	96	54	94
7	99	31	96	55	93
8	99	32	96	56	93
9	99	33	96	57	93
10	99	34	96	58	93
11	99	35	96	59	93
12	99	36	96	60	93
13	98	37	96	61	93
14	98	38	95	62	93
15	98	39	95	63	93
16	98	40	95	64	92
17	98	41	95	65	92
18	98	42	95	66	92
19	98	43	95	67	92
20	98	44	95	68	92
21	98	45	95	69	92
22	97	46	95	70	92
23	97	47	94	71	92
24	97	48	94	72	91

Retelling

Examiner: "Tell me about what you just read and what you thought of it."

If there is no spontaneous response, repeat the request to "Tell me what you thought about the passage."

Retelling Rubric

Story Structure:

1. **Key Characters and Setting:** Ron and his father.
2. **Character's Problem or Goal:** Ron is faced with a difficult decision about his future.
3. **Problem-Solving or Goal-Meeting Process:**
   - Ron is star athlete being recruited by college scouts.
   - Injury jeopardizes his scholarship and future.
   - Ron is aware of his father's regrets about his poor decisions and their consequences.
   - Ron agonizes over his decision.
   - Father tells Ron that he should not have spent so much time on regrets.
   - Father tells Ron that the most important thing is to make the best of your choices.
4. **Personal Response:** Any well-supported positive or negative response to the characters or events in the story; any reaction to the humor or sadness in the story; any well-supported positive or negative reaction to the story as a whole.

Rubric:

4 = Complete retelling includes characters, problem/goal, all six steps in the problem-solving process, and a well-supported personal response.

3 = Retelling includes characters, problem/goal, and five or six steps in the problem-solving process, but has no personal response.

2 = Retelling includes characters, problem/goal, and three or four steps in the problem-solving process; some key factual errors or omissions. Add ½ point for well-pointed personal response.

1 = Retelling omits either characters or problem; includes two or three steps in the problem-solving process, but the account is disjointed and includes factual errors or serious omissions. Add ½ point for well-pointed personal response.

0 = Provides a title or topic statement but shows no real awareness of the character's problem and how the problem is worked out.

Retelling Score: _____

Comprehension Questions

1. Why did so many people attend the final football game of the season at Franklin High School?

   Text-based: Recruiters from colleges had come to see Ron play.

2. Why was the torn rotator cuff such a serious injury for Ron?

   Text-based: He may not recover his athletic skills; he may lose his scholarship.

3. In what ways is Ron's personality like that of his father?

   Inference: Very thoughtful and reflective; afraid of regrets; wants to make the right decision.

4. Why would Ron seem to prefer that his father tell him what to do?

   Inference: He trusts his father's judgment; the decisions are serious ones; he won't have to accept the consequences alone that way.

5. Do you think his father should have given Ron more specific advice at the end of the story?

   Critical Response: Yes, he needs the guidance; he is still young to be making that kind of choice; he trusts his father. No, he will have to accept the consequences, not his father; he is old enough to make his own decisions at this point.

6. Why didn't Ron's father stay in college when he had the chance?

   Text-based: He was jealous of his friends who were earning money in their jobs.

7. Do you think, as Ron did, that his father would have been disappointed in Ron if he made the "wrong decision?"

   Inference: Probably not, too proud of his son; the father had reconsidered his own regrets and decisions.

8. Why was the football scholarship so important to Ron's father?

   Text-based: He could not afford to send his son to a private school.

9. Who do you think learned more from the experience of Ron's injury, Ron or his father? Explain.

   Critical Response: Ron—had to grow up fast and make some important decisions; learned about how to reconsider life decisions. Father—had to rethink his life and values; injury changed him almost completely.

10. Based on what you know about the situation, what do you think would be the best course of action for Ron and why?

    Critical Response: Stop sports and concentrate on academics since the injury is so serious; concentrate on baseball which isn't as dangerous a sport; get a loan and attend a state college.

Comprehension Analysis:

   Text-Based: /4
   Inference: /3
   Critical Response: /3

Total Comprehension %: _____

Section 10

Examiner's Copy of Informational Passages: Form B

Reader's copy on p. 47 of the Reader's Passages.

Introductory Statement: "Would you read this passage about trucks out loud for me? When you are finished, I'll take the passage away. Then I'll ask you to tell me about what you read and what you think of it. After that, I'll ask you some questions about the passage."

Story

A big, red fire truck goes fast.

It helps put out fires.

A small, green truck goes down the street.

It brings boxes to our store.

A tanker truck has a long, long hose.

It brings gas to our gas station.

A large, blue truck sprays water.

It cleans our street.

The best truck rings its bell and plays a song.

It brings me a treat. (66 words)

Miscues

_____ N of miscues that maintained meaning (checked). This is the MM.

_____ N of miscues that violated meaning (unchecked). This is the MV.

Reading Accuracy Index: _____ %
(N of words – N of miscues, checked and unchecked) / N of words

Meaning Maintenance Index: _____ %
(N of words – N of meaning-violating miscues, unchecked only) / N of words

All Kinds of Trucks: 66 words

Miscue Chart

Miscues	%	Miscues	%
1	98	7	89
2	97	8	88
3	95	9	86
4	94	10	85
5	92	11	83
6	91	12	82

Retelling

Examiner: "Tell me about what you just read and what you thought about it."

If there is no spontaneous response, repeat the request, "Tell me what you thought about the passage."

Retelling Rubric

Macro Concepts (numbered) and Micro Concepts (bulleted):

1. There are many kinds of trucks.
2. Trucks help people in many ways.
   - Fire trucks put out fires.
   - Trucks deliver boxes to the stores.
   - Tankers bring gas to the stations.
   - Trucks clean the streets.
3. Favorite truck is one that brings a treat.

Personal Response: Any well-supported positive or negative response to the content or ideas in the text; any reaction of humor or sadness in response to the ideas in the text; any well-supported positive or negative reaction to the text as a whole.

Rubric:

4 = All 3 macro concepts, 4 micro concepts, and a well-supported personal response.

3 = All 3 macro concepts, 3 or 4 micro concepts, no personal response.

2 = Two macro concepts, 2 or 3 micro concepts with some factual errors or omissions. Add ½ point for well-supported personal response.

1 = One or two macro concepts, 1 or 2 micro concepts, disjointed account with factual errors or omissions. Add ½ point for well-supported personal response.

0 = No or one macro concept, 1 micro concept; may provide a title or topic but shows little awareness of the relationships among key ideas in the text.

Retelling Score: _____

Comprehension Questions

1. Tell me one way that the passage tells us how trucks help people.

   Text-based: Put out fires; deliver boxes or gas; clean streets; bring ice cream.

2. What does the tanker truck use to pump gas?

   Text-based: Long hose.

3. Why do some trucks need to go fast?

   Inference: Going to put out fires.

4. Which truck in the story do you think helps people the most? Why?

   Critical Response: Fire truck—saves lives; tanker truck—delivers gas that people need; delivery truck—brings things people need.

5. Where does the child in the story probably live? Why?

   Inference: In or near a city: trucks, sidewalks, street cleaners, etc.

6. Why does the truck in the passage spray water?

   Text-based: It is cleaning the streets.

7. Why does the child in the story like the last truck best?

   Inference: He knows it is the ice cream truck.

8. The child in the story looks for trucks wherever he goes. Is that a good thing to do? Why?

   Critical Response: Yes, he likes trucks; he is interested in trucks No, he will miss other things that may be better; thinks too much about trucks.

Comprehension Analysis:

   Text-Based: __/3__
   Inference: __/3__
   Critical Response: __/2__

Total Comprehension %: _____

Reader's copy on p. 51 of the Reader's Passages.

Introductory Statement: "Would you read this passage about plants to yourself? When you are finished, I'll take the passage away. Then I'll ask you to tell me about what you read and what you think of it. After that, I'll ask you some questions about the passage."

Story

A man needs water.

He goes to the sink.

He gets a drink of water.

A cow needs water.

She goes to the stream.

She drinks water.

A plant needs water.

It can not move.

The plant has roots.

The roots grow in the soil.

The soil has water.

The soil has food.

The roots take in the water.

The roots take in food.

People eat the plants.

The plants are good for them.

They get food from the plants. (80 words)

Reading Accuracy Index: _____ %
   (N of words – N of miscues, checked and unchecked) /
   N of words

Meaning Maintenance Index: _____ %
   (N of words – N of meaning-violating miscues, unchecked
   only) / N of words

Plants: 80 words

Miscue Chart (for optional use as oral passage)

Miscues	%	Miscues	%
1	99	7	91
2	98	8	90
3	96	9	89
4	95	10	88
5	94	11	86
6	93	12	85

Retelling

Examiner: "Tell me about what you just read and what you thought about it."

If there is no spontaneous response, repeat the request, "Tell me what you thought about the passage."

Retelling Rubric

Macro Concepts (numbered) and Micro Concepts (bulleted):

1. Men and cows need water.
   • They can move to get water.
2. Plants cannot move.
   • They get their water from the soil.
   • They get their water through their roots.
   • They get their food from their roots too.
3. Plants are good for people.
   • People use plants for food.

Personal Response: Any well-supported positive or negative response to the content or ideas in the text; any reaction of humor or sadness in response to the ideas in the text; any well-supported positive or negative reaction to the text as a whole.

Rubric:

4 = All 3 macro concepts, 5 micro concepts, and a well-supported personal response.

3 = All 3 macro concepts, 4 or 5 micro concepts, no personal response.

2 = Two macro concepts, 3 or 4 micro concepts with some factual errors or omissions. Add ½ point for well-supported personal response.

1 = One or two macro concepts, 1 or 2 micro concepts, disjointed account with factual errors or omissions. Add ½ point for well-supported personal response.

0 = No or one macro concept, 1 or 2 micro concepts; may provide a title or topic but shows little awareness of the relationships among key ideas in the text.

Retelling Score: _____

Comprehension Questions

1. How does a plant get its water?

   Text-based: Roots take in water from the soil.

2. Why does a plant need roots? (Must identify one.)

   Text-based: To get water from the soil; to get food from the soil.

3. Why do plants die if there is no rain, but men and cows do not die?

   Inference: They can get water from other places; they can move to get water.

4. Who has an easier time getting the water it needs, a plant or a cow? Explain.

   Critical Response: Cow—it can walk to find water. Plant—it doesn't have to move or work at all.

5. Why can't plants get their water like cows do?

   Inference: They cannot move.

6. Why do people eat plants?

   Text-based: To get food

7. Could a cow ever have a problem getting water? Explain.

   Inference: Yes, if the streams dried up or if it could not move.

8. Which is more helpful to people, the roots or the soil?

   Critical Response: Roots—plant would not be able to get food or water without roots. Soil—if there were no water or food in the soil the plant could not live.

Comprehension Analysis:

   Text-Based: __/3__
   Inference: __/3__
   Critical Response: __/2__

Total Comprehension %: _____

Reader's copy on p. 52 of the Reader's Passages.

Introductory Statement: "Would you read this passage about turtles out loud for me? When you are finished, I'll take the passage away. Then I'll ask you to tell me about what you read and what you think of it. After that, I'll ask you some questions about the passage."

Story

Turtles can be big or small.

All turtles can crawl.

Some turtles can swim.

All turtles have hard shells.

A turtle can hide in its shell and be safe.

Small turtles make good pets.

They can live near a pond or a lake.

They eat worms, bugs, and grass.

Children often catch small turtles and take them home.

They can keep them in a large cage and take care of

    them.

They give the turtles water and food.

Large turtles live near the sea.

They catch their food in the sea.

They stay under the water for a long time.

They can swim very fast and can live a long

    time. (111 words)

Miscues

_____ N of miscues that maintained meaning (checked). This is the MM.

_____ N of miscues that violated meaning (unchecked). This is the MV.

Reading Accuracy Index: _____ %
    (N of words – N of miscues, checked and unchecked) / N of words

Meaning Maintenance Index: _____ %
    (N of words – N of meaning-violating miscues, unchecked only) / N of words

Turtles: 111 words

Miscue Chart

Miscues	%	Miscues	%	Miscues	%
1	99	7	94	13	88
2	98	8	93	14	87
3	97	9	92	15	86
4	96	10	91	16	86
5	95	11	90	17	85
6	95	12	89	18	84

Retelling

Examiner: "Tell me about what you just read and what you thought about it."

    If there is no spontaneous response, repeat the request, "Tell me what you thought about the passage."

NOTE: Use the Retelling Rubric on the next page to assess the child's retelling performance.

Retelling Rubric

Macro Concepts (numbered) and Micro Concepts (bulleted):

1. Turtles can be big or small.
2. Small turtles make good pets.
   - They are easy to take care of.
   - They are easy to find food for.
3. Large turtles do not always make good pets.
   - They live near the sea.
   - They catch their food in the sea.
   - They are hard to take care of.

Personal Response: Any well-supported positive or negative response to the content or ideas in the text; any reaction of humor or sadness in response to the ideas in the text; any well-supported positive or negative reaction to the text as a whole.

Rubric:

4 = All 3 macro concepts, 5 micro concepts, and a well-supported personal response.

3 = All 3 macro concepts, 4 or 5 micro concepts, no personal response.

2 = Two macro concepts, 3 or 4 micro concepts with some factual errors or omissions. Add ½ point for well-supported personal response.

1 = One or two macro concepts, 1 or 2 micro concepts, disjointed account with factual errors or omissions. Add ½ point for well-supported personal response.

0 = No or one macro concept, 1 or 2 micro concepts; may provide a title or topic but shows little awareness of the relationships among key ideas in the text.

Retelling Score: _____

Comprehension Questions

1. Why does a turtle need its shell?

   Text-based: The turtle hides inside; it keeps the turtle safe.

2. Where could you catch a small turtle?

   Text-based: Near a pond or lake

3. Would it be easy to find food for a small turtle? Why?

   Inference: Yes, bugs, worms, and grass are everywhere.

4. Which kind of turtle would be better to have for a pet and why?

   Critical Response: Small—easy to take care of; could keep him at home. Large—they live a long time; more work but worth it.

5. Which kind of turtle would be easier to catch if you wanted a pet?

   Inference: Small turtle—not as fast; do not live underwater; do not swim fast.

6. Why would it be hard to catch a large turtle?

   Text-based: They swim fast; they live in the sea.

7. Why don't we see large turtles as often as we see small ones?

   Inference: They live near the sea; they stay underwater for a long time.

8. Would it be right to keep a large turtle as a pet?

   Critical response: Yes, if you take care of it; if you have enough space. No, it needs too much water; it needs to be free; needs exercise.

Comprehension Analysis:

Text-based: __/3__
Inference: __/3__
Critical Response: __/2__

Total Comprehension %: _____

Reader's copy on p. 54 of the Reader's Passages.

Introductory Statement: "Would you read this passage about maps to yourself? When you are finished, I'll take the passage away. Then I'll ask you to tell me about what you read and what you think of it. After that, I'll ask you some questions about the passage."

Story

A pilot can fly an airplane.

He takes people from state to state.

He can go a long way but it does not take a long time.

He uses a map to find his way.

A lady can drive a truck.

She drives goods from state to state.

She goes a long way too, but it will take a long time.

Sometimes she needs a map.

We can take a trip in our car.

We do not always need a map.

But sometimes we can get lost.

Then a map can help.

Maps help people find the right way.

They keep people from going the wrong way.

(107 words)

Reading Accuracy Index: _____ %
(N of words – N of miscues, checked and unchecked) / N of words

Meaning Maintenance Index: _____ %
(N of words – N of meaning-violating miscues, unchecked only) / N of words

Maps: 107 Words

Miscue Chart (for optional use as oral passage)

Miscues	%	Miscues	%
1	99	8	93
2	98	9	92
3	97	10	91
4	96	11	90
5	95	12	89
6	94	13	88
7	93	14	87

Retelling

Examiner: "Tell me about what you just read and what you thought about it."

If there is no spontaneous response, repeat the request, "Tell me what you thought about the passage."

Retelling Rubric

Macro Concepts (numbered) and Micro Concepts (bulleted):

1. A pilot can fly an airplane.
   • Can go a long way in short time.
2. A lady can drive a truck.
   • Can go a long way but takes longer.
3. Both use maps to help them find their way.
   • We don't always need maps.
   • If we are lost, maps can help.

Personal Response: Any well-supported positive or negative response to the content or ideas in the text; any reaction of humor or sadness in response to the ideas in the text; any well-supported positive or negative reaction to the text as a whole.

Rubric:

4 = All 3 macro concepts, 4 micro concepts, and a well-supported personal response.

3 = All 3 macro concepts, 3 or 4 micro concepts, no personal response.

2 = Two macro concepts, 2 or 3 micro concepts with some factual errors or omissions. Add ½ point for well-supported personal response.

1 = One or two macro concepts, 1 or 2 micro concepts, disjointed account with factual errors or omissions. Add ½ point for well-supported personal response.

0 = No or one macro concept, 1 micro concept; may provide a title or topic but shows little awareness of the relationships among key ideas in the text.

Retelling Score: _____

Comprehension Questions

1. Where can both the pilot and the truck driver in the passage go?

   Text-based: Different states.

2. When would the people in the passage need to use a map?

   Text-based: If they were lost; to find their way.

3. Why wouldn't the truck driver need a map?

   Inference: She already knows the way.

4. If someone had to travel to another state, should he use a plane or a truck? Why?

   Critical Response: Truck—if it isn't far; safer. Plane—faster; can go longer distances faster.

5. Why would the pilot want to make sure that he does not get lost?

   Inference: He has a lot of people on board; does not want to run out of fuel.

6. How do maps help people?

   Text-based: They help them find their way.

7. Why should people keep a map in their car?

   Inference: To keep them from getting lost; to help them in case they get lost.

8. Who has the more important job, the pilot or the truck driver?

   Critical Response: Pilot—carries more people and truck driver only has herself and her goods. Truck driver—we need the things she carries; trucks move more goods than planes.

Comprehension Analysis:

Text-Based: __/3__
Inference: __/3__
Critical Response: __/2__

Total Comprehension %: _____

Reader's copy on p. 55 of the Reader's Passages.

Introductory Statement: "Would you read this passage about black bears out loud for me? When you are finished, I'll take the passage away. Then I'll ask you to tell me about what you read and what you think of it. After that, I'll ask you some questions about the passage."

Story

Black bears live in the U.S.

They live near woods or near mountains.

They live in dens.

The dens can be inside a tree or a cave.

They sleep all winter.

In spring, they wake up hungry.

Sometimes they can't find enough food.

They like to eat berries, honey, nuts, and acorns.

But they will eat almost anything.

If they don't find food close to home, they go out
    looking.

One bear and her cubs could not find enough to eat.

They came down the mountain.

They broke into someone's house.

This was very dangerous.

They took cookies, dog food, and honey.

The cubs took burgers off the grill.

People found them.

The cubs weighed only 20 pounds.

They should have weighed 50 pounds.

No wonder they were hungry. (129 words)

Miscues

_____ N of miscues that maintained meaning
(checked). This is the MM.
_____ N of miscues that violated meaning
(unchecked). This is the MV.

Reading Accuracy Index: _____ %
(N of words – N of miscues, checked and unchecked) /
N of words.

Meaning Maintenance Index: _____ %
(N of words – N of meaning-violating miscues, unchecked
only) / N of words

Black Bears: 129 words

Miscue Chart

Miscues	%	Miscues	%	Miscues	%
1	99	11	91	21	84
2	98	12	91	22	83
3	98	13	90	23	82
4	97	14	89	24	81
5	96	15	88	25	81
6	95	16	88	26	80
7	95	17	87	27	79
8	94	18	86	28	78
9	93	19	85	29	78
10	92	20	84	30	77

Retelling

Examiner: "Tell me about what you just read and what you thought about it."

If there is no spontaneous response, repeat the request, "Tell me what you thought about the passage."

NOTE: Use the Retelling Rubric on p. 214 to assess the child's retelling performance.

Macro Concepts (numbered) and Micro Concepts (bulleted):

1. Black bears live in the United States.
   • They live in dens.
   • They sleep all winter.
2. Black bears need to find food.
   • They wake up hungry.
   • They will eat anything.
3. Bears will come near people's homes to find food.
   • This can be very dangerous.

Personal Response: Any well-supported positive or negative response to the content or ideas in the text; any reaction of humor or sadness in response to the ideas in the text; any well-supported positive or negative reaction to the text as a whole.

Rubric:

4 = All 3 macro concepts, 5 micro concepts, and a well-supported personal response.

3 = All 3 macro concepts, 4 or 5 micro concepts, no personal response.

2 = Two macro concepts, 3 or 4 micro concepts with some factual errors or omissions. Add ½ point for well-supported personal response.

1 = One or two macro concepts, 1 or 2 micro concepts, disjointed account with factual errors or omissions. Add ½ point for well-supported personal response.

0 = No or one macro concept, 1 or 2 micro concepts; may provide a title or topic but shows little awareness of the relationships among key ideas in the text.

Retelling Score: _____

1. Why do black bears wake up hungry every spring?

   Text-based: They have been sleeping all winter; haven't eaten.

2. Why did the bears in the story leave their home in the mountain?

   Text-based: They couldn't find enough to eat.

3. Why don't we see black bears very often in the city?

   Inference: They live near mountains and woods; don't want their sleep to be disturbed.

4. Would bears rather eat people's food or food they could find nearer their homes? Why?

   Critical Response: Food near home—more familiar; less trouble; don't have to travel to eat. People's food—often better than wild food; often easier to find than food in the wild.

5. Is it a good idea for bears to break into homes looking for food?

   Inference: No, they could be shot and killed, do damage to the homes, or injure the people living there.

6. Why were the bear cubs in the story so thin?

   Text-based: They could not find enough to eat.

7. What could happen if the people came home and found the bears in their home?

Inference: Could panic; could be injured; could kill the bears.

8. Do you think the bears *should* sleep all winter instead of going out to find food? Why?

Critical Response: Yes, that is natural for them; they need to sleep in order to survive; there would be little food available in winter anyway. No, if they looked for food all winter they wouldn't be so hungry in the spring.

Comprehension Analysis:

Text-Based: __/3__
Inference: __/3__
Critical Response: __/2__

Total Comprehension %: _____

First Grade Silent: People in Groups

Reader's copy on p. 57 of the Reader's Passages.

Introductory Statement: "Would you read this passage about people living in groups to yourself? When you are finished, I'll take the passage away. Then I'll ask you to tell me about what you read and what you think of it. After that, I'll ask you some questions about the passage."

Story

Long ago people lived in groups.

They were called tribes.

They hunted and fished together.

They found plants and berries.

They moved on foot from place to place.

They followed the animals.

They killed only the animals they needed.

They did not grow their own food.

They had to work together to live.

Today people live in groups, too.

They live in cities and towns.

They still like to hunt and fish.

But now they grow their own food on farms.

They also raise their own animals.

But most people buy their food.

They have cars and planes to help them move.

But they still have to work together to live.

(111 words)

Reading Accuracy Index: _____ %
   (N of words – N of miscues, checked and unchecked) /
   N of words

Meaning Maintenance Index: _____ %
   (N of words – N of meaning-violating miscues, unchecked
   only) / N of words

People in Groups: 111 words

Miscue Chart (for optional use as oral passage)

Miscues	%	Miscues	%
1	99	8	93
2	98	9	92
3	97	10	91
4	96	11	90
5	95	12	89
6	95	13	88
7	94	14	87

Retelling

Examiner: "Tell me about what you just read and what you thought about it."

If there is no spontaneous response, repeat the request, "Tell me what you thought about the passage."

NOTE: Use the Retelling Rubric on the next page to assess the child's retelling performance.

Retelling Rubric

Macro Concepts (numbered) and Micro Concepts (bulleted):

1. Long ago people lived in tribes.
   - They moved from place to place.
   - They found food.
   - They hunted animals.
2. Today people live in cities or towns.
   - They grow their own food.
   - They buy it in stores.
3. But people must still work together.

Personal Response: Any well-supported positive or negative response to the content or ideas in the text; any reaction of humor or sadness in response to the ideas in the text; any well-supported positive or negative reaction to the text as a whole.

Rubric:

4 = All 3 macro concepts, 5 micro concepts, and a well-supported personal response.

3 = All 3 macro concepts, 4 or 5 micro concepts, no personal response.

2 = Two macro concepts, 3 or 4 micro concepts with some factual errors or omissions. Add ½ point for well-supported personal response.

1 = One or two macro concepts, 1 or 2 micro concepts, disjointed account with factual errors or omissions. Add ½ point for well-supported personal response.

0 = No or one macro concept, 1 or 2 micro concepts; may provide a title or topic but shows little awareness of the relationships among key ideas in the text.

Retelling Score: _____

Comprehension Questions

1. Why did people long ago have to move from place to place? (Must identify one.)

   Text-based: They needed to find food; they had to follow the animals; they had to catch fish.

2. Why don't people have to hunt and fish today?

   Text-based: They grow their own food; they raise their own animals; they can buy their own food.

3. Why did people long ago only kill the animals they needed?

   Inference: They didn't want to run out of food; they would starve if they killed too many.

4. Which group of people would need to work together more, people from long ago or people of today?

   Critical Response: Long ago; they would need to find hunting places; they would need to find fishing places; they would need to find berries and share their food. Today, people work in the stores to sell; not everybody grows food; we need people to fix the cars and planes.

5. Why didn't people from long ago live in cities and towns?

   Inference: They had to keep moving and they would have to leave their homes behind.

6. Why is it easier for people to find food today? (Must identify one.)

   Text-based: They can grow their own food; they can go to the store and buy it; they don't have to go out hunting.

7. Why do people who hunt for food need to work together?

   Inference: Better chance of catching an animal; they might feel safer.

8. When would you rather live, long ago or today? Why? (If reader responds on basis of background information only, use Examiner Probe it ask if there is information in the text to support their response.)

   Critical Response: Long ago—hunting and fishing would be fun. Today—safer and easier to get food, shelter.

Comprehension Analysis:

   Text-Based: __/3__
   Inference: __/3__
   Critical Response: __/2__

Total Comprehension %: _____

Reader's copy on p. 58 of the Reader's Passages.

Introductory Statement: "Would you read this passage about army ants out loud for me? When you are finished, I'll take the passage away. Then I'll ask you to tell me about what you read and what you think of it. After that, I'll ask you some questions about the passage."

Story

Do you ever run from ants? Some people in South America do. They run from the army ants. Army ants march in very large numbers looking for food. The ants are only about the size of your fingernail. But they have large and strong jaws. They march very slowly in a row four feet wide. But most armies are more than a mile long. All animals must get out of their way. They can bite and kill large animals and they can even kill men.

Army ants are hard to stop. They can climb over walls and trees. Not even water can stop them. They just hold onto each other with their jaws and then roll themselves into a ball. Then they can float across rivers and streams! Sometimes the ants march close to a village. Then the people must all move out. But some of the people are glad to see the ants. The ants clean up the town for them by killing small animals and pests. (168 words)

Miscues

_____ N of miscues that maintained meaning (checked). This is the MM.

_____ N of miscues that violated meaning (unchecked). This is the MV.

Reading Accuracy Index: _____%
   (N of words – N of miscues, checked and unchecked) / N of words

Meaning Maintenance Index: _____%
   (N of words – N of meaning-violating miscues, unchecked only) / N of words

Army Ants: 168 words

Miscue Chart

Miscues	%	Miscues	%	Miscues	%
1	99	11	93	21	88
2	99	12	93	22	87
3	98	13	92	23	86
4	98	14	92	24	86
5	97	15	91	25	85
6	96	16	90	26	85
7	96	17	90	27	84
8	95	18	89	28	83
9	95	19	89	29	83
10	94	20	88	30	82

Retelling

Examiner: "Tell me about what you just read and what you thought about it."

If there is no spontaneous response, repeat the request, "Tell me what you thought about the passage."

NOTE: Use the Retelling Rubric on p. 220 to assess the child's retelling performance.

Retelling Rubric

Macro Concepts (numbered) and Micro Concepts (bulleted):

1. Army ants in South America can be dangerous.
   - The armies have large numbers of ants.
   - The ants have strong jaws.
2. People can't avoid them so they must get out of the way.
   - The ants march in a row more than a mile long.
   - The ants can climb over walls.
   - The ants can float over streams.
3. Ants can do good as well as harm.
   - Ants clean up the town when they pass through.

Personal Response: Any well-supported positive or negative response to the content or ideas in the text; any reaction of humor or sadness in response to the ideas in the text; any well-supported positive or negative reaction to the text as a whole.

Rubric:

4 = All 3 macro concepts, 5 or 6 micro concepts, and a well-supported personal response.

3 = All 3 macro concepts, 4 to 6 micro concepts, no personal response.

2 = Two macro concepts, 3 or 4 micro concepts with some factual errors or omissions. Add ½ point for well-supported personal response.

1 = One or two macro concepts, 1 to 3 micro concepts, disjointed account with factual errors or omissions. Add ½ point for well-supported personal response.

0 = No or one macro concept, 1 or 2 micro concepts; may provide a title or topic but shows little awareness of the relationships among key ideas in the text.

Retelling Score: _____

Comprehension Questions

1. How big are army ants?

   Text-based: About the size of your fingernail.

2. How do the ants do something good for the people in the villages?

   Text-based: They clean up the village and remove pests.

3. Why can't animals just walk around the army of ants to get away from them?

   Inference: The row is more than a mile long.

4. Why don't people in the villages build a wall to protect themselves from the ants?

   Inference: The ants would be able to climb over the wall.

5. If you lived in a village, would you be happy or unhappy to see the ants coming? Explain.

   Critical Response: Unhappy—too much danger; very inconvenient to have to move out—where do they stay? Happy—the village and all the houses are free from pests; village is cleaner.

6. Why do the people in the villages move out when the ants are moving close by?

   Text-based: They would be bitten or killed by the ants.

7. If the army ants are so small, how would they be able to kill and eat a large animal?

   Inference: There are so many of them.

8. How do army ants cross rivers and streams?

   Text-based: They have to hold on to each other and float; they have to roll each other into a ball.

9. Would it be a good idea to jump into a river if the ants were biting you? Why or why not?

   Inference: Yes, the ants need their jaws to hold onto each other and they wouldn't be able to bite you.

10. Do you think it would be a good idea for the people in South America to kill all of the army ants?

    Critical Response: Yes, then there would be no danger to people and animals. No, the ants kill pests and without them there may be too many pests to control; some animals eats ants.

Comprehension Analysis:

   Text-Based: __/4__
   Inference: __/4__
   Critical Response: __/2__

Total Comprehension %: _____

Second Grade Silent: The Doctor Fish

Reader's copy on p. 59 of the Reader's Passages.

Introductory Statement: "Would you read this passage about a special kind of fish to yourself? When you are finished, I'll take the passage away. Then I'll ask you to tell me about what you read and what you think of it. After that, I'll ask you some questions about the passage."

Story

Some animals are a big help to other animals. One animal that helps others is the wrasse. The wrasse is a fish about four inches long. He is very brightly colored. He lives in the South Pacific Ocean. He is like a doctor to other fish.

His office is in the rocks called reefs. Many fish come to the doctor for help. These fish have animals that live on their bodies. They would like to have them taken off. The wrasse eats these tiny animals. He also uses his teeth to clean wounds. He helps the fish to get better.

The doctor can be very busy. Sometimes he works all day. But the doctor gets his pay too! The doctor gets the food he likes from his patients. They also protect the doctor from bigger fish. But the doctor and his patients must be careful. A fish called the blenny looks just like the wrasse. Some fish think they are coming to see the doctor. Then the blenny takes a bite out of them! That makes things worse. (178 words)

Reading Accuracy Index: _____%
  (N of words – N of miscues, checked & unchecked) /
  N of words

Meaning Maintenance Index: _____%
  (N of words – N of meaning-violating miscues, unchecked
  only) / N of words

The Doctor Fish: 178 words

Miscue Chart (for optional use as oral passage)

Miscues	%	Miscues	%
1	99	11	94
2	99	12	93
3	98	13	93
4	98	14	92
5	97	15	92
6	97	16	91
7	96	17	90
8	96	18	90
9	95	19	89
10	94	20	89

Retelling

Examiner: "Tell me about what you just read and what you thought about it."

If there is no spontaneous response, repeat the request, "Tell me what you thought about the passage."

NOTE: Use the Retelling Rubric on the next page to assess the child's retelling peformance.

Retelling Rubric

Macro Concepts (numbered) and Micro Concepts (bulleted):

1. The wrasse is like a doctor to other fish.
   - He eats little animals that live on fish.
   - He cleans their wounds.
2. The doctor fish is paid for his services.
   - Fish bring him food.
   - They protect the wrasse from harm.
3. The blenny fools fish into thinking he is a wrasse.
   - The blenny can be dangerous to fish.

Personal Response: Any well-supported positive or negative response to the content or ideas in the text; any reaction of humor or sadness in response to the ideas in the text; any well-supported positive or negative reaction to the text as a whole.

Rubric:

4 = All 3 macro concepts, all 5 micro concepts, and a well-supported personal response.

3 = All 3 macro concepts, 4 or 5 micro concepts, no personal response.

2 = Two macro concepts, 3 or 4 micro concepts with some factual errors or omissions. Add ½ point for well-supported personal response.

1 = One or two macro concepts, 1 to 2 micro concepts, disjointed account with factual errors or omissions. Add ½ point for well-supported personal response.

0 = No or one macro concept, 1 or 2 micro concepts; may provide a title or topic but shows little awareness of the relationships among key ideas in the text.

Retelling Score: _____

Comprehension Questions

1. How is the wrasse like a doctor? (Must identify two.)

   Text-based: He helps sick fish; he cleans wounds; he has an office; he gets paid.

2. How do fish pay the doctor for his help? (Must identify one.)

   Text-based: The animals that live on them are food for the wrasse; they will protect the wrasse from other fish.

3. How can fish find the wrasse when they need help?

   Inference: They know where the office is located; they can tell by the bright colors of the wrasse.

4. What advantages does the blenny have by looking just like the wrasse?

   Inference: Gets food from biting the fish; other fish may even protect him.

5. Would a human doctor accept the same kind of pay that the doctor fish does? Explain.

   Critical Response: No, doctors don't need protection from patients. Yes, doctors may accept food or other things in exchange for treatment.

6. Where is the doctor fish's office?

   Text-based: In the rocks; in the reefs.

7. Why would other fish protect the wrasse from harm?

   Inference: They may need his help one day.

8. Why would the doctor fish be very busy some days?

   Text-based: Some days there are many fish who need his help.

9. Why wouldn't the wrasse be able to help every kind of fish that lives in the ocean?

   Inference: He would be too big to help some and too small to help very large fish.

10. Who do you think gets the better deal, the wrasse or the fish that he helps? Tell why.

   Critical Response: The wrasse gets food that he likes; he gets protection from bigger fish. Fish he helps, they get the animals taken off; they get their wounds cleaned; they get better.

Comprehension Analysis:

   Text-Based: __/4__
   Inference: __/4__
   Critical Response: __/2__

Total Comprehension %: _____

Third Grade Oral: The Immigrants

Reader's copy on p. 60 of the Reader's Passages.

Introductory Statement: "Would you read this passage about immigrants out loud for me? When you are finished, I'll take the passage away. Then I'll ask you to tell me about what you read and what you think of it. After that, I'll ask you some questions about the passage."

Story

Between 1820 and 1920 many people moved to America. Some came to find better jobs. Others came because they were not free in their own lands. Others came because their country's leaders did not like them. Most people just came looking for a better life. They were called immigrants.

Most of these people came to America on sailing ships. Some trips took only a few weeks. Others took months. Some people could afford a cabin for themselves. They were lucky. The rest stayed in large rooms below the deck. The rooms were crowded and often dirty. The food was very poor. The ocean was sometimes rough. The trip was very dangerous.

The immigrants finally arrived in New York. Then they would wait in line for hours. They had to find out if they would be allowed to stay. There was a long line for most people. There was a short line for richer people.

Many of these new Americans were not welcome. They could not speak English. They were different and strange. They were willing to work for low wages. But some factory owners would not hire them at all. These owners all seemed to forget one thing. Almost everyone in America had family members who were immigrants themselves. (209 words)

Miscues

_____ N of miscues that maintained meaning (checked). This is the MM.
_____ N of miscues that violated meaning (unchecked). This is the MV.

Reading Accuracy Index: _____%
(N of words − N of miscues, checked and unchecked) / N of words

Meaning Maintenance Index: _____%
(N of words − N of meaning-violating miscues, unchecked only) / N of words

The Immigrants (220 words)

Miscue Chart

Miscues	%	Miscues	%	Miscues	%
1	100	12	95	23	90
2	99	13	94	24	89
3	99	14	94	25	89
4	98	15	93	26	88
5	98	16	93	27	88
6	97	17	92	28	87
7	97	18	92	29	87
8	96	19	91	30	86
9	96	20	91	31	86
10	95	21	90	32	85
11	95	22	90	33	85

Retelling

Examiner: "Tell me about what you just read and what you thought about it."

If there is no spontaneous response, repeat the request, "Tell me what you thought about the passage."

NOTE: Use the Retelling Rubric on p. 226 to assess the child's retelling performance.

Retelling Rubric

Macro Concepts (numbered) and Micro Concepts (bulleted):

1. People came to America to find a better life.
   - Some came looking for freedom.
   - Some came looking for jobs.
2. It was a difficult journey to America.
   - It was a long and dangerous trip by ship.
   - Conditions on the ship were poor.
3. Immigrants had hard lives when they arrived.
   - Many were not welcome.
   - They were mistreated by others.

Personal Response: Any well-supported positive or negative response to the content or ideas in the text; any reaction of humor or sadness in response to the ideas in the text; any well-supported positive or negative reaction to the text as a whole.

Rubric:

4 = All 3 macro concepts, 5 or 6 micro concepts, and a well-supported personal response.

3 = All 3 macro concepts, 4 to 6 micro concepts, no personal response.

2 = Two macro concepts, 3 or 4 micro concepts with some factual errors or omissions. Add ½ point for well-supported personal response.

1 = One or two macro concepts, 1 to 3 micro concepts, disjointed account with factual errors or omissions. Add ½ point for well-supported personal response.

0 = No or one macro concept, 1 or 2 micro concepts; may provide a title or topic but shows little awareness of the relationships among key ideas in the text.

Retelling Score: _____

Comprehension Questions

1. Why were rich people luckier than the poor people? (Must identify one.)

   Text-based: Could have their own cabins; did not have to wait in line.

2. Why did the immigrants have to wait in line when they got to New York?

   Text-based: To see if they would be allowed to stay.

3. Why would trips on some sailing ships take longer than others?

   Inference: Storms, bad weather, ill wind, longer distances.

4. Why would people who were already rich want to come to America?

   Inference: Probably were disliked by leaders or were not free in their countries.

5. Was it right for people with more money to be treated differently from the others?

   Critical Response: No, everyone should be treated as equals; money does not make you better. Yes, they did not need the services; they could pay for what they needed.

6. Why were there two lines in New York?

   Text-based: One for the rich and one for the poor.

7. Why were the trips across the ocean so dangerous?

Inference: Storms; bad food, and dirt caused illness.

8. How were many immigrants treated when they got to America?

Text-based: Badly; were not welcome; hard to find jobs.

9. Why should the United States continue to welcome immigrants?

Inference: People still need a better life; most of us have immigrants in our family history; differences among people can be good.

10. Would you hire an immigrant if you were a factory owner? Why or why not?

Critical Response: Yes, cheaper labor; give them a chance. No, could not speak English and would not understand instructions.

Comprehension Analysis:

Text-Based: __/4__
Inference: __/4__
Critical Response: __/2__

Total Comprehension %:____

Reader's copy on p. 61 of the Reader's Passages.

Introductory Statement: "Would you read this passage about child slaves to yourself? When you are finished, I'll take the passage away. Then I'll ask you to tell me about what you read and what you think of it. After that, I'll ask you some questions about the passage."

Story

Everyone knows that slavery is wrong. But slavery is still very common. And one of its worst forms is child slavery. Poor families are the most likely victims. Farm owners can make families pay for their food and shelter. The family cannot earn enough to pay the owners back. So everyone in the family works to try to pay the debt. Most of the time, they will never succeed. But the owners don't care! All those years of cheap work are too valuable.

Often the parents can no longer work. But the children must still work for the owners. The children can not go to school. They can never stop working to pay what they owe. Some owners are at least kind to the children. Then their life is a little better. But other owners are cruel. Children may not get enough food to stay healthy. If the child misses a day of work, the family must pay a fine. Then they will owe even more.

Many countries have laws against children working. But no one in the family knows about the laws. They don't know that their children have rights. And so it is very difficult to stop people from using children as slaves. (205 words)

Reading Accuracy Index: _____%
    (N of words – N of miscues, checked and unchecked) / N of words

Meaning Maintenance Index: _____%
    (N of words – N of meaning-violating miscues, unchecked only) / N of words

Child Slaves: 205 words

Miscue Chart (for optional use as oral passage)

Miscues	%	Miscues	%
1	100	12	94
2	99	13	94
3	99	14	93
4	98	15	93
5	98	16	92
6	97	17	92
7	97	18	91
8	96	19	91
9	96	20	90
10	95	21	90
11	95	22	89

Retelling

Examiner: "Tell me about what you just read and what you thought about it."

If there is no spontaneous response, repeat the request, "Tell me what you thought about the passage."

NOTE: Use the Retelling Rubric on the next page to assess the child's retelling performance.

Retelling Rubric

Macro Concepts (numbered) and Micro Concepts (bulleted):

1. Child slavery is a terrible thing.
   - Owners can be cruel to their slaves.
2. Child slavery usually happens to the poor.
   - Owners charge families for their food and shelter.
   - Families build up debt.
   - Everyone in family must work to pay off debt.
3. Child slavery is difficult to stop.
   - There are laws against child slavery.
   - Families often don't know about the laws.

Personal Response: Any well-supported positive or negative response to the content or ideas in the text; any reaction of humor or sadness in response to the ideas in the text; any well-supported positive or negative reaction to the text as a whole.

Rubric:

4 = All 3 macro concepts, 5 or 6 micro concepts, and a well-supported personal response.

3 = All 3 macro concepts, 4 to 6 micro concepts, no personal response.

2 = Two macro concepts, 3 to 4 micro concepts with some factual errors or omissions. Add ½ point for well-supported personal response.

1 = One or two macro concepts, 1 to 3 micro concepts, disjointed account with factual errors or omissions. Add ½ point for well-supported personal response.

0 = No or one macro concept, 1 or 2 micro concepts; may provide a title or topic but shows little awareness of the relationships among key ideas in the text.

Retelling Score: _____

Comprehension Questions

1. Why can't the families pay back what they owe and go work for someone else?

   Text-based: They don't earn enough money.

2. Why don't the owners care that the families cannot pay their debts?

   Text-based: They make more money from the families' work.

3. Why is it better for the farmers to keep the pay of families very low?

   Inference: So that they can never pay off their debt and they will have to work all of their lives.

4. What makes farmers think that they can get away with using children as slaves?

   Inference: Parents don't know about the laws.

5. Why would people think that slavery of children is worse than any other kind?

   Critical Response: Children are more helpless than adults; have no protection against stronger people; they won't be able to get a better job.

6. What happens if a child's parents become too old or sick to work?

   Text-based: The child must work to pay off the parents' debt.

7. Why are poor families the most likely to end up as slaves?

   Inference: They have no power to fight back; do not know about their rights by law; can be easily cheated by owners; have no other source of food or shelter.

8. Why are some poor families always in debt?

   Text-based: They owe the farmer money for their shelter and food; they never earn enough to pay him back.

9. Why will the child slaves never be able to get better jobs or have a better future?

   Inference: Without schooling, they would not be able to do anything else.

10. What would be the best way of stopping the use of children as slaves?

    Critical Response: Making children go to school; have laws against slavery; regulating the use of labor by owners; informing the workers of their rights; fining the owners who do these things; setting a minimum wage.

Comprehension Analysis:

   Text-Based: __/4__
   Inference: __/4__
   Critical Response: __/2__

Total Comprehension %: _____

Fourth Grade Oral: Frida Kahlo

Reader's copy on p. 62 of the Reader's Passages.

Introductory Statement: "Would you read this passage about an artist out loud for me? When you are finished, I'll take the passage away. Then I'll ask you to tell me about what you read and what you think of it. After that, I'll ask you some questions about the passage."

Story

Frida Kahlo was born in Mexico in 1907. She was an intelligent and beautiful young woman. She planned to become a doctor. But when she was 18 years old, she was hurt while riding a bus. The accident broke her back in three places. After a long time in the hospital, she had to stay in bed for months. To pass the time, Frida began to paint. She soon found her talent and her love.

Some of her friends saw that Frida's paintings were very interesting. They helped her to meet Diego Rivera, a famous Mexican painter. Diego helped Frida to develop as a painter. They soon fell in love and married. But their marriage was troubled and painful. Frida soon learned that painting helped her to deal with her feelings. She painted many pictures of herself. She often said that she was the subject she knew best of all.

Frida had many operations on her back. Her great pain and her great strength made their way into her paintings. She had a rare ability to express pain and unhappiness through art. For this reason Frida Kahlo is seen as one of the truly great talents of her time. A museum in Mexico shows only her works. She is one of very few women artists who have ever achieved that honor. (221 words)

Miscues

_____ N of miscues that maintained meaning (checked). This is the MM.

_____ N of miscues that violated meaning (unchecked). This is the MV.

Reading Accuracy Index: _____%
(N of words – N of miscues, checked and unchecked) / N of words

Meaning Maintenance Index: _____%
(N of words – N of meaning-violating miscues, unchecked only) / N of words

Frida Kahlo: 221 words

Miscue Chart

Miscues	%	Miscues	%	Miscues	%
1	100	12	95	23	90
2	99	13	94	24	89
3	99	14	94	25	89
4	98	15	93	26	88
5	98	16	93	27	88
6	97	17	92	28	87
7	97	18	92	29	87
8	96	19	91	30	86
9	96	20	91	31	86
10	95	21	90	32	85
11	95	22	90	33	85

Retelling

Examiner: "Tell me about what you just read and what you thought about it."

If there is no spontaneous response, repeat the request, "Tell me what you thought about the passage."

NOTE: Use the Retelling Rubric on p. 232 to assess the child's retelling performance.

Retelling Rubric

Macro Concepts (numbered) and Micro Concepts (bulleted):

1. Frida Kahlo had a serious accident.
   - She began painting to pass time in the hospital.
2. Frida met and married a Mexican painter.
   - He helped her grow as a painter.
   - They were often unhappy together.
3. Frida used painting to work out her feelings of pain and unhappiness.
4. Frida became one of the greatest talents of her time.
   - Has an entire museum that shows only her works.

Personal Response: Any well-supported positive or negative response to the content or ideas in the text; any reaction of humor or sadness in response to the ideas in the text; any well-supported positive or negative reaction to the text as a whole.

Rubric:

4 = All 4 macro concepts, 4 micro concepts, and a well-supported personal response.

3 = All 4 macro concepts, 3 or 4 micro concepts, no personal response.

2 = Three macro concepts, 2 or 3 micro concepts with some factual errors or omissions. Add ½ point for well-supported personal response.

1 = Two macro concepts, 1 or 2 micro concepts, disjointed account with factual errors or omissions. Add ½ point for well-supported personal response.

0 = No or one macro concept, 1 or 2 micro concepts; may provide a title or topic but shows little awareness of the relationships among key ideas in the text.

Retelling Score: _____

Comprehension Questions

1. Why did Frida Kahlo begin to paint?

   Text-based: Pass the time when she was recovering from the accident.

2. Why did Frida paint many pictures of herself?

   Text-based: She said she was the subject she knew best.

3. Why could Diego help Frida to become a better painter?

   Inference: He was already well-known and had more experience than Frida.

4. What would you think that Frida looked like in her pictures of herself?

   Inference: Sad, unhappy, in great pain.

5. Some people say that without her pain and unhappiness, Frida would never have become a great painter. Do you agree? Why or why not?

   Critical Response: Yes, the pain gave her the subject matter; she would not have discovered painting unless she was in the hospital. No, she had talent and she would probably have used it for different subjects.

6. Why did her friends introduce Frida to Diego Rivera?

   Text-based: Saw that her paintings were interesting; recognized her talent.

7. Why would people say that Frida had a great deal of strength as well as talent?

   Inference: She had to endure much pain and painted throughout the years of suffering.

8. How do we know that Mexico honors Frida as a great artist?

   Text-based: There is a museum there that shows only her work.

9. Why is it unusual for a woman to achieve the honor of her own museum?

   Inference: Women artists are not as well known; receive less attention; are not expected to be as good as male artists.

10. How does Frida's life show that the ability to draw and paint does not make anyone a great artist?

    Critical Response: Must be able to express emotions like pain and suffering; must enable people to see ideas in the paintings.

Comprehension Analysis:

  Text-Based: __/4__
  Inference: __/4__
  Critical Response: __/2__

Total Comprehension %:____

Fourth Grade Silent: Krakatoa (crack-uh-toe-uh)

Reader's copy on p. 63 of the Reader's Passages.

Introductory Statement: "Would you read this passage about a famous volcano to yourself? When you are finished, I'll take the passage away. Then I'll ask you to tell me about what you read and what you think of it. After that, I'll ask you some questions about the passage."

Story

Krakatoa was a small island volcano about five miles wide. Over many years it had grown bigger from dozens of small eruptions and lava flows. That was before the morning of August 27, 1883. At the end of that day there was almost no island left. The volcano had exploded. Almost three quarters of the island was gone. Much of it was blown miles into the sky. The dust in the air shaded the sun for months.

It was lucky that no people lived on the island. But there were many islands close by where people did live. The huge waves caused by the blast killed many people. Some waves were as high as twelve story buildings. They washed whole villages into the sea. Almost 36,000 people died.

The explosion of Krakatoa was heard 2,800 miles away. Windows in homes 100 miles away were broken. Many people think that the explosion was the biggest that ever happened on earth. Over the years a new volcano has risen. It is very close to the old island. Some people believe that it took Krakatoa's place. It has been named "Child of Krakatoa." Many people have read about that first great explosion. Some of them believe that we may not have heard the last of Krakatoa after all. (215 words)

Reading Accuracy Index: _____%
(N of words – N of miscues, checked and unchecked) / N of words.

Meaning Maintenance Index: _____%
(N of words – N of meaning-violating miscues, unchecked only) / N of words

Krakatoa: 214 words

Miscue Chart (for optional use as oral passage)

Miscues	%	Miscues	%
1	100	12	94
2	99	13	94
3	99	14	93
4	98	15	93
5	98	16	93
6	97	17	92
7	97	18	92
8	96	19	91
9	96	20	91
10	95	21	90
11	95	22	90

Retelling

Examiner: "Tell me about what you just read and what you thought about it."

If there is no spontaneous response, repeat the request, "Tell me what you thought about the passage."

NOTE: Use the Retelling Rubric on the next page to assess the child's retelling performance.

Retelling Rubric

Macro Concepts (numbered) and Micro Concepts (bulleted):

1. The Krakatoa volcano erupted in the 1800s.
   - Three quarters of the island was blown away.
2. Krakatoa caused much damage.
   - The volcano's eruption created huge waves.
   - 36,000 people were killed by the flooding from the waves.
   - Some believe it was the biggest explosion ever on earth.
3. A new volcano has taken Krakatoa's place.
   - There may be another great eruption some day.

Personal Response: Any well-supported positive or negative response to the content or ideas in the text; any reaction of humor or sadness in response to the ideas in the text; any well-supported positive or negative reaction to the text as a whole.

Rubric:

4 = All 3 macro concepts, all 5 micro concepts, and a well-supported personal response.

3 = All 3 macro concepts, 4 or 5 micro concepts, no personal response.

2 = Two macro concepts, 3 or 4 micro concepts with some factual errors or omissions. Add ½ point for well-supported personal response.

1 = One or two macro concepts, 1 or 2 micro concepts, disjointed account with factual errors or omissions. Add ½ point for well-supported personal response.

0 = No or one macro concept, 1 or 2 micro concepts; may provide a title or topic but shows little awareness of the relationships among key ideas in the text.

Retelling Score: _____

Comprehension Questions

1. How much of the island of Krakatoa disappeared in the explosion?

   Text-based: Three quarters.

2. How many people died in the explosion of Krakatoa?

   Text-based: 36,000; almost or nearly 36,000.

3. Why were there no people living on Krakatoa?

   Inference: Too many eruptions in the past.

4. Why didn't the people on the other islands get out of the way of the waves?

   Inference: Too big or came too quickly; no warning.

5. Which is more dangerous to people, volcanoes or huge waves?

   Critical Response: Huge waves—these actually killed the people rather than the volcano. Volcano—actually caused the tidal waves.

6. When did the explosion of Krakatoa take place?

   Text-based: 1883; at the end of the 1800s.

7. Why would people say that Krakatoa caused the biggest explosion on earth?

Inference: It was heard so far away.

8. Why was the new volcano named "Child of Krakatoa?"

Text-based: It grew up very close to the original volcano.

9. Would Krakatoa have had an effect on farmers in the nearby islands? Why?

Inference: Yes, the shading of the sun would affect crops.

10. If "Child of Krakatoa" exploded today, would it cause the same damage and death as Krakatoa did? Explain.

Critical Response: No, we have better communication and more warnings; better buildings. Yes, the islands have more people on them now and so more lives could be lost.

Comprehension Analysis:

Text-Based: __/4__
Inference: __/4__
Critical Response: __/2__

Total Comprehension %: _____

Fifth Grade Oral: The Mosquito

Reader's copy on p. 64 of the Reader's Passages.

Introductory Statement: "Would you read this passage about mosquitoes out loud for me? When you are finished, I'll take the passage away. Then I'll ask you to tell me about what you read and what you think of it. After that, I'll ask you some questions about the passage."

Story

The next time you smack a mosquito on your arm and say to yourself, "Got him!" you should think again. Actually you got *her!* Only the female mosquito does the biting. She is in search of fresh blood to feed the eggs that will soon become more little Draculas. The female mosquito finds her victims by following streams of carbon dioxide. This is the gas that is exhaled by the warm-blooded animals she seeks. The carbon dioxide guides the mosquito to her prey.

Once she has found you, she is hard to stop. Unless you hear the telltale buzzing of her wings, you will probably never know she is there. She lands very lightly on her feet. Once she has landed she inserts her long, needle-like nose into your skin. Her nose is so thin that most people never feel the needle at all. Before she can start sipping your blood, she injects a little saliva to make it thinner. Otherwise it is like trying to drink a thick milk shake through a straw. It is the saliva that the mosquito leaves behind that makes the skin itch and swell.

Some people are lucky enough to feel her and fast enough to smack her. She may leave a smear of blood on their bare arm. But they weren't fast enough. That blood they see is their own! It is no surprise that mosquitoes are not the most popular of insects, unless you happen to be a spider or a bat! In addition to being pests, they also carry and spread diseases like malaria and the West Nile virus. But until we think of a better way to control them, mosquitoes will continue to annoy any animal that has blood and thin skin. (292 words)

Miscues

_____ N of miscues that maintained meaning (checked). This is the MM.

_____ N of miscues that violated meaning (unchecked). This is the MV.

Reading Accuracy Index: _____%
(N of words – N of miscues, checked and unchecked) / N of words

Meaning Maintenance Index: _____%
(N of words – N of meaning-violating miscues, unchecked only) / N of words

The Mosquito: 292 words

Miscue Chart

Miscues	%	Miscues	%	Miscues	%
1	100	13	96	25	91
2	99	14	95	26	91
3	99	15	95	27	91
4	99	16	95	28	90
5	98	17	94	29	90
6	98	18	94	30	90
7	98	19	93	31	89
8	97	20	93	32	89
9	97	21	93	33	89
10	97	22	92	34	88
11	96	23	92	35	88
12	96	24	92	36	88

Retelling

Examiner: "Tell me about what you just read and what you thought about it."

If there is no spontaneous response, repeat the request, "Tell me what you thought about the passage."

NOTE: Use the Retelling Rubric on p. 238 to assess the child's retelling performance.

Retelling Rubric

Macro Concepts (numbered) and Micro Concepts (bulleted):

1. Only female mosquitoes bite.
   - They need blood to feed their eggs.
   - They find blood by following exhaled carbon dioxide.
2. It is hard to avoid being bitten by mosquitoes.
   - They land very lightly.
   - They have a very thin nose.
   - They inject saliva to thin the blood.
3. Mosquitoes spread diseases.
   - They spread malaria or West Nile virus.

Personal Response: Any well-supported positive or negative response to the content or ideas in the text; any reaction of humor or sadness in response to the ideas in the text; any well-supported positive or negative reaction to the text as a whole.

Rubric:

4 = All 3 macro concepts, 5 or 6 micro concepts, and a well-supported personal response.

3 = All 3 macro concepts, 4 to 6 micro concepts, no personal response.

2 = Two macro concepts, 3 to 4 micro concepts with some factual errors or omissions. Add ½ point for well-supported personal response.

1 = One or two macro concepts, 1 to 3 micro concepts, disjointed account with factual errors or omissions. Add ½ point for well-supported personal response.

0 = No or one macro concept, 1 or 2 micro concepts; may provide a title or topic but shows little awareness of the relationships among key ideas in the text.

Retelling Score: _____

Comprehension Questions

1. Why does a mosquito's bite itch?

   Text-based: The saliva she leaves behind irritates the skin.

2. Why does the female mosquito need fresh blood?

   Text-based: She needs the blood to feed her eggs.

3. When you kill a mosquito, how can you tell if it has bitten you?

   Inference: If you see blood, it has probably bitten you.

4. Why can't the mosquito drink your blood without thinning it first?

   Inference: The blood is too thick; her nose is too thin.

5. If you were a mosquito, would you be more likely to prey on a person or a dog? Why?

   Critical Response: Person—skin is easier to get to; there are more people around than dogs; dogs have fur to protect them. Dogs—they are less likely to feel the mosquito; can't swat them as easily as humans can.

6. How can you tell if a mosquito is a male or a female?

   Text-based: Only the female bites.

7. Why can't people avoid being bitten by mosquitoes?

   Inference: You can't stop breathing; mosquitoes are everywhere, even indoors; can't feel her when she lands.

8. Why does the mosquito inject saliva under your skin?

   Text-based: Needs to thin out the blood before she drinks it.

9. How could a mosquito possibly spread a disease from one person to another?

   Inference: Can spread blood in its saliva from one person to another.

10. If you must go outside in the summer, what is the best way to avoid being bitten by a mosquito?

    Critical Response: Cover up all exposed areas of skin; stay out for short periods of time; use mosquito repellant.

Comprehension Analysis:

Text-Based: __/4__
Inference: __/4__
Critical Response: __/2__

Total Comprehension %: _____

Reader's copy on p. 65 of the Reader's Passages.

Introductory Statement: "Would you read this passage about an oil spill to yourself? When you are finished, I'll take the passage away. Then I'll ask you to tell me about what you read and what you think of it. After that, I'll ask you some questions about the passage."

Story

On the night of March 24, 1989, a huge oil tanker named the *Exxon Valdez* ran into a reef in Prince William Sound in Alaska. It was carrying oil from the Alaska Pipeline to the mainland United States. More than 11 million gallons of crude oil spilled from the ship. This was the largest oil spill in U.S. history. The spill was a terrible shock to the residents and Coast Guard that night. They did not know that the spill would soon get much worse.

At first, the Coast Guard tried to burn up the oil. But bad weather made controlled burning difficult. Then cleanup crews tried to scoop the oil from the water. But their equipment quickly became clogged with seaweed and thick oil. To make matters even worse, the spill site could be reached only by boat or helicopter. Crews sent to help clean oil-coated animals were slow to arrive. Then they just could not work fast enough. There were too many birds and animals that needed to be cleaned. The oil spill is estimated to have killed 250,000 sea birds, including 250 bald eagles. Nearly 3,000 sea otters and 22 killer whales were lost in the spill as well.

All in all, 140 miles of coastline were soaked with oil. Nearly 1,500 miles had some oil. Exxon Corporation has spent an estimated 2.5 billion dollars in the clean-up of the spill. The fishing industry in Alaska is still not the same. Many fishermen feel that it never will

be. Experts predict that the effects of the spill will be felt for decades to come. (267 words)

Reading Accuracy Index: _____%
  (N of words – N of miscues, checked and unchecked) / N of words

Meaning Maintenance Index: _____%
  (N of words – N of meaning-violating miscues, unchecked only) / N of words

Oil Spill: 267 words

Miscue Chart (for optional use as oral passage)

Miscues	%	Miscues	%	Miscues	%
1	100	10	96	19	93
2	99	11	96	20	93
3	99	12	96	21	92
4	99	13	95	22	92
5	98	14	95	23	91
6	98	15	94	24	91
7	97	16	94	25	91
8	97	17	94	26	90
9	97	18	93	27	90

Retelling

Examiner: "Tell me about what you just read and what you thought about it."

If there is no spontaneous response, repeat the request, "Tell me what you thought about the passage."

NOTE: Use the Retelling Rubric on the next page to assess the child's retelling performance.

Retelling Rubric

Macro Concepts (numbered) and Micro Concepts (bulleted):

1. *Exxon Valdez* spilled a huge amount of oil.
   • The ship ran into a reef in Alaska.
2. The oil was very difficult to clean up.
   • There were equipment problems.
   • Bad weather prevented clean-up.
   • Crews arrived late to help.
3. The cost of the spill was huge.
   • 2.5 billion dollars in costs
   • Damage to the area's fishing industry and wildlife.

Personal Response: Any well-supported positive or negative response to the content or ideas in the text; any reaction of humor or sadness in response to the ideas in the text; any well-supported positive or negative reaction to the text as a whole.

Rubric:

4 = All 3 macro concepts, 5 or 6 micro concepts, and a well-supported personal response.

3 = All 3 macro concepts, 4 to 6 micro concepts, no personal response.

2 = Two Macro Concepts, 3 to 4 micro concepts with some factual errors or omissions. Add ½ point for well-supported personal response.

1 = One or two macro concepts, 1 to 3 micro concepts, disjointed account with factual errors or omissions. Add ½ point for well-supported personal response.

0 = No or one macro concept, 1 or 2 micro concepts; may provide a title or topic but shows little awareness of the relationships among key ideas in the text.

Retelling Score: _____

Comprehension Questions

1. What caused the *Exxon Valdez* to spill her oil?

   Text-based: The ship hit a reef.

2. Why didn't burning the oil work?

   Text-based: Bad weather made it difficult.

3. Why did it cost Exxon Corporation so much money to clean up after the spill?

   Inference: All the men and equipment were required to clean hundreds of miles of shoreline.

4. Why couldn't volunteers who wanted to help clean the animals get to the oil spill very quickly?

   Inference: The site could be reached only by boat and helicopter.

5. If you were in charge, would you allow tankers to carry oil on the oceans? Why or why not?

   Critical Response: No, too much chance of disaster; dangerous to sail near rocks and reefs. Yes, must get the oil from Alaska to the United States and there is no other way; one disaster doesn't mean that most shipping is not safe.

6. Why couldn't the volunteers save more birds than they did?

   Text-based: There were too many birds; they could not work fast enough.

7. Why wasn't the Coast Guard able to deal with the problem as soon as it happened?

Inference: Spill was too large; they weren't equipped to deal with it; everything went wrong.

8. What happened when the Coast Guard tried to scoop the oil from the water?

Text-based: Their equipment became clogged with oil and seaweed.

9. Why would the fishing industry be affected so many years after the spill?

Inference: Oil would affect the breeding grounds of the fish; loss of so many fish-eating mammals would affect the fish as well; disturbance of food chain is serious.

10. Was it right to make the Exxon Corporation pay for the total cost of oil cleanup? Why or why not?

Critical Response: Yes, it was their ship; they had responsibility for any damage that was done. No, it was an accident; really no one's fault.

Comprehension Analysis:

Text-Based: __/4__
Inference: __/4__
Critical Response: __/2__

Total Comprehension %: _____

Sixth Grade Oral: A Community of Wolves

Reader's copy on p. 66 of the Reader's Passages.

Introductory Statement: "Would you read this passage about wolves out loud for me? When you are finished, I'll take the passage away. Then I'll ask you to tell me about what you read and what you think of it. After that, I'll ask you some questions about the passage."

Story

Wolves are probably one of the most misunderstood animals on our planet. Many myths and legends depict wolves as tricky, cunning, and dangerous. Who doesn't remember "The Big Bad Wolf" and "Little Red Riding Hood" or the "Werewolf" legend? This image, however, couldn't be further from the truth. Wolves may be dangerous . . . to rabbits, deer, pigs, sheep, and cattle. But you don't have to worry that one will eat you or your granny up!

Actually wolves are part of a closely-knit family that consists of 2 to 10 adults and any young pups. All of the wolves in the pack share responsibility for the young. The wolves travel in packs for the sake of more successful hunting, for mutual protection, and for companionship. Wolves are also territorial. They usually travel within a specific range, sometimes up to 50 square miles.

Many experts believe that it is the wolf's eerie howl that plays on the fears of man. In fact, their howl is part of a sophisticated communication system within their group. Howling is the wolves' way of "staying in touch" over long distances. If a wolf is separated from her pack, she will begin howling. This is a cry for help as well as a call to reunite. It can, however, be very costly. If a competing pack is within her range, they may seek her out and kill her. Pups are especially vulnerable. They have not yet learned the appropriate times and places for howling.

Other purposes for howling include warning rival packs to keep moving or staking a claim on fresh-killed prey. The so-called "chorus howls" are used to make competing packs think that there are really more wolves in the pack. The next time you hear a wolf howl, you will know it is not a werewolf howling at the moon. Perhaps it is only a lost wolf looking for its pack.

(315 words)

Miscues

_____ N of miscues that maintained meaning (checked). This is the MM.
_____ N of miscues that violated meaning (unchecked). This is the MV.

Reading Accuracy Index: _____%
    (N of words – N of miscues, checked and unchecked) / N of words

Meaning Maintenance Index: _____%
    (N of words – N of meaning-violating miscues, unchecked only) / N of words

A Community of Wolves: 315 words

Miscue Chart

Miscues	%	Miscues	%	Miscues	%
1	100	13	96	25	92
2	99	14	96	26	92
3	99	15	95	27	91
4	99	16	95	28	91
5	98	17	95	29	91
6	98	18	94	30	90
7	98	19	94	31	90
8	97	20	94	32	90
9	97	21	93	33	90
10	97	22	93	34	89
11	97	23	93	35	89
12	96	24	92	36	89

Retelling

Examiner: "Tell me about what you just read and what you thought about it."

If there is no spontaneous response, repeat the request, "Tell me what you thought about the passage."

Retelling Rubric

Macro Concepts (numbered) and Micro Concepts (bulleted):

1. Wolves are misunderstood and feared by people.
   - Wolves live in close-knit families.
   - Wolves work together and protect each other.
2. Howling may be part of the reason for fear of wolves.
3. Howling is a means of communication among wolves.
   - If a wolf is separated from the pack, howling can be a call for help.
   - Howling can be dangerous to wolves.
   - Other pack may hear the howl and kill the lone wolf.

Personal Response: Any well-supported positive or negative response to the content or ideas in the text; any reaction of humor or sadness in response to the ideas in the text; any well-supported positive or negative reaction to the text as a whole.

Rubric:

4 = All 3 macro concepts, 5 micro concepts, and a well-supported personal response.

3 = All 3 macro concepts, 4 or 5 micro concepts, no personal response.

2 = Two macro concepts, 3 or 4 micro concepts with some factual errors or omissions. Add ½ point for well-supported personal response.

1 = One or two macro concepts, 1 or 2 micro concepts, disjointed account with factual errors or omissions. Add ½ point for well-supported personal response.

0 = No or one macro concept, 1 or 2 micro concepts; may provide a title or topic but shows little awareness of the relationships among key ideas in the text.

Retelling Score: _____

Comprehension Questions

1. What advantages are there for wolves traveling in a pack? (Must identify one.)

   Text-based: Better hunting, protection, companionship.

2. Why would ranchers or farmers fear and dislike wolves?

   Text-based: Wolves will kill their livestock for food.

3. How is the wolf pack similar to a human family?

   Inference: Stay together; take care of each other; communicate with each other.

4. Why would chorus howling be a way for wolves to solve their problems with competing packs?

   Inference: Would make a competing pack less likely to attack; makes it seem that they have more wolves.

5. Is it a good idea for a wolf to howl and let others know that he had found food? Why or why not?

   Critical Response: Yes, that way the wolf can share his kill with the pack.; should howl only if the rest of the pack is nearby. No, other wolves may hear the howl and take the kill; may even kill the wolf.

6. What purposes does howling serve? (Must identify one.)

   Text-based: Communication with the pack; cry for help; attempt to reunite with pack.

7. What advantages are there for wolves killing off another pack of wolves?

   Inference: Can take over their territory; more food and better hunting.

8. Why is killing one wolf usually not the solution to the problem if a rancher is losing his livestock to wolf attacks?

   Text-based: There are many wolves in the pack; they are territorial and will stay wherever there is food.

9. Do wolves ever do anything good for farmers and ranchers?

   Inference: Yes, they kill rabbits and deer that may eat the farmers' crops.

10. Do you think that the stories about wolves are fair? Why or why not?

    Critical Response: Yes, wolves are clever hunters; they do try to deceive other packs. No, wolves are really families who help and support each other.

Comprehension Analysis:

Text-Based: /4
Inference: /4
Critical Response: /2

Total Comprehension %: _____

Sixth Grade Silent: Are You Afraid of Sharks?

Reader's copy on p. 67 of the Reader's Passages.

Introductory Statement: "Would you read this passage about sharks to yourself? When you are finished, I'll take the passage away. Then I'll ask you to tell me about what you read and what you think of it. After that, I'll ask you some questions about the passage."

Story

Every summer in the United States, we hear about shark attacks. On some beaches, it is even common to see sharks swimming offshore. Other beaches will be closed because there are so many sharks swimming near the shore. But how likely is it that if you go for a dip in the ocean you will be attacked by a shark? Not very likely at all!

We are far more likely to be killed by another person than by a shark. Most scientists believe that the few shark attacks that occur are really mistakes. When we tan, the top portion of our foot turns brown while the bottom remains white. This shading is similar to that of many fish. Others think sharks mistake us for sea lions or seals, which are some of their favorite food. When they realize that they have made a mistake, most sharks simply spit out their victims and leave. Just think about it . . . if sharks wanted to have us for dinner on a regular basis, they could just come to any shore in the United States and help themselves.

Sharks should probably be more afraid of us than we are of them. The total shark population is in decline as a result of human hunting. For example, in some countries, shark fin soup is a delicacy and the fins are very much in demand. The shark fin itself is often used in ceremonial dinners. When local fishermen capture the shark, they will use the entire body, but commercial fishers have been known to follow the practice of "finning."

They cut off the fins of any sharks caught in their nets. They then throw the sharks back into the sea, leaving them to bleed to death. And *we're* afraid of *them*?

Because we do not have "shark farms" as we do for catfish or shrimp, constant fishing leads to over-killing of certain kinds of sharks. They simply cannot reproduce quickly enough to keep up with the demand. Although we may fear sharks with good cause, destroying them beyond rescue may be even more harmful to us all in the long run. (353 words)

Reading Accuracy Index: _____%
   (N of words – N of miscues, checked and unchecked) / N of words.

Meaning Maintenance Index: _____%
   (N of words – N of meaning-violating miscues, unchecked only) / N of words.

Are You Afraid of Sharks?: 353 words

Miscue Chart (for optional use as oral passage)

Miscues	%	Miscues	%	Miscues	%
1	100	14	96	27	92
2	99	15	96	28	92
3	99	16	95	29	92
4	99	17	95	30	92
5	99	18	95	31	91
6	98	19	95	32	91
7	98	20	94	33	91
8	98	21	94	34	90
9	97	22	94	35	90
10	97	23	93	36	90
11	97	24	93	37	90
12	97	25	93	38	89
13	96	26	93	39	89

Retelling

Examiner: "Tell me about what you just read and what you thought about it."

If there is no spontaneous response, repeat the request, "Tell me what you thought about the passage."

Retelling Rubric

Macro Concepts (numbered) and Micro Concepts (bulleted):

1. We hear about shark attacks every summer.
   - But attacks are very unlikely.
2. Scientists believe that most attacks are mistakes.
   - Sharks mistake us for seals or sea lions.
   - They spit us out when they realize the mistake.
3. Sharks have more to fear from humans.
   - Men hunt sharks.
   - "Finning" of sharks is common in some places.
   - Sharks can't reproduce fast enough to keep up with demand.

Personal Response: Any well-supported positive or negative response to the content or ideas in the text; any reaction of humor or sadness in response to the ideas in the text; any well-supported positive or negative reaction to the text as a whole.

Rubric:

4 = All 3 macro concepts, 5 or 6 micro concepts, and a well-supported personal response.

3 = All 3 macro concepts, 4 to 6 micro concepts, no personal response.

2 = Two macro concepts, 3 or 4 micro concepts with some factual errors or omissions. Add ½ point for well-supported personal response.

1 = One or two macro concepts, 1 to 3 micro concepts, disjointed account with factual errors or omissions. Add ½ point for well-supported personal response.

0 = No or one macro concept, 1 or 2 micro concepts; may provide a title or topic but shows little awareness of the relationships among key ideas in the text.

Retelling Score: _____

Comprehension Questions

1. Why are some beaches in the United States closed every summer?

   Text-based: Sharks can be seen swimming offshore.

2. Why would sharks spit out humans after just one bite?

   Text-based: They probably do not like the taste; they realize that they have made a mistake.

3. Why would fishermen bother to cut the fins from sharks that they've caught?

   Inference: They sell them for profit.

4. How would the local fishermen feel about commercial fishermen finning sharks? Why?

   Inference: They would probably disapprove of the waste of the sharks.

5. Do you think it would be a good idea for people to start shark farms as a solution to the shark-fishing problem? Why or why not?

   Critical Response: Yes, it may reduce some of the fishing of sharks that goes on. No, probably wouldn't work; takes too long to reproduce sharks.

6. What is the greatest danger to sharks?

   Text-based: Humans and hunting.

7. Is the author afraid of sharks? Why do you think that?

   Inference: Probably not, seems to know that there is little danger from sharks.

8. What is the explanation that most scientists give for shark attacks?

   Text-based: Mistaken identity.

9. Do we really know why sharks attack humans?

   Inference: No, it is a theory; we cannot be sure.

10. Should finning of sharks be banned? Why or why not?

    Critical Response: No, it is a cultural practice to eat shark fin soup; there are still many sharks in the sea. Yes, the shark populations are low; the sharks are being wasted by careless people.

Comprehension Analysis:

Text-Based: __/4__
Inference: __/4__
Critical Response: __/2__

Total Comprehension %: _____

Junior High Oral (Grades 7–9): Mary Jemison

Reader's copy on p. 68 of the Reader's Passages.

Introductory Statement: "Would you read this passage about an Indian captive out loud for me? When you are finished, I'll take the passage away. Then I'll ask you to tell me about what you read and what you think of it. After that, I'll ask you some questions about the passage."

Story

Mary Jemison was born in 1743 on board a ship sailing to America. Her family settled in a rural community near what is now Gettysburg, Pennsylvania. Mary's father showed no fear of the reports of Indian raids that he heard from their neighbors. Her mother, however, had always felt differently. On April 5th, 1758, her fears came true. A party of French soldiers and Indians raided the Jemison farm. Her terrified mother told Mary to obey her captors, remember her English language, and never forget who she was. Mary was taken away by her captors. Unknown to her, Mary's parents and most of the rest of her family were killed. Mary would have to rely only on her mother's words throughout the long days of captivity.

Mary was given to a pair of Seneca Indian women whose brother had been killed in battle. The women had a simple choice. They could kill Mary in revenge for their lost brother. Or they could adopt her to replace him. They chose to adopt Mary and treated her as their own sister, with a great deal of kindness. Mary missed her parents and family and could not at first be happy. She prayed and practiced her English language every day. But she eventually came to appreciate and respect her two new sisters. At the same time, she began to recognize the qualities that the Indian tribe demonstrated in their daily life. She characterized the Indians as extremely faithful to each other, very honest and honorable in all that they did. Mary married a Seneca warrior in 1765 and had several children of her own.

After the Revolutionary War, Mary was offered her freedom by the tribe. Her son was anxious to see his mother go and live with her own people. Mary, however, could not bring herself to leave her son. She also worried about how she and her family would be treated by white people. She was afraid they might view her as a traitor. And so she chose to remain with her Indian family and spend the remainder of her days with them. Mary Jemison died in 1831, having spent more than 70 years as an Indian captive. (367 words)

Miscues

_____ N of miscues that maintained meaning (checked). This is the MM.

_____ N of miscues that violated meaning (unchecked). This is the MV.

Reading Accuracy Index: _____%
   (N of words – N of miscues, checked and unchecked) / N of words

Meaning Maintenance Index: _____%
   (N of words – N of meaning-violating miscues, unchecked only) / N of words

Mary Jemison: 367 words

Miscue Chart

Miscues	%	Miscues	%	Miscues	%	Miscues	%
1	100	13	96	25	93	37	90
2	99	14	96	26	93	38	90
3	99	15	96	27	93	39	89
4	99	16	96	28	92	40	89
5	99	17	95	29	92	41	89
6	98	18	95	30	92	42	89
7	98	19	95	31	92	43	88
8	98	20	95	32	91	44	88
9	98	21	94	33	91	45	88
10	97	22	94	34	91	46	87
11	97	23	94	35	90	47	87
12	97	24	93	36	90	48	87

Retelling

Examiner: "Tell me about what you just read and what you thought about it."

If there is no spontaneous response, repeat the request, "Tell me what you thought about the passage."

Retelling Rubric

Macro Concepts (numbered) and Micro Concepts (bulleted):

1. Mary Jemison was taken from her family by Indians.
   - Her family was killed.
2. Two Indian sisters took Mary into their home.
   - They had a choice: kill her or take her into the family.
   - They took her in and treated her with kindness.
3. Mary accepted the Indian way of life.
   - She came to appreciate the Indians as honest and faithful.
   - She married an Indian warrior.
   - She chose to stay with the Indians and her son when she had the chance to return to her own people.

Personal Response: Any well-supported positive or negative response to the content or ideas in the text; any reaction of humor or sadness in response to the ideas in the text; any well-supported positive or negative reaction to the text as a whole.

Rubric:

4 = All 3 macro concepts, 5 or 6 micro concepts, and a well-supported personal response.

3 = All 3 macro concepts, 4 to 6 micro concepts, no personal response.

2 = Two macro concepts, 3 or 4 micro concepts with some factual errors or omissions. Add ½ point for well-supported personal response.

1 = One or two macro concepts, 1 to 3 micro concepts, disjointed account with factual errors or omissions. Add ½ point for well-supported personal response.

0 = No or one macro concept, 1 or 2 micro concepts; may provide a title or topic but shows little awareness of the relationships among key ideas in the text.

Retelling Score: _____

Comprehension Questions

1. Why was Mary given to the two Indian women?

   Text-based: To replace their brother who was killed.

2. Why did Mary choose to stay with the Indians when she was offered her freedom? (Must identify one.)

   Text-based: She could not leave her son; she was worried about how people would treat her.

3. What would make us think that Mary respected and appreciated her Indian companions?

   Inference: She married one of the Indian warriors.

4. Why would her own people treat Mary as if she were a traitor?

   Inference: She joined an Indian tribe and married one of its members; many people saw the Indians as dangerous enemies.

5. What reasons could Mr. Jemison have for not taking the warning about Indians seriously?

   Critical Response: He might have thought the reports were exaggerated; may have thought the military would protect them; may have thought it couldn't happen to his family.

6. Why was Mary unhappy even though the two women treated her with kindness?

   Text-based: She missed her family and her own home.

7. Why would Mary's mother tell her to always obey her captors?

   Inference: So that she could avoid being mistreated, punished, or killed.

8. Why could the sisters have chosen to kill Mary instead of adopt her?

   Text-based: To avenge the death of their brother.

9. Why would Mary's son be anxious to see his mother rejoin her own people?

   Inference: He thought she would be happy with them; wanted to see her captivity come to an end.

10. What would make Mary think that Indians were kind and honorable after they had killed her family?

    Critical Response: They adopted her and treated her with kindness; she observed their everyday dealings with each other.

Comprehension Analysis:

   Text-Based: __/4__
   Inference: __/4__
   Critical Response: __/2__

Total Comprehension %: _____

Reader's copy on p. 69 of the Reader's Passages.

Introductory Statement: "Would you read this passage about the Mississippi River to yourself? When you are finished, I'll take the passage away. Then I'll ask you to tell me about what you read and what you think of it. After that, I'll ask you some questions about the passage."

Story

For many Midwestern Americans living along the floodplains of the Mississippi River, the Great River was the source of their livelihood. The commercial traffic that flowed daily on the river provided goods and employment for thousands of people. But as William Faulkner wrote, the river was like a mule that would work for you for ten years just for the privilege of kicking you once.

And one of the river's hardest kicks was delivered in 1993. A huge flood left 74,000 people without homes in nine states. It caused over 15 billion dollars in damage. To be sure, the Mississippi had flooded before. Old-timers in the town could remember many flood years in their lifetimes. But 1993 seemed to almost everyone to be the worst of them all. This flood broke high-water records all across the Midwest. But to the people living along the floodplains, the Great Flood of 1993 was simply another of life's challenges to be met and overcome. They would rebuild their homes with help from the Federal Emergency Management Agency (FEMA). Life would go on just as it had so many times in the past.

But this time things were different. The U.S. Congress was apparently tired of flood emergency claims year after year. Instead, they announced a grand social experiment. They would no longer help the citizens living on floodplains to rebuild their homes in the same place. Congress instructed FEMA to help them rebuild their homes and towns in locations that were not as prone to flooding. In 1993 alone, over 10,000 homes were relocated. But hardships, as always, seemed to relocate along with the homes. Many citizens complained that their new homes, built on more expensive land, drove up their mortgage debt. Others felt the loss of friends as towns and communities went their separate ways rather than relocating together.

But there were also many success stories. Many towns managed to stay intact and to plan newer and better communities. Many local leaders emerged to help their friends and fellow townspeople ease the stresses of the drastic changes in their lives. It is too early to tell whether the experiment has worked for the greater good of all. Only one thing is certain. The U.S. Congress will probably never again help flood victims to stay in the same places just to wait for the next Great Flood to strike. (396 words)

Reading Accuracy Index: _____%
   (N of words – N of miscues, checked and unchecked) /
   N of words

Meaning Maintenance Index: _____%
   (N of words – N of meaning-violating miscues, unchecked
   only) / N of words

Old Man River: 396 words

Miscue Chart (for optional use as oral passage)

Miscues	%	Miscues	%	Miscues	%
1	100	14	96	27	93
2	99	15	96	28	93
3	99	16	96	29	93
4	99	17	96	30	92
5	99	18	95	31	92
6	98	19	95	32	92
7	98	20	95	33	92
8	98	21	95	34	91
9	98	22	94	35	91
10	97	23	94	36	91
11	97	24	94	37	91
12	97	25	94	38	90
13	97	26	93	39	90

Retelling

Examiner: "Tell me about what you just read and what you thought about it."

If there is no spontaneous response, repeat the request, "Tell me what you thought about the passage."

Retelling Rubric

Macro Concepts (numbered) and Micro Concepts (bulleted):

1. The Mississippi River flooded in the 1900s.
   - Worst flood ever.
   - Left thousands homeless.
   - They expected that the government would help them rebuild as always.
2. Government decided to help people move, not rebuild.
   - This was a social experiment.
   - Many were unhappy but there were many successes too.
3. Too early to tell if the experiment was a success.
   - But government will probably never just rebuild homes again.

Personal Response: Any well-supported positive or negative response to the content or ideas in the text; any reaction of humor or sadness in response to the ideas in the text; any well-supported positive or negative reaction to the text as a whole.

Rubric:

4 = All 3 macro concepts, 5 or 6 micro concepts, and a well-supported personal response.

3 = All 3 macro concepts, 4 to 6 micro concepts, no personal response.

2 = Two macro concepts, 3 or 4 micro concepts with some factual errors or omissions. Add ½ point for well-supported personal response.

1 = One or two macro concepts, 1 to 3 micro concepts, disjointed account with factual errors or omissions. Add ½ point for well-supported personal response.

0 = No or one macro concept, 1 or 2 micro concepts; may provide a title or topic but shows little awareness of the relationships among key ideas in the text.

Retelling Score: _____

Comprehension Questions

1. What was different about the 1993 flood from those that went before? (Must identify one.)

   Text-based: It was more serious; families did not move back to the same place.

2. Why weren't all of the people happy about getting a new home after the flood? (Must identify one.)

   Text-based: Mortgages were higher; land was more expensive.

3. What made many people think that the relocation experiment would succeed?

   Inference: Leaders emerged who helped people and helped keep communities together; people came together to help each other.

4. What did William Faulkner mean when he said "The river is like a mule that will work for you for 10 years just for the privilege of kicking you once?"

   Inference: River provided many good things but then became a huge problem when it was least expected.

5. Do you think that Faulkner was right? (Explain concept if child got previous item incorrect.)

   Critical Response: Yes, the problems that occurred with the flood outweighed the good that had been done before it; the flood was worse than the good things. No, the river had provided many years of jobs and good things and one incident couldn't outweigh them all.

6. What did the people along the river expect FEMA to do after the 1993 floods?

   Text-based: Help them rebuild their homes in the same place.

7. Why wouldn't the government just help people to rebuild their homes wherever they wanted?

   Inference: It cost too much to keep rebuilding after every flood.

8. What did Congress tell FEMA to do instead?

   Text-based: Help them rebuild in different locations away from the river.

9. Why would people want to rebuild along the river after so many floods?

   Inference: It was their home town; they knew their neighbors and were comfortable where they were.

10. Do you think that the U.S. Congress was right to experiment with people's lives? Explain.

    Critical Response: Yes, if it worked, they would save a great deal of money; the idea was a good one and would make things better for everyone. No, people should be free to live where they want; government should not be playing with people's lives.

Comprehension Analysis:

Text-Based: __/4__
Inference: __/4__
Critical Response: __/2__

Total Comprehension %: _____

Reader's copy on p. 70 of the Reader's Passages.

Introductory Statement: "Would you read this passage about America's search for Pancho Villa out loud for me? When you are finished, I'll take the passage away. Then I'll ask you to tell me about what you read and what you think of it. After that, I'll ask you some questions about the passage."

Story

America's hunt for the infamous Mexican revolutionary Pancho Villa in 1916 was in reality the result of a series of botched political, economic, and military decisions. The United States had huge business interests in Mexico, interests that were threatened by the Mexican Revolution of 1910. Anxious to protect these interests, President Woodrow Wilson decided to throw his support behind Venustiano Carranza as the Mexican president. Carranza was the man he believed to be most sympathetic to the American agenda. But Carranza was fearful of alienating his own people by showing favor to the hated neighbor to the north. He refused to give in to some of Wilson's demands. Wilson then began to supply another revolutionary, Pancho Villa, with arms and supplies. It was Wilson's hope that Villa would be more favorably inclined to the United States if he came into power.

But Villa's potential as a threat to the Mexican leader failed to materialize. Wilson decided to make his peace with Carranza and recognize his government. Villa was infuriated at the desertion of Wilson. In retaliation, he and his men killed 16 Americans traveling on a train in Mexico. But his boldest attack occurred on American soil in the town of Columbus, New Mexico, and left 19 Americans dead. Villa hoped that by provoking a counterattack by the Americans, he could turn popular opinion against Carranza and expose his ties to the United States. Then Villa would be waiting in the wings to assume the leadership of all of Mexico.

America, in its turn, launched what came to be known as the Punitive Expedition against Villa and his men. Wilson sent General John J. Pershing and 5,000 soldiers, equipped with trucks, armored vehicles, and even airplanes into Mexico to hunt down Villa and his army. But Pershing underestimated Villa's enormous support and popularity among the Mexican people. They consistently protected their local Robin Hood, giving Villa advance notice of Pershing's movements. They even supplied false information about Villa's whereabouts to Pershing's troops. After nearly two years of trying, Pershing had nothing to show for his efforts. He had not even come close to locating Villa. The Punitive Expedition was finally called off.

Despite the miserable failure of the Expedition in achieving its primary end, many historians consider it a resounding success in the larger scheme of things. With the threat of World War I looming, American troops had the chance to familiarize themselves with their new weapons and technology. In particular, their use of reconnaissance aircraft, despite its failure in the short term, led to a great deal of success in the preparation for the war against Germany. (439 words)

Miscues

_____ N of miscues that maintained meaning (checked). This is the MM.
_____ N of miscues that violated meaning (unchecked). This is the MV.

Reading Accuracy Index: _____%
(N of words – N of miscues, checked and unchecked) / N of words

Meaning Maintenance Index: _____%
(N of words – N of meaning-violating miscues, unchecked only) / N of words

The Search for Pancho Villa: 439 words

Miscues	%	Miscues	%	Miscues	%	Miscues	%
1	100	13	97	25	94	37	91
2	100	14	97	26	94	38	91
3	99	15	97	27	94	39	91
4	99	16	96	28	94	40	91
5	99	17	96	29	93	41	91
6	99	18	96	30	93	42	90
7	98	19	96	31	93	43	90
8	98	20	95	32	93	44	90
9	98	21	95	33	92	45	90
10	98	22	95	34	92	46	89
11	97	23	95	35	92	47	89
12	97	24	94	36	92	48	89

Retelling

Examiner: "Tell me about what you just read and what you thought about it."

If there is no spontaneous response, repeat the request, "Tell me what you thought about the passage."

Macro Concepts (numbered) and Micro Concepts (bulleted):

1. The U.S. problem with Villa was the result of a series of mistakes.
   - The United States first supported Carranza for Mexican president.
   - When he did not cooperate, Wilson began to support Villa.
   - When Villa did not become strong enough, Wilson returned to Carranza.
2. Villa retaliated against Wilson's disloyalty.
   - Villa attacked Americans on American soil.
3. U.S. sent General Pershing and 5000 troops to find Villa.
   - The people protected Villa.
   - Punitive Expedition never found Villa but it did help the United States prepare for World War I.

Personal Response: Any well-supported positive or negative response to the content or ideas in the text; any reaction of humor or sadness in response to the ideas in the text; any well-supported positive or negative reaction to the text as a whole.

Rubric:

4 = All 3 macro concepts, 5 or 6 micro concepts, and a well-supported personal response.

3 = All 3 macro concepts, 4 to 6 micro concepts, no personal response.

2 = Two macro concepts, 3 or 4 micro concepts with some factual errors or omissions. Add ½ point for well-supported personal response.

1 = One or two macro concepts, 1 to 3 micro concepts, disjointed account with factual errors or omissions. Add ½ point for well-supported personal response.

0 = No or one macro concept, 1 or 2 micro concepts; may provide a title or topic but shows little awareness of the relationships among key ideas in the text.

Retelling Score: _____

Comprehension Questions

1. What would President Carranza gain by refusing to give in to President Wilson's demands?

   Text-based: He would show his people that he was not favoring the United States.

2. Why did President Wilson abandon Pancho Villa after first giving him arms and supplies?

   Text-based: He did not become a threat to the Mexican President; it became clear that Villa would not become Mexico's leader.

3. What did Presidents Wilson and Carranza have in common with respect to their political decisions?

   Inference: Both had their own interests in mind at all times; neither one trusted the other.

4. Did Mexico have any reason for hating the United States?

   Inference: Yes, the United States was interfering in their affairs; the U.S. president did not seem to care about who was in charge of Mexico, but only if they were favorable to the United States.

5. Was Pancho Villa successful in his quest for power in Mexico? Explain.

   Critical Response: Yes, he achieved success with the people and through his popularity; he had power because Pershing could not locate him. No, he did not attain his ultimate goal of the presidency; he was on the run constantly from the U.S. troops and could not even show his face without being in danger.

6. How did the United States benefit from the Punitive Expedition?

   Text-based: They learned to use their new technology and equipment; learned about aerial surveillance techniques; practiced for the first World War.

7. Why would the people of Mexico consider Pancho Villa another Robin Hood?

   Inference: He was hunted down by more powerful enemies; he was much loved by the common people; people saw him as a hero who would protect them.

8. Why did Pancho Villa turn against the United States?

   Text-based: The United States recognized the government of Carranza; it stopped providing him with aid.

9. With 20–20 hindsight, how should Pershing have gone about finding and arresting Villa?

   Critical Response: He could have used spies to infiltrate his organization; could pay Mexican people for information on Villa's whereabouts; could have tried to undermine the trust people had in Villa; could have offered bribes for information.

10. How does the saying "You reap what you sow" fit both President Wilson and Pancho Villa?

    Inference: Wilson strengthened Villa and then had to pay the price; Villa's lack of political skill kept him from becoming a threat to Carranza.

Comprehension Analysis:

Text-Based: __/4__
Inference: __/4__
Critical Response: __/2__

Total Comprehension %: _____

Reader's copy on p. 72 of the Reader's Passages.

Introductory Statement: "Would you read this passage about quasars to yourself? When you are finished, I'll take the passage away. Then I'll ask you to tell me about what you read and what you think of it. After that, I'll ask you some questions about the passage."

Story

Ever since the dawn of humanity, searching the skies with more and more sophisticated instruments has led to a spate of new discoveries almost too breathtaking to keep up with. In the 1940s, for example, radio astronomers found that many objects in the night sky were emitting radio waves; most of these sources were common stars. But some faint blue-colored objects in the celestial landscapes were very difficult to explain. They looked like stars but they emitted a huge quantity of very intense radio and ultraviolet waves, much more than could be expected from a typical star.

It was not until 1963 that Dr. Maarten Schmidt explained the phenomenon. Examining the strange light spectrum emitted by one of the "stars," Schmidt deduced that the unusual red-shifted spectrum lines (the measure of an object's recession velocity) were part of a simple hydrogen spectrum. However, the only way that the objects could produce this type of spectrum is if they were traveling away from Earth at a speed of almost 30,000 miles per second! And if that were correct, the objects would be more than 3 billion light years away, making them the most distant and, arguably, the most fascinating objects ever discovered in our universe. Because they were not true stars, scientists dubbed the strange objects *quasars* (for quasi-stellar radio sources).

Scientists were at a loss to explain how telescopes on earth could still detect such distant objects. To be detectable from earth, quasars would have to emit light as intense as that produced by 1,000 entire galaxies but yet take up space only about the size of our own solar system. But scientists today believe that the brightness of a quasar can be accounted for by the presence of super-sized black holes in the midst of huge galaxies. Black holes suck in passing stars and clouds of gas and, in doing so, heat huge amounts of matter to such an extent that it emits stupendous amounts of light.

Because quasars are so distant, they must have been created in the very early stages of the development of the universe. Indeed, it would be logical to conclude that since it is taking 3 billion years for the light of some quasars to reach us, those quasars are no longer in existence. Only their light, still traveling over the vast expanses of the universe, is reaching us today. It is certainly true that quasars still raise more questions than scientists have answers. But quasars are objects that unquestionably challenge the imagination of scientists and laymen alike as we seek more and more answers to the mysteries of the universe. (437 words)

Reading Accuracy Index: _____%
  (N of words – N of miscues, checked and unchecked) / N of words
Meaning Maintenance Index: _____%
  (N of words – N of meaning-violating miscues, unchecked only) / N of words
Quasars: 437 words

Miscue Chart (for optional use as oral passage)

Miscues	%	Miscues	%	Miscues	%
1	100	15	97	29	93
2	100	16	96	30	93
3	99	17	96	31	93
4	99	18	96	32	93
5	99	19	96	33	92
6	99	20	95	34	92
7	98	21	95	35	92
8	98	22	95	36	92
9	98	23	95	37	92
10	98	24	95	38	91
11	97	25	94	39	91
12	97	26	94	40	91
13	97	27	94	41	91
14	97	28	94	42	90

Retelling

Examiner: "Tell me about what you just read and what you thought about it."

If there is no spontaneous response, repeat the request, "Tell me what you thought about the passage."

Retelling Rubric

Macro Concepts (numbered) and Micro Concepts (bulleted):

1. Scientists discovered objects in the sky emitting large amounts of radio waves.
   - Schmidt interpreted the red-shift lines in the spectrum of the light from these objects.
   - Concluded that they were 3 billion light years away.
   - They were not true stars so they were called quasars.
2. Quasars would have to be incredibly bright to be seen from so far away.
   - Quasars produce the light of 1,000 galaxies.
   - Scientists believe they are black holes heating up matter as they suck it in.
3. Many quasars are no longer in existence.
   - Only the light is still traveling toward us for 3 billion years.

Personal Response: Any well-supported positive or negative response to the content or ideas in the text; any reaction of humor or sadness in response to the ideas in the text; any well-supported positive or negative reaction to the text as a whole.

Rubric:

4 = All 3 macro concepts, 5 or 6 micro concepts, and a well-supported personal response.

3 = All 3 macro concepts, 4 to 6 micro concepts, no personal response.

2 = Two macro concepts, 3 or 4 micro concepts with some factual errors or omissions. Add ½ point for well-supported personal response.

1 = One or two macro concepts, 1 to 3 micro concepts, disjointed account with factual errors or omissions. Add ½ point for well-supported personal response.

0 = No or one macro concept, 1 or 2 micro concepts; may provide a title or topic but shows little awareness of the relationships among key ideas in the text.

Retelling Score: _____

Comprehension Questions

1. What did the passage say was so different about quasars that first made scientists curious about them?

   Text-based: They emitted huge amounts of radio waves.

2. Why aren't quasars considered true stars?

   Text-based: They are the size of the entire solar system.

3. Why would scientists find it hard to believe that quasars were 3 billion light years from the earth?

   Inference: Their light was still visible from earth.

4. Why would the distance of quasars cause scientists to conclude that they were formed in the early stages of the universe?

   Inference: They must have been created early to have traveled such a huge distance; if they were moving at 30,000 miles per second, it would have taken huge amounts of time to travel 3 billion light years.

5. Based on the information in this passage, how much progress do you think scientists have made in explaining the mysteries of the universe?

   Critical Response: Not much, we don't even know what else is out there to be discovered; we can not yet see all of the universe. A great deal, scientists have discovered and explained many new phenomena; our technology has improved tremendously and so has our understanding.

6. How could we see quasars if most of them are no longer in existence?

   Text-based: Their light is still traveling for billions of years.

7. If many quasars are not in existence today, how could scientists explain how they died?

   Inference: Black holes ran out of materials to suck in.

8. How does the name fit the nature of quasars?

   Text-based: They are not real stars—they are quasi-stars.

9. Why didn't astronomers discover the existence of quasars before the 1940s?

   Inference: Radio technology had not yet been invented.

10. Some commentators have observed that it is a good thing that quasars are so far from the earth. Do you agree? Why or why not?

    Critical Response: Agree, so much heat and light would be dangerous; don't want to be too close to a black hole; might get sucked in by the black hole. Disagree, they would be easier to study if they were closer; we might uncover more of the mysteries of the universe.

Comprehension Analysis:

Text-Based: __/4__
Inference: __/4__
Critical Response: __/2__

Total Comprehension %: _____

Sample Scoring of Comprehension Questions

In this section of the CRI we provide a sample of actual children's responses to the comprehension questions that follow the second grade oral passage entitled *The Race*. These responses illustrate the wide range of creative (and not so creative) thinking that children can do in response to any text. You will notice that there are times when an examiner-probe question is used, times when a probe question should have been used but was not, and even times when a probe question was used but was actually unnecessary. Individual variations in testing technique and expectations for responses must be an accepted part of any informal measure. You will also note that when you are evaluating the responses gathered by a colleague, it is sometimes necessary to utilize the partial credit convention for responses that are less than clear. We provide with each response a suggested score and a rationale for that score.

Text: *The Race*

   Spencer was the fastest animal in the jungle. All of the other animals knew it. Spencer made sure of that. He would say, "No one can beat me! You are all too afraid to race!" It was true. No one wanted to race against Spencer. He always won. Then he would brag even more.

   One day another family of cats moved in. Spencer ran up to the new family. He said, "I'm the fastest animal in the jungle. Do you want to race?" The father said, "No, thank you. But maybe our daughter Annie will race with you." Annie smiled and said, "Yes. I'd love to race." Soon the two cats were running for the finish line. Spencer was winning as always. But Annie was very fast. She raced past him and crossed the finish line first.

   The other animals cheered in surprise. But Spencer cried, "I want another chance!" They raced again and again. But the result was still the same. There was a new champion in the jungle and her name was Annie.

   All the animals came over to talk to Annie. But Spencer went away angry. Annie was a little sad. She hoped that Spencer would be her friend. "Well, at least we won't have to listen to him brag again," said the fox. The next day Spencer was back. The first thing he said was, "I can jump higher than anybody in the jungle! No one can beat me!" The other animals groaned and rolled their eyes. Nothing had changed after all.

Comprehension Questions

1. Why didn't any of the animals want to race against Spencer?

   Text-based: He always won and he bragged afterwards.

Child A: "He always won the races and then bragged." +10
This response is correct based on the text content.

Child B: "He bragged a lot." Examiner probe: But why wouldn't they want to race against him? "They didn't want to hear him bragging after the race." +10
The initial response suggests that the reader has comprehended the text and many examiners would consider the probe question unnecessary. The probe question gives the child the chance to successfully clarify the relationship between bragging and racing.

Child C: "They thought he would always win." +10
This is a correct response based on text content.

Child D: "Because they wanted to be better than him." Examiner probe: But why wouldn't they race with him? "So they could brag when they won." +0
The reader confuses who is doing the bragging after the races.

Child E: "Because they didn't want him to brag." +10
Based on the content of the text, the response is correct. Note that we should accept text-based responses if the reader replies with a single idea that is stated or strongly implied in the text. The ability to link text-based information and draw conclusions on the basis of those links is assessed in inferential and critical response items.

2. What did the animals do when Annie won the race? (Must identify one.)

Text-based: They cheered; talked with her.

Child A: "They were happy because Spencer was no longer the fastest." Examiner probe: But what did they do? "They don't have to listen to him brag anymore." +0
The reader was unable to clarify a vague response with information from the text, the essence of a text-based item.

Child B: "They were surprised." Examiner probe: But what did they do? "I don't remember." +0
The reader could not recall what the other animals did after the race.

Child C: "They talked to her. They were glad she was the champion." +10
The passage states clearly that the other animals talked to Annie after the race. It is not necessary for the child to include both parts of the answer in the response.

Child D: "They clapped and cheered." +10
The passage states that they cheered; clapping is a plausible accompaniment to cheering.

Child E: "They cheered for her but then she felt bad for her brother." +5
This is a tricky item to score because of the presence of both accurate and inaccurate information. When in doubt, half credit may be the better scoring strategy.

Child F: "They clapped, cheered, and they were surprised." +10
The response provides more than is needed, strictly speaking. However, it is completely accurate and the fact that it accurately paraphrases the text may be a good sign.

Child G: "They cheered, 'Hurrah, hurrah!'" +10
Once again, the response is accurate with a touch of creativity as well.

3. Why would Spencer want to race against Annie again?

Inference: He couldn't accept the fact that someone was faster; thought he could win.

Child A: "He wanted to prove he was still the fastest." +10
This is a plausible reason for wanting a rematch.

Child B: "Because he wouldn't want her to win." +0

    It is too late for that consideration; the race is over and Annie has already won.

Child C: "He wanted to see if he was faster than her." +0

    The race has already occurred in the story and she has already demonstrated that she is faster.

Child D: "He thought he could beat her with another chance." +10

    Response is right to the point and accurate.

Child E: "Because he wanted to win against Annie." +5

    Here the reader may have the right idea or she may be indicating that she doesn't remember that Spencer also wanted to win the first race. We really need an examiner probe question to determine what the child means but in the absence of such a probe, half credit is our best choice.

Child F: "Because he thought he was better than a girl; he thought he could win." +10

    Here we have gender-consciousness rearing its head, but the reader does finish with the right idea.

Child G: "Because he wanted to win this one because then they would be tied and they could have raced again to break the tie." +10

    This is a reader who dives into the story with both feet and uses past experience to flesh out the text. Good response!

4. Why did Annie agree to race against Spencer when no one else would?

Inference: She knew she was very fast; she probably knew she could beat him.

Child A: "She wanted to see if she could win." +10

    This is a plausible motivation for Annie's wanting to race.

Child B: "She never raced against him and she wanted a friend." +10

    It is true that Annie may have raced against Spencer because she wanted him to become her friend. The first part of the response is connected only a bit tenuously to the question but the overall response is a good one and provides a plausible motivation for Annie's actions.

Child C: "She was brave and she wanted to race. She loved to race." +0

    This response is too vague to justify even partial credit, but it does illustrate the need for an examiner-probe question to clarify what the reader meant.

Child D: "Because the other animals didn't because they just wanted to watch them." +0

    Annie would have no way of knowing whether the other animals wanted to race against Spencer. In any case, it seems to have little to do with Annie's motivation.

Child E: "Because she never knew she was the fastest and she wanted to be friends." +10

    Both parts of the response are plausible motivations for Annie's actions.

Child F: "Because she knew she was faster than him." +10

    This response is clear and right to the point.

Child G: "Annie didn't know he was fast. She just moved there." +0

    This response contradicts the passage content. Annie was there when Spencer bragged; she had to know he was fast.

Child H: "Because she was the fastest in her family." +0

    There is no indication from passage content that Annie was the fastest runner in her family.

5. What would have been the best thing for Spencer to do after Annie beat him? Why?

Critical Response: Be a good loser and admit that she was faster; try to be her friend since he didn't have any friends; stop bragging about himself to the other animals.

Child A: "To say, 'nice race' because it would be more polite than getting angry." +10
    This response captures the spirit of being a good sport and accepting one's defeats.

Child B: "He could just say, 'good race' and move on with his life." +10
    Good response from a future psychologist.

Child C: "Congratulate her and stop racing." +10
    This response again seems to suggest being a good sport. To stop racing is not as necessary as to stop bragging but the latter is not essential in response to this question. The examiner might have asked a probe question to see if the child could clarify the response but even in the absence of the probe, the response seems solid.

Child D: "Say, 'Thank you for racing.'" Examiner probe: What do you mean? "That would be the polite thing to do." +10
    The child successfully clarifies the initial response after the examiner-probe question. There is, of course, no penalty involved with the probe.

Child E: "He should have said, 'good job' so she would like him." +10
    Here the reader links Spencer's response with Annie's desire for a friend.

Child F: "Take it like a man and still be friends with Annie and not mad at her." +5
    This response has several dimensions to it. The fact is that Spencer and Annie were never friends and there is no clear indication that he is angry with her. It is far more likely that he is angry with the animals who cheered when she defeated him. However, the "take it like a man" element is very close to the response that we would like to see.

Child G: "Say, 'Good job' because he had bad sportsmanship." +10
    Despite the less than optimal syntactic structure of the response, it seems clear that the reader did not approve of Spencer's lack of sportsmanship.

Child H: "Cheer for her." Examiner probe: Why would they do that? "Because she won." +0
    While we could make a case that cheering for Annie would at least have been an acknowledgment of her victory, it is difficult to see how the second part of the response addresses the question.

6. What did Spencer do when he came back the next day?

Text-based: Started bragging about something else; bragged that he could jump higher than anyone else.

Child A: "He said he could jump higher than anyone." +10
    This is an accurate text-based response.

Child B: "He raced against Annie." +0
    This did not happen in the story; Annie was not specifically mentioned on the second day.

Child C: "They were friends." +0
    While they may indeed become friends someday, there is nothing in the story to suggest that this is imminent.

Child D: "He just sat around the jungle and tried to race her till he won." +0
    There is no indication of this in the story.

Child E: "He bragged again." Examiner probe: What did he brag about? "This time something about jumping higher." +10
    The first response is not entirely adequate. The probe question is justified and the clarified correct response is accepted without penalty.

7. Do you think that this was the first time Annie had ever raced against anyone? Why or why not?

Inference: No, she smiled when Spencer challenged her; she probably knew she could beat him.

Child A: "No, because if she could beat Spencer she could beat anyone." +0
   This response really does not address the point of the question.

Child B: "No, because maybe she played and raced other kids where she lived before." +5
   Here the reader clearly links background experience to the text and although it is speculation, it is somewhat plausible. The examiner may have asked a probe question to elicit more details but in the absence of such a question, half credit would seem to be most appropriate.

Child C: "Yes, because she hadn't raced anybody but Spencer." +0
   There is nothing in the passage to support this conclusion.

Child D: "No, because she said she hadn't raced in a long time." +0
   There is nothing in the passage to support this statement.

Child E: "Yes, because she was afraid he would beat her." +0
   This response contradicts the confidence that Annie expressed through her smile.

Child F: "She probably raced where she used to live and she knew she would win." +10
   This response provides a plausible rationale for Annie's confidence.

Child G: "Yes, because she just moved there." +0
   This response provides no support for the opinion stated.

Child H: "No. She knew she was fast or she wouldn't be smiling." +10
   Good, clear response with a clear supporting explanation.

8. What did the other animals hope would happen after Spencer lost the race?

Text-based: That Spencer would stop bragging.

Child A: "That he wouldn't challenge them anymore." +10
   Since challenging them to race was clearly related to Spencer's bragging, we can accept this response.

Child B: "He would not brag anymore." +10
   This is clearly stated in the text.

Child C: "They would be happy." +0
   This is a very vague response that suggests little real understanding of the situation described in the story.

Child D: "A fox said, 'At least he doesn't have to be such a show-off.'" Examiner probe: But what did the animal hope would happen? "That he wouldn't show off." +10
   The examiner-probe question gave the reader an opportunity to explain her linkage of ideas; in the absence of such a clarification, the response was too vague to score very easily.

Child E: "They were hoping he would win one day." +0
   This response contradicts the essence of the text.

Child F: "They thought they could beat him." +0
   Apparently no one thought that they could beat Spencer.

Child G: "That he would change and be Annie's friend." +0
   Apparently this was Annie's wish but not necessarily the wish of the other animals.

Child H: "That he would win but Annie did." +0
   This response suggests a great deal of confusion about the facts of the story.

9. If another new family moved into the jungle, do you think Spencer would ask them to race or not?

Critical Response: Yes, he did not seem to have learned anything; still bragged even after he lost. No, he has lost once; he may still brag but he didn't like to lose and he may not be as confident as he was once.

Child A: "Yes, to see if he could beat one of them." +0
   This response seems to be based on pure experience and speculation and not on information gleaned from the passage.

Child B: "Maybe he would challenge them to a jumping contest." +10
   This is actually a plausible possibility, given Spencer's past behavior and his need to brag.

Child C: "Yes, because he wants others to know he is the fastest again." +0
   Beating others will not establish that Spencer is the fastest again; he will need to beat Annie in order to accomplish that.

Child D: "To see if he is still the second fastest." +10
   This represents a plausible and creative motivation for challenging others to race and suggests a clear understanding of the essence of the story.

Child E: "No, because he might lose again. Then it would be worse." +10
   This response captures one of the potentially unpleasant consequences that Spencer just recently suffered.

Child F: "Yes, because he still wants to brag that he's the fastest in the jungle." +0
   The problem with this response is that Spencer has already lost and can no longer brag that he is the fastest unless he beats Annie.

Child G: "No. If they beat him there would be a new champion in the jungle." +0
   Here the child has forgotten that there already was a new champion in the jungle, at least as far as racing is concerned.

Child H: "No. They will probably be faster than him." +0
   Based on past experience with racing, they will probably not be faster than Spencer.

Child I: "No, because he lost the race and he doesn't want to lose again." +10
   This response implies a loss in confidence on Spencer's part, a change that has occurred because of his initial loss to Annie.

10. If Spencer stopped bragging, do you think he would be a good friend for Annie or would he still have to change?

Critical Response: Yes, he wouldn't annoy people; others would give him a chance; others would like him better. No, has to be a better loser; shouldn't be so selfish; must admit she is a better runner.

Child A: "No. He would be better but he would still have to change." +5
   This response should have been followed by a probe question to determine if the reader had any idea of the changes that Spencer would need to make. In the absence of clarification, half credit appears to be the fairest assessment.

Child B: "Yes. He has to be the best and beat everyone at everything." +0
   This response addressed the issue of bragging but does not address Spencer's role as a potential friend.

Child C: "Yes, because they could just race for fun." +0
   This response does not really address the question. If they race for fun, there would be no need to brag, but the issue of friendship is not addressed.

Child D: "He should be a good friend to Annie." +0

    This simply asserts that he should be Annie's friend but does not address what he needs to do to be a friend.

Child E: "Yes, he would say polite things and not mean things to Annie." +0

    This response suggests that if Spencer stopped bragging he would automatically say polite things. This cause–effect relationship is not supported by the text and does not address the question.

Child F: "Yes, Annie would like him." +0

    Response does not explain why Annie would like him if he stopped bragging.

Child G: "He would be a better friend if he didn't brag anymore." +0

    Does not respond to the question about whether Spencer would be a good friend; instead the reader simply restates the question.

Child H: "Yes. He doesn't seem like he wants to be friends with her now." +10

    This response recognizes that Spencer does not appear to be interested in anything but winning races and bragging.

Child I: "Yes. I think people would like him more if he stopped bragging and bothering everyone about always winning." +10

    Good overall response that seems to recognize that Spencer might behave differently if he thought that others liked him.

Appendix B

Sample Retellings and Use of Scoring Rubric

These sample retellings are designed for use by individuals or groups to develop familiarity with the scoring of retellings based on Retelling Rubrics. The sample retellings are based on the second grade oral story entitled *The Race*.

Text: *The Race*

Spencer was the fastest animal in the jungle. All of the other animals knew it. Spencer made sure of that. He would say, "No one can beat me! You are all too afraid to race!" It was true. No one wanted to race against Spencer. He always won. Then he would brag even more.

One day another family of cats moved in. Spencer ran up to the new family. He said, "I'm the fastest animal in the jungle. Do you want to race?" The father said, "No, thank you. But maybe our daughter Annie will race with you." Annie smiled and said, "Yes. I'd love to race." Soon the two cats were running for the finish line. Spencer was winning as always. But Annie was very fast. She raced past him and crossed the finish line first.

The other animals cheered in surprise. But Spencer cried, "I want another chance!" They raced again and again. But the result was still the same. There was a new champion in the jungle and her name was Annie.

All the animals came over to talk to Annie. But Spencer went away angry. Annie was a little sad. She hoped that Spencer would be her friend. "Well, at least we won't have to listen to him brag again," said the fox. The next day Spencer was back. The first thing he said was, "I can jump higher than anybody in the jungle! No one can beat me!" The other animals groaned and rolled their eyes. Nothing had changed after all.

Retelling 1

"It was about a cat who thought he was really fast. And he bragged a lot. And all the animals got mad at him and they hoped he would stop." *Examiner: Is there anything else you remember about the story?* "Um . . . he bragged about jumping high too but that's all I remember." *Examiner: Tell me what you thought about the passage.* "I liked that story . . . I just thought it was funny."

Scoring and Discussion

This retelling fails to identify all of the key characters or the central event of the race with Annie. Thus the reader recalls the first and last part of the story but completely omits the middle as well as the steps the characters take in their attempt to resolve the problem. This type of retelling is characteristic of children who see their task as providing a faithful recall of details. They are often successful at recalling the details of passages at or near their independent level. But when the material becomes more challenging, longer and more detailed, their memories become overloaded and they can often produce no more than very sketchy outlines. The reader has provided a personal response but cannot support it.

Score: 0

Retelling Rubric

Story Structure:	
1. **Key Characters and Setting:** Spencer, other animals, and Annie who moved into jungle.	0
2. **Character's Problem or Goal:** Spencer wants to be the fastest runner in the jungle and to brag about it.	0
3. **Problem-Solving or Goal-Meeting Process:**	
• Spencer brags and gets others to race with him so that he can brag more.	0
• Annie moves in and Spencer races with her.	0
• Spencer loses the race.	0
• Spencer walks away angrily and Annie is sad because she had wanted a friend.	0
• Spencer returns the next day brags about jumping.	0
4. **Personal Response:** Any well-supported positive or negative response to the characters or events in the story; any reaction to the humor or sadness in the story; any well-supported positive or negative reaction to the story as a whole.	0

Rubric:

4 = Complete retelling includes characters, problem/goal, all five steps in the problem-solving process, and a well-supported personal response.

3 = Retelling includes characters, problem/goal, and all five steps in the problem-solving process, but has no personal response.

2 = Retelling includes characters, problem/goal, and three or four steps in the problem-solving process; some key factual errors or omissions. Add ½ point for well-supported personal response.

1 = Retelling omits either characters or problem; includes one or two steps in the problem-solving process, but the account is disjointed and includes factual errors or serious omissions. Add ½ point for well-supported personal response.

0 = Provides a title or topic statement, but shows no real awareness of the character's problem and how the problem is worked out.

Retelling 2

"Spencer was the fastest animal in the jungle. Everybody knew it. He would tell them and ask them if they wanted to race but no one wanted to. Then he lost a race to Annie and went away. But he came back the next day and said, 'I can jump higher than any animal in the jungle.'" *Examiner: Tell me what you thought about the passage.* "I liked how the cat didn't give up. He just kept trying to win, no matter what the others said."

Scoring and Discussion

Here the reader identifies the two key characters in the story as well as three of the steps in the problem-solving process. But the reader seems intent on relating events rather than linking them in a logical relationship. She does not discuss, for example, why Spencer went away after his loss, why he returned the next day bragging again, or why the animals were disappointed that he had not changed as a result of his experiences. The fact that there is a clear personal response to the story is surprising, given that there is little indication of an understanding of the cause–effect relationships that comprise the story. We may want to consider the possibility that this child's level of understanding is greater than her ability to express it verbally. We add ½ point to her score for the personal response.

Score: 1.5

Retelling Rubric

Story Structure:

1. **Key Characters and Setting:** Spencer, other animals, and Annie who moved into jungle. **+1**
2. **Character's Problem or Goal:** Spencer wants to be the fastest runner in the jungle and to brag about it. **0**
3. **Problem-Solving or Goal-Meeting Process:**
   - Spencer brags and gets others to race with him so that he can brag more. **0**
   - **0**
   - Annie moves in and Spencer races with her. **+1**
   - Spencer loses the race. **0**
   - Spencer walks away angrily and Annie is sad because she had wanted a friend. **0**
   - Spencer returns the next day brags about jumping. **+1**
4. **Personal Response:** Any well-supported positive or negative response to the characters or events in the story; any reaction to the humor or sadness in the story; any well-supported positive or negative reaction to the story as a whole. **+1**

Rubric:

4 = Complete retelling includes characters, problem/goal, all five steps in the problem-solving process, and a well-supported personal response.

3 = Retelling includes characters, problem/goal, and all five steps in the problem-solving process, but has no personal response.

2 = Retelling includes characters, problem/goal, and three or four steps in the problem-solving process; some key factual errors or omissions. Add ½ point for well-supported personal response.

1 = Retelling omits either characters or problem; includes one or two steps in the problem-solving process, but the account is disjointed and includes factual errors or serious omissions. Add ½ point for well-supported personal response.

0 = Provides a title or topic statement, but shows no real awareness of the character's problem and how the problem is worked out.

Retelling 3

"It's about Spencer who was very fast and bragged a lot. And he raced against another cat named Annie and at first he won but then he lost and the other animals laughed at him because he always bragged and they wanted him to go away. But he wouldn't go away because he wanted to show them that he could be a good friend. And so he and Annie became friends and they were happy in the jungle." *Examiner: Tell me what you thought about the passage.* "I really didn't like the story much." Examiner Probe: Rephrased the question. "I just didn't like it."

Scoring and Discussion

This reader identifies the key characters and hints at Spencer's goal. From that point the retelling wanders a great distance from the ideas in the text. The reader seems to be using background experiences to fill in those parts of the story that she cannot recall. The reader is clearly not using text clues as a support for her conclusions. Consequently, the retelling is disjointed and includes several serious factual errors.
Score: 1.0

Retelling Rubric

Story Structure:

1. **Key Characters and Setting:** Spencer, other animals, and Annie who moved into jungle. +1
2. **Character's Problem or Goal:** Spencer wants to be the fastest runner in the jungle and to brag about it. +½
3. **Problem-Solving or Goal-Meeting Process:**
   - Spencer brags and gets others to race with him so that he can brag more. +1
   - Annie moves in and Spencer races with her. +1
   - Spencer loses the race. +1
   - Spencer walks away angrily and Annie is sad because she had wanted a friend. 0
   - Spencer returns the next day brags about jumping. 0
4. **Personal Response:** Any well-supported positive or negative response to the characters or events in the story; any reaction to the humor or sadness in the story; any well-supported positive or negative reaction to the story as a whole. 0

Rubric:

4 = Complete retelling includes characters, problem/goal, all five steps in the problem-solving process, and a well-supported personal response.

3 = Retelling includes characters, problem/goal, and all five steps in the problem-solving process, but has no personal response.

2 = Retelling includes characters, problem/goal, and three or four steps in the problem-solving process; some key factual errors or omissions. Add ½ point for well-supported personal response.

1 = Retelling omits either characters or problem; includes one or two steps in the problem-solving process, but the account is disjointed and includes factual errors or serious omissions. Add ½ point for well-supported personal response.

0 = Provides a title or topic statement, but shows no real awareness of the character's problem and how the problem is worked out.

Retelling 4

"It's about two cats, Spencer and Annie, who both liked to race and one of them wanted to be the best so he could brag. Then they raced and the first cat lost. Everybody was happy when he lost. He got mad at them all and Annie was sad to see him go. He bragged about how fast he was and that's why the other animals got mad at him and they wouldn't race with him. Then he came back and started bragging about how high he could jump too. It was a good story and tells people about what can happen if they brag too much."

Scoring and Discussion

This retelling identifies the key characters and includes five steps in the problem-solving process. The retelling is not sequential but the reader does appear to be able to logically connect the ideas in the text. The personal response is brief but well-supported.

Score: 4.0

Retelling Rubric

Story Structure:	
1. **Key Characters and Setting:** Spencer, other animals, and Annie who moved into jungle.	+1
2. **Character's Problem or Goal:** Spencer wants to be the fastest runner in the jungle and to brag about it.	+1
3. **Problem-Solving or Goal-Meeting Process:**	
• Spencer brags and gets others to race with him so that he can brag more.	+1
• Annie moves in and Spencer races with her.	+1
• Spencer loses the race.	+1
• Spencer walks away angrily and Annie is sad because she had wanted a friend.	+1
• Spencer returns the next day brags about jumping.	+1
4. **Personal Response:** Any well-supported positive or negative response to the characters or events in the story; any reaction to the humor or sadness in the story; any well-supported positive or negative reaction to the story as a whole.	+1

Rubric:

4 = Complete retelling includes characters, problem/goal, all five steps in the problem-solving process, and a well-supported personal response.

3 = Retelling includes characters, problem/goal, and all five steps in the problem-solving process, but has no personal response.

2 = Retelling includes characters, problem/goal, and three or four steps in the problem-solving process; some key factual errors or omissions. Add ½ point for well-supported personal response.

1 = Retelling omits either characters or problem; includes one or two steps in the problem-solving process, but the account is disjointed and includes factual errors or serious omissions. Add ½ point for well-supported personal response.

0 = Provides a title or topic statement, but shows no real awareness of the character's problem and how the problem is worked out.

Retelling 5

"Spencer bragged all the time about how fast he was and no one wanted to race him because it was true. But then a new family moved into the jungle and one of the cats named Annie raced against him. Spencer thought he was going to win but then she beat him and he got mad and went away. Annie was sad 'cause she wanted to be friends. All the animals were happy because they thought he would stop bragging. But he came back the next day and started bragging about how high he could jump. He never changed at all. That was a pretty funny story. It just shows how some things don't really change that much when maybe they should."

Scoring and Discussion

This is an excellent retelling that includes every element in the rubric and a personal response to the story as well.
Score: 4.0

Retelling Rubric

Story Structure:

1. **Key Characters and Setting:** Spencer, other animals, and Annie who moved into jungle. +1
2. **Character's Problem or Goal:** Spencer wants to be the fastest runner in the jungle and to brag about it. +1
3. **Problem-Solving or Goal-Meeting Process:**
   - Spencer brags and gets others to race with him so that he can brag more. +1
   - Annie moves in and Spencer races with her. +1
   - Spencer loses the race. +1
   - Spencer walks away angrily and Annie is sad because she had wanted a friend. +1
   - Spencer returns the next day brags about jumping. +1
4. **Personal Response:** Any well-supported positive or negative response to the characters or events in the story; any reaction to the humor or sadness in the story; any well-supported positive or negative reaction to the story as a whole. +1

Rubric:

4 = Complete retelling includes characters, problem/goal, all five steps in the problem-solving process, and a well-supported personal response.

3 = Retelling includes characters, problem/goal, and all five steps in the problem-solving process, but has no personal response.

2 = Retelling includes characters, problem/goal, and three or four steps in the problem-solving process; some key factual errors or omissions. Add ½ point for well-supported personal response.

1 = Retelling omits either characters or problem; includes one or two steps in the problem-solving process, but the account is disjointed and includes factual errors or serious omissions. Add ½ point for well-supported personal response.

0 = Provides a title or topic statement, but shows no real awareness of the character's problem and how the problem is worked out.

Retelling 6

"Spencer likes to brag a lot about how fast he is and it gets on everyone's nerves. When a new cat named Annie comes along and beats him, everyone hopes he will stop bragging. But he doesn't; he walks away and just finds something else to brag about." *Examiner: Tell me what you thought about the passage.* "It was pretty good." *Anything else?* "No, not really."

Scoring and Retelling

This retelling, despite its brevity, manages to identify the key characters as well as Spencer's goal. It then briefly but clearly describes nearly all of the steps in the problem-solving process, although it includes no personal response. While the reader does not qualify for a full 3.0 score, he has no key factual errors. It is clear from the retelling that the reader has comprehended the key elements and relationships included in the story.

Score: 2.5

Retelling Rubric

Story Structure:	
1. **Key Characters and Setting:** Spencer, other animals, and Annie who moved into jungle.	+1
2. **Character's Problem or Goal:** Spencer wants to be the fastest runner in the jungle and to brag about it.	+1
3. **Problem-Solving or Goal-Meeting Process:**	
• Spencer brags and gets others to race with him so that he can brag more.	+1
• Annie moves in and Spencer races with her.	+1
• Spencer loses the race.	+1
• Spencer walks away angrily and Annie is sad because she had wanted a friend.	+½
• Spencer returns the next day brags about jumping.	+1
4. **Personal Response:** Any well-supported positive or negative response to the characters or events in the story; any reaction to the humor or sadness in the story; any well-supported positive or negative reaction to the story as a whole.	0

Rubric:

4 = Complete retelling includes characters, problem/goal, all five steps in the problem-solving process, and a well-supported personal response.

3 = Retelling includes characters, problem/goal, and all five steps in the problem-solving process, but has no personal response.

2 = Retelling includes characters, problem/goal, and three or four steps in the problem-solving process; some key factual errors or omissions. Add ½ point for well-supported personal response.

1 = Retelling omits either characters or problem; includes one or two steps in the problem-solving process, but the account is disjointed and includes factual errors or serious omissions. Add ½ point for well-supported personal response.

0 = Provides a title or topic statement, but shows no real awareness of the character's problem and how the problem is worked out.

Retelling 7

"It's about a cat who is very fast until a new family moves in. Then he finds out that he is not as fast as he thinks he is. He races against the girl and loses and then goes away. The girl wanted him to be her friend so she is sad. But he comes back the next day so maybe they will become friends. It's nice to have a friend when you've just moved into a new place."

Scoring and Discussion

The reader in this case focused upon an issue in the text that was of interest to her: the possible friendship of Spencer and Annie. She even includes a personal response in the course of the retelling by speculating on whether they will become friends and commenting on the importance of friends in Annie's situation. But the retelling still misses the key element of Spencer's bragging and the consequences of that bragging. Thus the reader omits the character's goal and cannot identify the characters by name. These omissions clearly weaken the retelling score, but the reader gives evidence of an emerging view of reading that is sound and encouraging.
Score: 1.5

Retelling Rubric

Story Structure:	
1. **Key Characters and Setting:** Spencer, other animals, and Annie who moved into jungle.	$+\frac{1}{2}$
2. **Character's Problem or Goal:** Spencer wants to be the fastest runner in the jungle and to brag about it.	0
3. **Problem-Solving or Goal-Meeting Process:**	
• Spencer brags and gets others to race with him so that he can brag more.	0
• Annie moves in and Spencer races with her.	+1
• Spencer loses the race.	+1
• Spencer walks away angrily and Annie is sad because she had wanted a friend.	+1
• Spencer returns the next day brags about jumping.	0
4. **Personal Response:** Any well-supported positive or negative response to the characters or events in the story; any reaction to the humor or sadness in the story; any well-supported positive or negative reaction to the story as a whole.	+1

Rubric:
4 = Complete retelling includes characters, problem/goal, all five steps in the problem-solving process, and a well-supported personal response.
3 = Retelling includes characters, problem/goal, and all five steps in the problem-solving process, but has no personal response.
2 = Retelling includes characters, problem/goal, and three or four steps in the problem-solving process; some key factual errors or omissions. Add ½ point for well-supported personal response.
1 = Retelling omits either characters or problem; includes one or two steps in the problem-solving process, but the account is disjointed and includes factual errors or serious omissions. Add ½ point for well-supported personal response.
0 = Provides a title or topic statement, but shows no real awareness of the character's problem and how the problem is worked out.

Retelling 8

"Spencer brags to the other animals about how fast he is and tries to get them to race so he can brag more. Then a new family moves in and he asks them to race and Annie races him and wins. All the animals were happy 'cause they thought he would stop bragging but Spencer was mad and he went away. He came back the next day and bragged about how high he could jump and all the animals rolled their eyes and groaned." *Examiner: Tell me what you thought about the passage.* "It was about a cat who bragged a lot."

Scoring and Discussion

This is a very good retelling that includes the key characters, the character's goal, and nearly all five steps in the problem-solving process. The fact that the reader misses the element of Annie's disappointment is not enough to drop the retelling to 2.0, but it is not quite enough for a 3.0. The only piece that is missing is the personal response.

Score: 2.5

Retelling Rubric

Story Structure:	
1. **Key Characters and Setting:** Spencer, other animals, and Annie who moved into jungle.	+1
2. **Character's Problem or Goal:** Spencer wants to be the fastest runner in the jungle and to brag about it.	+1
3. **Problem-Solving or Goal-Meeting Process:**	
• Spencer brags and gets others to race with him so that he can brag more.	+1
• Annie moves in and Spencer races with her.	+1
• Spencer loses the race.	+1
• Spencer walks away angrily and Annie is sad because she had wanted a friend.	+1
• Spencer returns the next day brags about jumping.	+1
4. **Personal Response:** Any well-supported positive or negative response to the characters or events in the story; any reaction to the humor or sadness in the story; any well-supported positive or negative reaction to the story as a whole.	0

Rubric:

4 = Complete retelling includes characters, problem/goal, all five steps in the problem-solving process, and a well-supported personal response.

3 = Retelling includes characters, problem/goal, and all five steps in the problem-solving process, but has no personal response.

2 = Retelling includes characters, problem/goal, and three or four steps in the problem-solving process; some key factual errors or omissions. Add ½ point for well-supported personal response.

1 = Retelling omits either characters or problem; includes one or two steps in the problem-solving process, but the account is disjointed and includes factual errors or serious omissions. Add ½ point for well-supported personal response.

0 = Provides a title or topic statement, but shows no real awareness of the character's problem and how the problem is worked out.

Passage Length and Readability Data
for *The Critical Reading Inventory*

Narrative Passages: Form A

Level	Title	N of Words	Readability*
PP Oral	At the Library	95	0.0
PP Silent	The Baker	120	0.0
P Oral	The Little Fish	175	0.4
P Silent	Learning to Fish	157	0.5
1 Oral	Where Is the Dog?	216	1.5
1 Silent	The Pigs Get a Job	195	1.7
2 Oral	The Race	256	2.4
2 Silent	The Roller Coaster Ride	244	2.3
3 Oral	The Farm Vacation	417	3.5
3 Silent	The Championship Game	399	3.7
4 Oral	The Vacation	412	4.4
4 Silent	Autumn Leaves	447	4.3
5 Oral	Getting What You Want	404	5.6
5 Silent	The Player	473	5.4
6 Oral	The Motor Bike	497	6.6
6 Silent	The Tutor	498	6.5
JH Oral	The Magician	419	7.3
JH Silent	The Friend	507	7.1
SH Oral	Differences	782	10.6
SH Silent	The Injury	845	10.0

*Readability levels determined using the Flesch-Kincaid formula (Microsoft Word, 1997).

Informational Passages: Form B

Level	Title	N of Words	Readability
PP Oral	All Kinds of Trucks	66	0.0
PP Silent	Plants	80	0.0
P Oral	Turtles	111	0.6
P Silent	Maps	107	0.5
1 Oral	Black Bears	129	1.6
1 Silent	People in Groups	111	1.3
2 Oral	Army Ants	168	2.4
2 Silent	The Doctor Fish	178	2.6
3 Oral	The Immigrants	209	3.8
3 Silent	Child Slaves	205	3.4
4 Oral	Frida Kahlo	221	4.7
4 Silent	Krakatoa	214	4.9
5 Oral	The Mosquito	292	5.4
5 Silent	Oil Spill	267	5.7
6 Oral	A Community of Wolves	315	6.4
6 Silent	Are You Afraid of Sharks?	353	6.1
JH Oral	Mary Jemison	367	7.6
JH Silent	Old Man River	396	7.8
SH Oral	The Search for Pancho Villa	439	11.9
SH Silent	Quasars	441	11.6

Appendix D

Directions for Using the Demonstration CD

The audio CD that accompanies *The Critical Reading Inventory* is designed to provide practice in scoring miscues, retellings, and comprehension questions for users who are unfamiliar with informal reading inventories. But it can also serve as a springboard for the interpretation of test results and classroom discussion about the interaction between word recognition and comprehension.

The CD includes the entire administration of the test to Eileen, a sixth grade student who is struggling with word recognition and has been placed in special education classrooms since first grade. Her instructional program consists primarily of the development of a sight vocabulary and practice in word recognition skills. In both cases this practice takes place primarily outside the context of actual text. Her view of the instruction she receives is "working with lists of words."

While this brief recap of background knowledge cannot serve as the basis for a Level Three Comprehensive Interpretation of results, the contents of the CD can certainly serve to promote discussion leading to a Level Two Analytical Interpretation.

Table of Contents

Second Grade Oral: The Race

:40	Oral Reading
3:02	Retelling
3:59	Comprehension Questions

Second Grade Silent: The Roller Coaster Ride

7:05	Retelling
7:54	Comprehension Questions

Third Grade Oral: The Farm Vacation

11:00	Oral Reading
16:32	Retelling
17:25	Comprehension Questions

Third Grade Silent: The Championship Game

20:31   Retelling
21:13   Comprehension Questions

Fourth Grade Oral: The Vacation

27:02   Oral Reading
33:30   Retelling
35:16   Comprehension Questions

Fourth Grade Silent: Autumn Leaves

38:40   Retelling
39:55   Comprehension Questions

Fifth Grade Oral: Getting What You Want

42:52   Oral Reading
49:41   Retelling
50:36   Comprehension Questions

Fifth Grade Silent: The Player

53:35   Retelling
54:40   Comprehension Questions

Sixth Grade Oral: The Motor Bike

58:28   Oral Reading
67:40   Retelling
69:10   Comprehension Questions

Sixth Grade Silent: The Tutor

73:05   Retelling
73:57   Comprehension Questions

References

Adams, M. J. (1990). *Beginning to read: Thinking and learning about print.* Cambridge, MA: MIT Press.

Allen, D. D., & Swearingen, R. A. (1991, May). *Informal reading inventories: What are they really asking?* Paper presented at the Annual Meeting of the International Reading Association (ERIC Document Reproduction Service No. ED341953)

Allington, R. L. (1983). Fluency: The neglected goal of the reading program. *The Reading Teacher, 36,* 556–561.

Allington, R. L. (2001). *What really matters for struggling readers.* NY: Addison-Wesley.

Allington, R. L., & Johnston, P. (2000, April). *Exemplary fourth grade reading Instruction.* Paper presented at the American Educational Research Association, New Orleans, LA.

Alvermann, D. (1988). Effects of spontaneous and induced lookbacks on self-perceived high-and low-ability comprehenders. *Journal of Educational Research, 8*(6), 325–331.

Alvermann, D. E. & Guthrie, J. T. (1993). The national reading research center. In A. P. Sweet & J. I. Anderson (Eds.), *Reading research into the year 2000* (pp. 129–150). Hillsdale, NJ: Erlbaum.

American Educational Research Association (2000). AERA position statement concerning high-stakes testing in pre-K–12 education. Retrieved 8/15/2002 from http://www.aera.net/about/policy/ stakes.htm

Anastasi, A., & Urbina, S. (1997). *Psychological testing, (7th ed.).* Upper Saddle River, NJ: Prentice Hall.

Anderson, R. C. (1984). Role of the reader's schema in comprehension, learning and memory. In R. C. Anderson, J. Osborn, & R. J. Tierney (Eds.). *Learning to read in American schools: Basal readers and content texts.* Hillsdale, NJ: Erlbaum.

Anderson, R. C., & Freebody, P. (1981). Vocabulary knowledge. In J. T. Guthrie, (Ed.). *Comprehension and teaching: Research perspectives.* Newark, DE: International Reading Association.

Anderson, R. C., Osborn, J., & Tierney, R. J. (Eds.) (1984). *Learning to read in American schools: Basal readers and content texts.* Hillsdale, NJ: Erlbaum.

Anderson, R. C., Wilkinson, I.A.G., & Mason, J. M. (1991). A microanalysis of small group, guided reading lesson: Effects of an emphasis on global story meaning. *Reading Research Quarterly, 26*(4), 417–441.

Anderson, R. C., Wilson, P., & Fielding, L. (1988). Growth in reading and how children spend their time outside of school. *Reading Research Quarterly, 23*(3), 285–303.

Applegate, M. D., Quinn, K. B., & Applegate, A. J. (2002). Levels of thinking required by comprehension questions in informal reading inventories. *The Reading Teacher, 56*(2), 174–180.

Armbruster, B. B., & Wilkinson, I. A. (1991). Silent reading, oral reading, and learning from text. *The Reading Teacher, 45,* 154–155.

Athey, I. (1976). Reading research in the affective domain. In H. Singer & R. Ruddell (Eds.). *Theoretical models and processes of reading,* (2nd ed.). Newark, DE: International Reading Association.

Ausubel, D. P. (1968). *Educational psychology: A cognitive view.* NY: Holt, Rinehart, Winston.

Bader, L. A. (1998). *Reading and language inventory* (3rd ed.). Upper Saddle River, NJ: Prentice Hall.

Bader, L. A., & Wiesendanger, K. D. (1989). Realizing the potential of Informal Reading Inventories. *Journal of Reading, 32,* 404–408.

Baker, L., & Wigfield, A. (1999). Dimensions of children's motivation for reading and their relationship to reading activity and reading achievement. *Reading Research Quarterly, 34*(4), 452–477.

Baumann, N. (1995). Reading millionaires—it works! *The Reading Teacher, 48,* 730.

Bean, R. M., Cassidy, J., Grumet, J. E., Shelton, D. S., Wallis, S., & Rose, R. (2002). What do reading specialists do? Results from a national survey. *The Reading Teacher, 55,* pp. 736–745.

Bean, R. M., Swan, L., & Knaub, R. (2003). Reading specialists in schools with exemplary reading programs: Functional, versatile, and prepared. *The Reading Teacher, 56,* pp. 446–456.

Beck, I. L., & McKeown, M. G. (1991). Reasons social studies texts are hard to understand: Mediating some of the difficulties. *Language Arts, 68*(6), 482–490.

Betts, E. (1954). *Foundations of reading instruction.* NY: American Book.

Biemiller, A. (1994). Some observations on beginning reading instruction. *Educational Psychologist, 29*(4) 203–209.

Black, P. (2000). Research and the development of educational assessment. *Oxford Review of Education, 26*(3/4), 407–419.

Black, P., & Wiliam, D. (1998). Assessment and classroom learning. *Assessment in Education, 5*(1), 7–71.

Boodt, G. M. (1984). Critical listeners become critical readers in remedial reading class. *The Reading Teacher, 37,* 390–394.

Bossert, T. S., & Schwantes, F. M. (1995–96). Children's comprehension monitoring: Training children to use rereading to aid comprehension. *Reading Research and Instruction, 35,* 109–121.

Bransford, J. D. (1984). Schema activation and schema acquisition: Comments on Richard C. Anderson's remarks. In R. C. Anderson, J. Osborn, & R. J. Tierney (Eds.), *Learning to read in American schools: Basal readers and content texts.* Hillsdale, NJ: Erlbaum.

Brophy, J. (1985). Teacher-Student interaction. In J. B. Dusek (Ed.), *Teacher expectancies,* (pp. 303–328). Hillsdale, NJ: Erlbaum.

Brown, R. G. (1991). *Schools of thought: How the politics of literacy shape thinking in the classroom.* San Francisco: Jossey-Bass.

Burns, P. C., & Roe, B. (1993). *Informal reading inventory.* Boston: Houghton Mifflin.

Carnine, D., & Kindler, B. D. (1985). Teaching low performing students to apply generative and schema strategies to narrative and expository material. *Remedial and Special Education, 6*(1), 20–30.

Cazden, C. (1988). *Classroom discourse: The language of teaching and learning.* Portsmouth, NH: Heinemann.

Chomsky, N. (1986). *Knowledge of language: Its nature, origin, and use.* NY: Praeger.

Cipielewski, J., & Stanovich, K. E. (1992). Predicting growth in reading ability from children's exposure to print. *Journal of Experimental Child Psychology, 54,* 74–89.

Clay, M. (1979). *Reading: The patterning of complex behavior,* (2nd ed.). Portsmouth, NH: Heinemann.

Cross, D. R., & Paris, S. G. (1988). Developmental and instructional analysis of children's metacognition and reading comprehension. *Journal of Education Psychology, 80,* 131–140.

CTB McGraw Hill (2002). TerraNova performance assessments: Product detail. Retrieved 9/21/2002 from http://www.ctb.com/products_detail.jsp

Cunningham, A. E., & Stanovich, K. E. (1997). Early reading acquisition and its relation to reading experience and ability 10 years later. *Developmental Psychology, 33,* 934–945.

Davis, Z. T. (1994). Effects of pre-reading story mapping on elementary readers' comprehension. *Journal of Educational Research, 87*(6), 353–360.

Delpit, L. (1995). *Other people's children: Cultural conflict in the classroom.* NY: Free Press.

Dolch, E. W. (1948). *Problems in reading.* Champaign, IL: Garrard Books.

Donahue, P. L., Voelkl, K. E., Campbell, J. R., & Mazzeo, J. (1999). NAEP 1998 reading report card for the nation and the states. (NCES 1999–500). National Center for Educational Statistics, Office of Educational Research and Improvement, U.S. Department of Education.

Driscoll, M. (1994). *Psychology of learning for instruction.* Boston: Allyn & Bacon.

Duffelmeyer, R. A., Robinson, S. S. & Squier, S. E. (1989). Vocabulary questions on informal reading inventories. *The Reading Teacher, 43,* 142–48.

Durkin, D. (1978–79). What classroom observations reveal about reading comprehension instruction. *Reading Research Quarterly, 14,* 481–538.

Ekwall, E. E., & Shanker, J. L. (2000). *Ekwall-Shanker reading inventory* (4th ed.). Boston: Allyn & Bacon.

Eldredge, J. L., Quinn, B., & Butterfield, D. D. (1990). Causal relationships between phonics, reading comprehension, and vocabulary achievement in the second grade. *Journal of Educational Research, 83* (4), 201–214.

Elmore, R. S., Peterson, P. L., & McCarthey, S. J. (1996). Restructuring in the classroom: Teaching, learning, and school organization. San Francisco: Jossey-Bass.

Flippo. R. E. (2001). Reading researchers in search of common ground. Newark, DE: International Reading Association.

Flynt, E. S., & Cooter, R. B. (2001). *Reading inventory for the classroom* (4th ed.). Upper Saddle River, NJ: Prentice Hall.

Foorman, B. R., Novy, D., Francis, D., & Liberman, D. (1991). How letter-sound instruction mediates progress in first grade reading and spelling. *Journal of Educational Psychology, 83,* 456–469.

Fountas, I. C., & Pinnell, G. S. (1996). *Guided Reading.* Portsmouth, NH: Heinemann.

Frances, W. N., & Kucera, H. (1982). *Frequency analysis of English usage.* Boston: Houghton Mifflin.

Freppon, P. (1991). Children's concepts of the nature and purpose of reading in different instructional settings. *Journal of Reading Behavior, 23*(2), 139–163.

Fuchs, L. S., Fuchs, D., & Deno, S. L. (1982). Reliability and validity of curriculum-based informal reading inventories. *Reading Research Quarterly, 18*, 6–26.

Gagne, E. D. (1985). *The cognitive psychology of school learning.* Boston: Little, Brown.

Gambrell, L. B. (1996). Creating classroom cultures that foster reading motivation. *The Reading Teacher, 50*, 14–25.

Gambrell, L. B., Palmer, B. M., Codling, R. M., & Mazzoni, S. A. (1996). Assessing motivation to read. *The Reading Teacher, 49* (7), 518–533.

Gerke, R. (1980). Critique of informal reading inventories: Can a valid instructional level be obtained? *Journal of Reading Behavior, 12*, 155–157.

Gillis, M. K., & Olson, M. W. (1986, Jan–Feb.). Informal reading inventories and test type/structure. Paper presented at the Annual Meeting of the Southwest Regional Conference of the International Reading Association (ERIC Document Reproduction Service No. ED276971)

Goodman, K. S. (1970). Reading: A psycholinguistic guessing game. In H. Singer & R. B. Ruddell (Eds.), *Theoretical models and processes of reading* (pp. 259–271). Newark, DE: International Reading Association.

Goodman, Y. (1997). Reading diagnosis—Qualitative or quantitative. *Reading Teacher, 50*(7), 534–540.

Goodman, Y. M., & Burke, C. (1972). *The reading miscue inventory.* Portsmouth, NH: Heinemann.

Goodman, Y. M., & Goodman, K. S. (1994). To err is human: Learning about language processes by analyzing miscues. In R. B. Ruddell, M. R. Ruddell, & H. Singer (Eds.), *Theoretical models and processes of reading* (4th ed.) (pp. 104–123). Newark, DE: International Reading Association.

Gottfried, A. E. (1990) Academic intrinsic motivation in young elementary school children. *Journal of Educational Psychology, 82*, 525–538.

Gray, J. A., & Moody, D. B. (2000). Effects of reading excellence model on children's reading. *Commerce Business Daily Issue.* Retrieved 5/16/2000 from: http:alerts.sciencewise.com/swalert/doed/opp/05150017.htm

Guthrie, J. T. (2001). Benefits of opportunity to read and balanced instruction on the NAEP. *Journal of Educational Research, 94*, 145–163.

Guthrie, J. T., Wigfield, A., Metsala, J. L., & Cox, K. E. (1999). Motivational and cognitive predictors of text comprehension and reading amount. *Scientific Studies of Reading, 3*(3), 231–257.

Hansen, J. (1981). The effects of inference training and practice on young children's reading comprehension. *Reading Research Quarterly, 16*, 391–417.

Harcourt (2002). Stanford 9 open-ended reading. Retrieved 12/12/2002 from http://www.hbem.com/trophy/schvtest/o-eread.htm

Harris, A. J., & Sipay, E. (1990). *How to increase reading ability* (10th ed.). White Plains, NY: Longman.

Harris, L. A., & Lalik, R. M. (1987). Teachers' use of informal reading inventories: An example of school constraints. *The Reading Teacher, 40*, 624–30.

Heath, S. B. (1983). *Way with words.* New York: Cambridge University Press.

Helgren-Lempesis, V. A., & Mangrum, C. T., II. (1986). An analysis of alternate-form reliability of three commercially-prepared informal reading inventories. *Reading Research Quarterly, 21*, 209–15.

Hunt, L. C., Jr. (1970). The effect of self-selection, interest, and motivation upon independent, instructional, and frustrational levels. *The Reading Teacher, 24*, 146–151.

Idol, L., & Croll, V. (1987). Story map training as a means of improving reading comprehension. *Learning Disabilities Quarterly, 10*, 214–230.

International Reading Association. (1999). *High-stakes assessment in reading: A position statement.* Newark, DE: International Reading Association.

International Reading Association Disabled Reader Subcommittee. (1991). *A nationwide U.S. survey of classroom teachers' and remedial reading teachers' perceptions and knowledge about assessment of disabled readers: A quantitative analysis.* Newark, DE: International Reading Association. (ERIC Document Reproduction Service No. ED337764)

Jitendra, A. K., Nolet, V., Xin, Y. P., Gomez, O., Renouf, K., Iskold, L., et al. (2001). An analysis of middle school geography textbooks: Implications for students with learning disabilities. *Reading & Writing Quarterly, 17*, 151–173.

Johns, J. (1994). *Basic reading inventory.* Dubuque, IA: Kendall-Hunt.

Johns, J. L. (1991). Emmett A. Betts on informal reading inventories. *Journal of Reading, 34*, 492–493.

Johns, J. L., & Maglieri, A. M. (1989). Informal reading inventories: Are the Betts criteria the best criteria? *Reading Improvement, 26*, 124–132.

Johnson, M. S., Kress, R. A., & Pikulski, J. J. (1987). *Informal reading inventories* (2nd ed.). Newark, DE: International Reading Association.

Johnson, S. (1982). Listening and reading: The recall of 7- to 9-year-olds. *British Journal of Educational Psychology, 52*, 24–32.

Johnston, P. (1997). *Knowing literacy.* Portland, ME: Stenhouse.

Jongsma, K. S., & Jongsma, E. A. (1981). Test review: Commercial informal reading inventories. *The Reading Teacher, 34,* 697–705.

Juel, C. (1988). Learning to read and write: A longitudinal study of 54 children from 1st to 4th grades. *Journal of Educational Psychology, 80,* 437–447.

Kameenui, E. J., Carnine, D. W., & Freschi, R. (1982). Effects of text construction and instructional procedures for teaching word meanings on comprehension and recall. *Reading and Research Quarterly, 17,* 367–388.

Kim , Y. H., & Goetz, E. T. (1994). Context effects on word recognition and reading comprehension of good and poor readers: A test of the interactive-compensatory hypothesis. *Reading Research Quarterly, 29,* 179–188.

Kinder, D., Bursuck, B., & Epstein, M. H. (1992). An evaluation of history textbooks. *Journal of Special Education, 25,* 472–92.

Klesius, J. P., & Homan, S. P. (1985). A validity and reliability update on the informal reading inventory with suggestions for improvement. *Journal of Learning Disabilities, 18,* 71–76.

Knapp, M. S. (1995). Teaching for meaning in high-poverty classrooms. New York: Teachers College Press.

Langer, J. A. (1995). *Envisioning literature: Literary understanding and literature instruction.* International Association, Teachers College, Columbia University.

Leslie, L., & Caldwell, J. (2001). *Qualitative reading inventory* (3rd ed.). New York: Longman.

Lewis, C. S. (1961). *An experiment in criticism.* Cambridge, UK: Cambridge University Press.

Lowell, R. E. (1969, Apr.-May). Problems in identifying reading levels with informal reading inventories. Paper presented at the International Reading Association conference, Kansas City, MO (ERIC Document Reproduction Service No. ED032199)

Lynch, D. J. (1988). Reading comprehension under listening, silent, and round robin reading conditions as a function of text difficulty. *Reading Improvement, 25,* 98–104.

Manning, M., & Manning G. (1994). Reading: Word or meaning centered? *Teaching Pre-K–8, 25,*(2) 98–100.

Manzo, A. V., Manzo, U. C., & McKenna, M. C. (1995). *Informal reading-thinking inventory.* Fort Worth, TX: Harcourt Brace.

McKenna, M. C. (1983). Informal reading inventories: A review of the issues. *The Reading Teacher,* 670–679.

Meece, J. L., Blumenfeld, P. C., & Hoyle, R. H. (1988). Students' goal orientation and cognitive engagement in classroom activities. *Journal of Educational Psychology, 85,* 582–590.

Miller, S. D., & Smith, D. E. (1990). Relations among oral reading, silent reading, and listening comprehension of students at differing competency levels. *Reading Research & Instruction, 29,* 73–84.

Morrow, L. M., Tracey, D. H., Woo, D. G., & Pressley, M. (1999). Characteristics of exemplary first-grade literacy instruction. *The Reading Teacher, 52,* 462–476.

Nagy, W. (1988–89). *Teaching vocabulary to improve reading comprehension.* Urbana, IL: National Council of Teachers of English.

National Center for Education Statistics (2002). Distribution of questions by reading stance, 2000 NAEP, Grade 4. Retrieved 12/12/2002 from http://nces.ed.gov/nationsreportcard/reading/distributequest.asp

Nessel, D. (1987). Reading comprehension: Asking the right questions. *Phi Delta Kappan, 68,* 442–45.

Ogbu, J. (1992). Adaptation to minority status and impact on school success. *Theory into Practice, 31,* 287–295.

Oliver, J. E., & Arnold, R. (1978). Comparing a standardized test, an informal inventory and teacher judgment on third grade reading. *Reading Improvement, 15,* 56–59.

Olson, M. W., & Gillis, M. K. (1987). Text type and text structure: An analysis of three secondary informal reading inventories. *Reading Horizons, 28,* 70–80.

Parker, R., & Hasbrouck, J. E. (1992). Greater validity for oral reading fluency: Can miscues help? *Journal of Special Education, 25*(4) 492–503.

Pearson, P. D. (1992). Reading. In *The Encyclopedia of Educational Research,* (pp. 1075–1085).

Pearson, P. D., & Camperell, K. (1994). Comprehension of text structures. In R. R. Ruddell, M. R. Ruddell, & H. Singer (Eds.), *Theoretical models and processes of reading* (4th ed.). Newark, DE: International Reading Association.

Pearson, P. D., Hansen, J., & Gordon, C. (1979). The effective background knowledge on young children's comprehension of explicit and implicit information. *Journal of Reading Behavior, 11,* 201–209.

Piaget, J. (1973). *The language and thought of the child.* New York: World Books.

Pikulski, J. J. (1990). Informal reading inventories. *The Reading Teacher, 43,* 514–516.

Pressley, M., Wharton-McDonald, R., Allington, R. L., Block, C. C., Morrow, L., Tracey, D., et al. (2001). Strategy instruction for elementary students searching informational text. *Scientific Studies of Reading, 5*(1), 35–58.

Quinn, K. B., Slowik, C. C., & Hartman, G. (2000). The relationship between motivation to read and reading achievement. *The Pennsylvania Psychologist, 60*, 23–25.

Rasinski, T. (1989). Fluency for everyone: Incorporating fluency instruction in the classroom. *The Reading Teacher, 42*(9), 690–693.

Report of the National Reading Panel (2000). *Teaching children to read.* Retrieved 11/15/2002 from http://www.nichd.nih.gov/publications/nrp/members/htm

Rosenblatt, L. M. (1978). *The reader, the text, the poem: The transactional theory of literary work.* Carbondale, IL: Southern Illinois University Press.

Rosenblatt, L. M. (1983). *Literature as exploration* (4th ed.). New York: Modern Language Association (originally published in 1938).

Rosenthal, R. (1985). From unconscious experimenter bias to teacher expectancy effects. In J. B. Dusek (Ed.), *Teacher Expectancies,* (pp. 37–65). Hillsdale, NJ: Erlbaum.

Rosenthal, R., & Jacobson, L. (1968). *Pygmalion in the classroom: Teacher expectations and pupils' intellectual development.* New York: Holt, Rinehart, Winston.

Ruddell, R. B., Draheim, M. E., & Barnes, J. (1990). A comparative study of the teaching effectiveness of influential and noninfluential teachers and reading comprehension development. In J. Zutell & S. McCormick (Eds.), *Literacy theory and research: Analyses from multiple paradigms* (pp. 153–162). Chicago: National Reading Conference.

Rumelhart, D. E. (198). Toward an interactive model of reading. In H. Singer & R. R. Ruddell (Eds.), *Theoretical models and processes of reading* (3rd ed.). Newark, DE: International Reading Association.

Samuels, S. J. (1988). Decoding and automaticity. *The Reading Teacher, 41*, 756–760.

Schiefele, U. (1991). Interest, learning, and motivation. *Educational Psychologist, 26*, 299–324.

Schraw, G., & Bruning, R. (1999). How implicit models of reading affect motivation to read and reading engagement. *Scientific Studies of Reading, 3*(3), 281–302.

Shanker, J. L., & Ekwall, E. E. (2000). *Ekwall-Shanker reading inventory* (4th ed.). Boston: Allyn & Bacon.

Silvaroli, N. J., & Wheelock, W. H. (2001). *Classroom reading inventory* (9th ed.). New York: McGraw-Hill.

Singer, H., & Donlan, W. (1982). Active comprehension: Problem solving with question generation for comprehension of complex short stories. *Reading Research Quarterly, 17*, 166–186.

Stahl, S. A., Duffy-Hester, A. M., & Stahl, K.A. (1998). Theory and research into practice: Everything you wanted to know about phonics (but were afraid to ask). *Reading Research Quarterly, 33*, 338–355.

Stanovich, K. (1986). Matthew effects in reading. *Reading Research Quarterly, 21*, 360–406.

Stanovich, K. E. (1980). Toward an interactive compensatory model of individual differences in the development of reading fluency. *Reading Research Quarterly, 16*, 32–71.

Stauffer, R. G. (1969). *Directing reading maturity as a cognitive process.* New York: Harper & Row.

Swanson, P. N., & De La Paz, S. (1998). Teaching effective comprehension strategies to students with learning and reading disabilities. *Intervention in School and Clinic, 33*(4), 209–218.

Taylor, B., Pearson, D., Clark, K., & Walpole, S. (2000). Beating the odds in teaching all children to read. (Report #2–006). East Lansing, MI: Center for Improving Early Reading Achievement.

Tharp, R. G., & Gallimore, R. (1989). Rousing schools to life. *American Educator, 13*(2), 20–25, 46–52.

Thorndike, E. L. (1917). Reading as reasoning: A study of mistakes in paragraph reading. *Journal of Educational Psychology, 8*, 323–332.

Vygotsky, L. (1978). *Mind in society.* Cambridge, MA: Harvard University Press.

Warren, T. S. (1985). Informal reading inventories—A new format. (ERIC Document Reproduction Service No. ED269740)

Weaver, C., & Smith, L. (1979). A psycholinguistic look at the informal reading inventory Part II: Inappropriate inferences from an informal reading inventory. *Reading Horizons, 19*, 103–111.

Wigfield, A., & Guthrie, J. T. (1997). Relations of children's motivation for reading to the amount and breadth of their reading. *Journal of Educational Psychology, 89*, 420–432.

Woods, M. L., & Moe, A. J. (1999). *Analytical reading inventory* (6th ed.). Upper Saddle River, NJ: Prentice Hall.